Inside *Fame* on Television

Inside *Fame* on Television

A Behind-the-Scenes History

MICHAEL A. HOEY

McFarland & Company, Inc., Publishers
Jefferson, North Carolina, and London

LIBRARY OF CONGRESS CATALOGUING-IN-PUBLICATION DATA

Hoey, Michael A.
    Inside Fame on television : a behind-the-scenes history /
by Michael A. Hoey.
        p.   cm.
    Includes bibliographical references and index.

    ISBN 978-0-7864-4665-0
    softcover : 50# alkaline paper ∞

    1. Fame (Television program)   I. Title.
PN1992.77.F25H64   2010
791.45'72 — dc22   2009047854

British Library cataloguing data are available

On the cover: Jesse Borrego and Nia Peeples in *Fame* television
series, 1982–1987 (NBC/Photofest)

Manufactured in the United States of America

*McFarland & Company, Inc., Publishers
    Box 611, Jefferson, North Carolina 28640
    www.mcfarlandpub.com*

For Katie, the love of my life.
And for my daughters, Lauren and Karin,
and my son, Dennis

Table of Contents

Prologue

On January 7, 1982, *Fame* made its debut on the NBC television network. The first episode, titled "Metamorphosis," was in fact, a drastically revised version of an earlier pilot shot in New York City the previous year by director Bob Kelljan, and based on the 1980 film written by Christopher Gore and directed by Alan Parker. *Fame*, the television series, would earn twelve Emmy nominations and six awards in its first season, barely survive for two years on NBC before being cancelled, and then rise from the ashes to become a highly successful syndicated series for four more years and a total of 361 episodes. It would generate best-selling record albums, numerous sold-out concert appearances in the United States, London and Israel, and garner a total of nine Emmy awards and twenty-nine nominations, as well as three Golden Globe Awards and numerous other accolades. Its cast and crew would bond over the years until in due course they became a family.

This is our story.

1

How It All Began

As usual, it started with a phone call. It seems that for most of my professional life any movement, or the lack of it, was inexorably coupled to a phone that would ring when least expected, or remain silent no matter how hard I willed it to ring. This time it was a phone call from a producer friend of mine named William Blinn. Bill was also a very talented writer who had written such television whoppers as *Roots* and *Brian's Song*, and for whom I had previously worked as a writer and producer on a number of projects. He was calling to ask a favor. Would I come over to MGM and work with him for a couple of weeks restructuring a pilot for a new television series based on the movie *Fame*? It would mean becoming an editor again, even though Bill knew that I was trying desperately to remain above the line as a writer or producer and possibly one day become a director. "On the other hand," he teased, "it might be an interesting project." He suggested that I come to the studio and view the existing pilot and then meet with him to discuss what needed to be done. Since I had just recently married my second wife, was still paying alimony to my first, and was at that moment out of work, Bill's offer seemed like a good idea at the time.

I had seen the movie *Fame* and absolutely loved it. As an enthusiast of movie musicals dating all the way back to my childhood (I think the first musical I ever viewed was the Gene Kelly–Rita Hayworth 1944 Columbia Pictures Technicolor production *Cover Girl*), I appreciated the vitality of the performers in *Fame* and the way the songs were integrated into the action. Since my father was an actor and I had begun my career as a struggling actor, I could still relate to the dreams and aspirations of students such as those at New York's High School of Performing Arts, the actual school upon which the film and the television series was based. When I was very young and still living in New York City I was a student at the Professional Children's School, a similar school founded in 1914 and dedicated to the education of young actors. Some of the school's celebrated alumni over the years were Ruby Keeler, Milton Berle, Christopher Walkin and Uma Thurman, while the High School of Performing Arts alumni included Liza Minnelli and Al Pacino.

I had virtually made up my mind to accept the assignment even before I drove over to MGM Studios in Culver City, California, to take a look at the pilot. A good friend of mine, Sven Libaek, accompanied me to the studio that day. Sven, who was Norwegian and a gifted musician, had co-starred in the Cinerama film *Windjammer: The Voyage of the Christian Radich*, in which he guest conducted the Boston Pops Orchestra. Sven had studied at the Juilliard School of the Arts in New York City and then moved to Australia, where he became a successful film composer. He had recently done a terrific job composing and conducting the score for *Those Were the Days*, a short film I had written and directed in an attempt to showcase my talents as a director. I asked Sven, who has since returned to Australia, to describe his impressions of the television series. He remembers that he was

> very impressed from the word go. I think it was one of the most important TV series that U.S. television ever produced. The music was brilliant all the way through the series, and the acting hit home for me as a graduate of Juilliard. Not only was the series very correct about "art schools," but very inspiring as well.

I could see that the pilot had a few problems, particularly in focusing on the characters, but all in all it grabbed me with its youthful enthusiasm and exciting musical numbers. So, needless to say, I quickly accepted the assignment and reported the following week to a cutting room at MGM studios.

This would be my third time at MGM. My first was way back in 1954 when I was just starting in the business. I'd managed to get myself into the film editors union, after spending a few years trying unsuccessfully to be an actor, and the union had sent me out to Culver City to work as an apprentice editor at MGM. I was assigned to the splicing room, and my job was to splice film together by operating a heavy splicing machine with my hands and feet. It was very tedious, doing the same thing over and over again — a bit like the classic routine that Charley Chaplin did in *Modern Times*, but nowhere near as imaginative. To keep from going crazy I'd escape whenever possible and sneak into one of the sound stages to watch the filming. By 1954 most of MGM's big stars had left the studio, but Gene

Kelly was still there, and he was filming a musical called *It's Always Fair Weather*, with Dan Dailey and Michael Kidd, and the incredibly beautiful and talented Cyd Charisse. I'd had a crush on Cyd from the time I first saw her dance with Kelly in the finale of *Singin' in the Rain*, and in the late eighties I would have the pleasure of directing her on location in Hawaii in an episode of Angela Landsbury's series *Murder, She Wrote*. She was just as gorgeous as ever and absolutely charming. Back in '54 I'd managed to sneak onto the *Fair Weather* stage once and watched as she filmed a portion of one of her musical numbers, "Baby, You Knock Me Out," with a group of punch-drunk boxers. I'll also never forget watching Kelly, Dailey and Kidd dancing with garbage can lids hooked to their feet up and down the New York Street set on Lot 2. Man, was that exciting!

My second tenure at MGM had been in the mid-sixties when I spent three years there off-and-on making five of the six films I did with Elvis Presley. I had previously managed to escape the cutting rooms and move into producing, thanks to the fortuitous whim of Jack L. Warner, who,

Michael Hoey (left) with Norman Taurog as he directs Elvis and Nancy Sinatra in *Speedway*.

after I had made a few suggestions on how to survive the censor cuts demanded for a forgettable film called *The Chapman Report*, promoted me from assistant film editor to producer. I had met Norman Taurog when he directed my first producing effort, *Palm Springs Weekend*, at Warner Bros. Norman had previously directed Elvis in four films and would go on to direct him in five more, and I had the good fortune to join him, first at Paramount Studios, where I met Elvis for the first time on *Tickle Me*, and then at MGM Studios, where I joined Taurog on three more Presley films as a writer and idea man, and then as the author of two screenplays, *Stay Away, Joe* and *Live a Little, Love a Little*.

Now, thirteen years later, here I was back for a third time and about to embark on what would become over the next five years the most exciting and rewarding period of my life. Somehow the fact that I was reverting back to the position of film editor didn't bother me at all; in fact, I looked upon it as a challenge and an opportunity to work again with Bill Blinn, a man I greatly admired.

William Blinn, a five-time Emmy nominee, was born and raised in Toledo, Ohio. After graduating from high school he left for New York City and enrolled in the American Academy of Dramatic Arts. Upon com-

Bill Blinn (right) and Michael Gleason in 2009.

pleting a two-year course he remained at the Academy for four more years as a stage manager and, as he puts it, "Jack-of-all-trades." In his words, here's what happened next:

> I then hooked up with a guy who'd been a classmate of mine, Michael Gleason. Mike and I, having looked at a lot of television, decided that television was dreadful and we could be that dreadful too. So we proceeded to write some truly embarrassingly awful scripts that went nowhere. Then we came out to Hollywood, wrote some more truly awful scripts, and then in a three week period we sold two speculative scripts, one to *Rawhide* and one to *Laramie*. Neither of us could remember exactly which one sold first, but we were in pig heaven. After that it was *My Favorite Martian* and a series called *It's a Man's World*, and after that we split up. Michael went on to do a number of seasons on the television series *Peyton Place*, and I went back to work at the Academy in New York. Then I sold a spec script to *Bonanza* and they asked me to come out to Hollywood and do a rewrite on another script for them, which I did. After that I was put on staff.

Blinn goes on to describe his time on *Bonanza* as a great learning experience. His boss on *Bonanza,* the story editor Denne Petitclerc, was hired to produce a new television series based on the Paramount feature *Shane*, to star David Carradine. Petitclerc asked Blinn to be his story editor, and he accepted the challenge. "We were babes in the woods, Denne and I," Blinn continued, "but we were lucky enough to get around people who were kind enough to entertain our stupidity. And after *Shane* got cancelled I did a series at Columbia's television subsidiary Screen Gems, called *Here Come the Brides*, and then a couple of years on *The Interns*." After that Blinn wrote several episodes for *Gunsmoke* and then returned to Screen Gems to write the pilot for a television series based on the 1965 film *Cat Ballou*. Interestingly enough, NBC developed two separate pilots based on that film and aired them on two consecutive evenings.

As it turned out, neither Blinn's nor the other pilot was bought for series, but his career took a major upswing on his next assignment when Paul Junger Witt, Blinn's producer on *Here Come the Brides*, hired him to write the screenplay for *Brian's Song*. This tragic story of Chicago Bears running back Brian Piccolo and his teammate Gayle Sayers, and the deep-rooted friendship they developed as Piccolo slowly succumbed to cancer, won Emmys for both the film and Bill Blinn's screenplay. The *Brian's Song* screenplay was also honored with the Peabody Award in 1972. Blinn's star rose rapidly after that, with a second Emmy win for Outstanding Writing on the seminal television mini-series *Roots*, and the creation of the highly popular action series *Starsky and Hutch*. Bill and I "hooked up," as he put it, when he later formed a partnership with director Jerry Thorpe. I became their associate producer on seven television movies and a couple of series over the next few years, and that's when Bill and I became good friends. We were often invited to his home for parties, particularly every year at Super Bowl time when he would install extra TV sets to watch the game and serve everyone a terrific chili. In working with Bill, I was impressed not only with his talent as a writer, but also his amazing ability to maintain his concentration while creating a scene. Any number of times I would have to interrupt his writing to deal with a production problem, and the very instant our conversation ended, before I was even out the door, I would hear his typewriter chattering away as if I'd never broken his train of thought. If that had been me, I'd have been sitting there for half an hour trying to get my brain back on track. Shortly after he and Thorpe retired their partnership in 1981, Blinn's agent asked him, "Did you ever see that motion picture called *Fame?*" And that's how it started.

Fame, the motion picture, burst onto the scene in 1980. Similar in some ways to its highly successful predecessor *Saturday Night Fever*, its musical numbers and diverse cast of characters resonated with young moviegoers. The movie's director, Alan Parker, and producer, Alan Marshall, had previously formed a production company back in 1970 to produce television commercials. Their first endeavor in filmmaking was *Bugsy Malone*, an imaginative 1976 musical based on the prohibition era, with a cast of children playing the gangsters and their molls. Then along came 1978's highly successful *Midnight Express*, followed by *Fame* in 1980. Parker's eclectic directorial style blended with Christopher Gore's screenplay and the dynamic music of Michael Gore, Dean Pitchford and Leslie Gore to produce a memorable film experience. Despite initially receiving mixed reviews, *Fame* went on to gross over 21 million dollars domestically and to be awarded two Oscars by the Academy of Motion Picture Arts and Sciences (for its score and title song), as well as winning three other awards, including a Hollywood Foreign Press Association Golden Globe Award, and garnering sixteen additional nominations. Roger Ebert of the *Chicago Sun–Times*, who was one of the initial few that wrote a glowing review of the film, had this to say: "The movie has the kind of sensitivity to the real lives of real people that we don't get much in Hollywood productions anymore. Anyone who ever went to high school will recognize some of *Fame*'s characters."

The author of the film's screenplay, Christopher Gore, was 36 years old when he wrote *Fame*. Born in Florida and a graduate of Northwest-

ern University, his somewhat check-
ered career had taken him to New
York, where he wrote the book and
lyrics for several unsuccessful productions, including a rock musical
called *Via Galactica*, and another
musical about the Egyptian queen
Nefertiti. Gore claimed that his inspiration for *Fame* came from seeing a performance of *A Chorus Line*
and hearing one of the characters
speak about attending the High
School of Performing Arts.

   The man who takes credit for
Fame's original concept is David de
Silva, a New York City native with
some background in education. In
speaking with David, he told me
that he originally planned to become
a history teacher, but his love of theater altered his goal. Somewhere

**David De Silva (courtesy David De
Silva).**

along the way he became aware of the city's High School of Performing
Arts and in 1976 came up with the idea of making a film based on the
school and its talented students. "It was a good idea waiting to happen,"
De Silva is quoted as saying. "If I hadn't done it, somebody else would
have." Apparently somebody else had tried.

   A young actor named Barry Robins, who had starred in Stanley
Kramer's 1971 production of *Bless the Beasts and Children* as the troubled
teenager Cotton, had in 1978 written a spec pilot for a television series.
Robins had attended the High School of Performing Arts in New York,
and his script was based on his experiences at the school. Having been
denied the right to identify the school by its real name in his screenplay,
he christened his the "High School of Music, Acting and Dance," and his
script *Our Days at M.A.D.* According to Barry's sister Elizabeth, with
whom I communicated by email and who manages a community theater
company in Tampa, Florida, sometime in 1979 Barry registered his script
with the Writers Guild and then, with the help of his agent, the legendary
Ruth Webb, contacted a literary lawyer, whose name she cannot remember, and began shopping his manuscript around Hollywood. According

to Elizabeth, the lawyer apparently died while the script was still being submitted, and the project lost momentum.

When the movie *Fame* opened in New York City on May 16, 1980, according to his sister, Barry was shocked to see what he believed to be his idea up on the screen. He considered filing a lawsuit, but according to Elizabeth it was never filed. In my research I also discovered that De Silva and Gore, and later Parker, had been working on various drafts of the screenplay since 1977, and the movie had begun an 18-week shooting schedule in Manhattan in the early summer of 1979, which meant that the script was in development long before Robbins' script had been completed. Having read a draft of Robbins' screenplay that his sister sent me, it is difficult to see where the parallels lie with the film, short of the obvious school setting and the student characters that inhabit it. It would appear, as is so often the case, that two writers simply were inspired with the same springboard and developed their stories in vastly different directions. As an example of this, De Siva told me that Ray Stark's production company at Columbia Pictures had been developing a film "about the kids that went to the Brooklyn Academy of Music, entitled *BAM*," which was abandoned when MGM announced its plans to go forward with *Fame*. Barry Robbins died of AIDS in Los Angeles on April 1, 1986, April Fools Day — one of the many associated with *Fame* who would ultimately die of this loathsome disease.

David De Silva knew Christopher Gore from his days as an agent: "He had written a play called, I think, *Mary Queen of Scots* that was being done in Florida, and I had put two stars into it." De Silva went down to Florida to watch a performance and liked what he saw. When Christopher Gore indicated that he wanted to move to New York, De Silva helped him find an agent. Sometime later De Silva approached Gore about collaborating on an idea he had that he called *Hot Lunch*. Having become aware of the High School of Performing Arts, De Silva had spent time at the school observing the students in action:

> I really had the idea of the whole structure of it, you know, to go from auditions to graduation and to involve all the departments and to bring in a really strong mixture of rich, poor, black and white; this could only happen in a democracy. It was not about parents being able to afford to train these kids. Kids could audition and be in this great school. It was just inspirational, the idea of it. I called it *Hot Lunch* because the lunchtime was such an exciting part of the school day.

As De Silva described it, Gore had never written a screenplay before:

"He was more interested in doing theater, not in doing anything on the screen." De Silva claims that from the very beginning it was a work for hire, that he gave Christopher Gore his structure and story ideas, and even his ideas for some of the characters. Once they had a completed screenplay things moved quite rapidly. "CAA, which was a very powerful agency," declared De Silva, "was forming at that time, and they wanted to represent it. They felt so strongly about it that they created a little bit of a bidding war, and four or five studios wanted to do it."

De Silva and CAA finally determined to give the production rights to MGM. "It was the best deal that was offered," admitted De Silva. "And there was that old connection with Mickey and Judy, and the timing just seemed to be right to do it there." The contract called for De Silva to have mutual approval of a director, and he was given a list of ten directors to choose from. "I zoomed in on Alan Parker," he said. "I had recently seen *Midnight Express*, which really impressed me, and he happened to be looking for his first American movie." So Alan Parker officially became part of the creative team, and he and Christopher Gore began working together on a new draft of the screenplay, still called *Hot Lunch*. There's no question that director Alan Parker, himself a writer, contributed to many of the moments in the film. By his own account he took inspiration from students and incidents that he observed while visiting the school on several occasions, and incorporated them into the film. David De Silva maintains that he and Alan Parker had an agreement that Christopher Gore would receive sole credit as author of the screenplay. Notwithstanding the above, and since the Writers Guild of America Credit Department's confidentiality ruling prohibits releasing information as to whether there was any arbitration held regarding the credits for the film, Gore's screenplay remains unquestionably the blueprint upon which the film was built.

Divided into four sections, comprising the freshman through senior years of seven diverse students attending the High School of Performing Arts, the film delved into the emotional underpinnings of their characters. Alan Parker has said that he strived to "push reality as far as it could go," that the film was his version of what happened at the school. "It wasn't just about having fun and games as a performer," he commented, "but actually about the pain and sweat that goes into it." Moving the story into darker areas created a source of conflict between the director and David De Silva. "That was one of our areas we disagreed on at times," noted De Silva. "I was really motivated and interested in the joy of what the school represented for these kids, and he was really much more interested in where the pain was in going to the school, and so we had our little conflicts based on that area." De Silva went on to expand on his relationship with Parker, "I recognized his talent and knew that he was the boss. Once I agreed to a director, I had my own opinion about things and we would share them, but ultimately he was in charge."

In early 1979 the production moved to New York City, where Parker continued his preparations for filming. The studio had given him carte blanche, and he had brought over from England his entire team from his previous films to work with him, including producer Alan Marshall, cinematographer Michael Seresin, production designer Geoffrey Kirkland and editor Gerry Hambling. Parker says that he interviewed hundreds of potential cast members, many of whom were students or graduates of the High School of Performing Arts. David De Silva describes Parker's casting methods:

> Every day he would change his mind about this role or that role. He picked these Polaroid shots, and he had them up like a horse race on his bulletin board. I liked the casting pretty much; my only reservation was the casting of Maureen Teefy as Doris Finsecker because I'd envisioned this as a 16- or 17-year-old Barbra Streisand from Brooklyn, and when he cast this Irish actress that was a trouble. In fact, he then wrote a line about it into the script. But that was my only reservation; I really had envisioned she was a young Barbra Streisand, a Jewish girl.

Alan Parker says that he spent quite a bit of time trying to convince the High School of Performing Arts to allow them to film on their premises, but to no avail. The head of the school declared that she didn't want him to do to her school what he did to *Midnight Express*. "I didn't quite understand what she was talking about," Parker later said. MGM made other arrangements for filming the interiors at a deserted high school on 59th street, which was later torn down. The exteriors of the school were filmed across the street from the actual high school at St. Mary's Catholic Church. David De Silva fondly remembers the filming of the "Fame" number: "That was an exciting day when we had the cooperation of the city and were able to control the traffic a little bit and shoot that scene with the dancing on the taxi, very impressive." Interestingly enough, the title song had not yet been written when Alan Parker filmed this sequence, and a temporary piece of music was used merely to set the tempo. Michael Gore, who is no relation to Christopher Gore and had originally been hired as music coordinator for the film, came to Parker and asked him for permission to try his hand at writing a piece to use in the sequence. Thus was the song "Fame" written and laid in over the sequence at a later time. Alan Parker admits that at first he hated the song but eventually grew to like it, and Michael Gore went on not only to compose the score for the film, but also win two Oscars as well, one for the score and the other for the title song that he and Dean Pitchford co-wrote. He and his sister, the singer Leslie Gore, were also nominated for an Oscar for their song "Out Here on My Own."

The initial success of the film, although somewhat moderate, was enough to start people thinking about a follow-up. The idea of a television series seemed like the right approach, and Gerald Isenberg, whose production company, the Jozak Company, had produced an impressive sixteen television movies over a five year span (from 1974 to 1978), made a deal with MGM, and subsequently with NBC, to produce a pilot. As executive producer, Isenberg hired Stan Rogow to produce, and together they developed a pilot script with Christopher Gore. Some of the film's original cast members, including Lee Curreri, Gene Anthony Ray, Debbie Allen and Albert Hague, were signed to appear in the pilot. Bob Kelljan, an experienced television director who had first made a name for himself directing a series of vampire movies in the early '70s, was hired to direct the pilot on location in New York in the spring of 1981. Tragically, Kelljin would die of cancer shortly after completing his work on the project.

2

Metamorphosis

Christopher Gore's teleplay for "Metamorphosis," the aptly-titled pilot for the television series, is nothing more than a rehash of the basic plot of the feature film, complete with identical scenes of debate between Bruno and Mr. Shorofsky over the merits of traditional orchestras vs. synthesized music; Miss Sherwood and Leroy battling over his missing class assignments; and, of course, Lydia Grant's continual dispute with Leroy over his not wearing tights in dance class. When the network first viewed the original version of "Metamorphosis" they had serious reservations. As the title unwittingly suggested, the pilot would go through a major transformation before it would be seen by the public.

Bill Blinn became involved with the project in the summer of 1981 when his agent, Leonard Hanser, phoned him to say that NBC wanted to meet with him. In Blinn's own words, here's how it happened:

> A lot of times you get hired, but you're not at the meeting where they decide to hire you. Anyhow, the guy in charge of NBC at that time, Fred Silverman, liked the pilot, but he wasn't in love with it. He said to one of the program people, "If you can get x or y or z to produce this show I'll put it on the air." Well, I was either x or y or z, and x and y weren't available. I had remained on the Board of Trustees of the American Academy of Dramatic Arts for over thirty five years and had just recently resigned, so the notion of being involved with a show that was about young people in a performing arts program appealed to me. I always found going to the Academy and dealing with the kids energizing and rejuvenating. And a lot went on there that people just weren't aware of. There was so much passion involved, it was almost heartbreaking. The feature certainly showed most of that, and the pilot was very good, but it lacked that kind of commonality of thrust, or spine. We kept probably 75 percent of the pilot, it was well done; it was just that it was a director's pilot, as opposed to an audience's pilot. I think the director was so in love with the musical numbers; understand that I don't quarrel with that, but the story line lost some focus.

So that brings us back to my return to MGM. As I moved into a temporary cutting room on the second level of what was affectionately known as "Cutting Alley" and began to re-edit the pilot according to my discussions with Bill Blinn, he and the line producer, Mel Swope, took the cast back to New York City to film background shots and some montage sequences. While I worked on the editing, crews were busy building the giant set that would be our home for the next six years. Our art director, Ira Diamond, created the entire interior for the school, including Miss Sherwood's classroom, staircases, hallways and lockers, Lydia Grant's dance rehearsal room, the teacher's lounge and the main office where the teachers picked up their mail and Mrs. Berg held sway. It was so realistic, complete with authentic-looking water stains on the walls, that you could almost hear the El roaring by outside. It reminded me of the school set that was built for *Blackboard Jungle*, the 1955 film that I had worked on as an assistant film editor during my first tenure at MGM.

Upon his return from New York, Bill and I continued working on the pilot through the month of August, dropping scenes and discussing ideas for new ones. In September, Thomas Carter, a young actor who had only recently given up his SAG card to move behind the camera, was hired to direct the added scenes for "Metamorphosis" that Bill had written. Carter had appeared as part of the ensemble cast of the CBS television series *The White Shadow*, and had won the DGA Award the previous year for his direction of an episode of *Hill Street Blues*.

Blinn proposed to add subtext to the character's back story. As he described it, "We shot, I think, an additional two days — no more than three — to add in our little sub-plots. So we were able to do that — not that we ended up with *Othello*, but we were able to make it more easily coherent." In point of fact we replaced the entire first act with new material, including an audition sequence that introduced most of the characters, and also two new scenes that introduced Julie's mother, played by Judy Farrell. There was also some recasting that needed to be done for the upcoming series, including dropping the character of Rhonda (played by a young Fran Drescher), although Bill Blinn admitted that he seriously considered keeping her in the series. This would prove to be merely a minor blip in Drescher's career trajectory, as by 1993 she was starring in, writing and directing her own production of *The Nanny* on CBS, and earning several Emmy nominations for her performance as the title character. The character of Ralph Garcy, which had been played in the film by Barry Miller and in the pilot by Tommy Aguilar, was replaced by Carlo Imperato's Danny Amatullo. As Blinn described it:

> I had someone else in mind for the part of the boy who wanted to be the nightclub comic, Danny Amatullo. Then the casting guy at NBC said you've got to read this kid from New York, Carlo Imperato, and I was pouting up and down the hall. Carlo came in and read, and I said that's it, there was no question about it. It's always hard to admit when the network's right.

You always read about "Sunny California," but in actual fact Southern California is generally foggy in the mornings, particularly if you are anywhere near the ocean — and MGM Studios is only a few short miles from Santa Monica Bay and the Pacific Ocean. Whenever I think of MGM I always conjure up an image of the studio at the beginning of a workday, its main street blanketed in early morning fog, with large, black Chrysler limousines busily ferrying stars from their dressing rooms to the sound stages. Each production had its own limousine, with a small identification

Thomas Carter and Debbie Allen filming added scenes for "Metamorphosis" (Donna Lee Collection).

placard on the front windshield that made it known it was assigned to "The Minnelli Company," "The Cukor Company," or "The Kelly/Donen Company." This was as it was when I first worked at the studio in 1954, and how I described it in my book *Elvis, Sherlock and Me: How I Survived Growing Up in Hollywood* but now many things had changed. There were no more limousines, and, in fact, no more Cukor, Minnelli or Kelly. Part of the studio now housed Columbia/Tri Star and there was a brand new four-story parking structure behind a brand new gate at the opposite end of the studio on Overland Avenue that was designed with sloping ramps that seemed to cross one another and were impossible to navigate. I grew to hate that structure intensely, as I repeatedly lost track of where I had parked my car, not to mention that it was also a twenty minute walk from the parking structure to my cutting room.

As we started gearing up to begin filming, two additional film editors came on board to share the editing assignments with me on a rotating basis of every third episode. The first editor became a close friend; his full name was Buford F. Hayes, but everyone called him Bud, and he and I would work together on many projects after we left *Fame*. The other editor was a very talented young man named Mark Melnick, and between the three of us we turned out 16 episodes over the next few months.

The day before we were scheduled to begin filming, a charter bus arrived at the studio and we all piled on board, making our way downtown to the Dorothy Chandler Pavilion's restaurant in the Los Angeles Music Center for a welcoming luncheon for the cast and crew, hosted by Bill Blinn and Mel Swope. It was a lovely gesture, as it gave all of us a chance to meet and get to know one another, and it marked the beginning of many warm friendships that have lasted through the years. I believe that I first introduced myself to Debbie Allen as we were standing in line waiting to fill our plates at the buffet table. Most of the cast members were new to Los Angeles and to filmmaking in general, and those of us who were experienced tried to help make the impending challenge appear less formidable for them. We truly became a family as we worked on what for all of us was a labor of love; and the ensuing five years would be for me, and for many of the others, like a dream come true.

I used to enjoy bragging to people that I was being paid to go to MGM studios every day and make musicals. My favorite time of all was when I was editing the big production numbers that usually concluded each episode. I would lock myself in my cutting room and work from early morning to late into the evening sorting out the various camera angles and constructing an exciting editing pattern to match Debbie Allen's dynamic choreography. I was always very proud of the finished product, although as it turned out, it was a simple pas de deux (danced by Lydia Grant, played by Debbie Allen, and Erica Gimpel's Coco) in an episode titled "Passing Grade" that was responsible for one of my Emmy nominations and for my winning an Eddie Award from the American Cinema Editors. "Passing Grade" was written by Bill Blinn and Lee H. Grant, and directed by Nicholas Sgarro, and was actually the third episode that was filmed, following "Tomorrow's Farewell" and "Alone in a Crowd." In "Passing Grade" Lydia and Coco had both auditioned for a role in a Broadway show, and while they had both lost the role to a less qualified actress who just happened to be the producer's girlfriend, their close relationship had also been damaged. In a deserted classroom Lydia tries to restore the rapport they once shared in a beautifully staged dance of friendship, accompanied by their voices singing "I Still Believe in Me." The song was co-written by Gary Portnoy who that year had also written the theme from *Cheers* "Where Everybody Knows Your Name" that would go on to win the ASCAP award seven years in a row. Debbie Allen, who also choreographed the number, had shot some of the dance with a slow-motion camera. I decided to try intercutting the slow-motion footage with real-time footage, going back and forth between the two, and the result was quite effective.

I was nervous as hell the day Debbie came down to my cutting room to look at my version for the first time, but she loved it and made only a couple of simple changes. Everybody liked the show, and it was decided to move it up to play after "Metamorphosis" as the first of the new episodes. I think the fact that the show had a subplot about Danny Amatullo taking a job as a busboy in order to meet Johnny Carson, which was a good way to introduce Carlo as Danny Amatullo, was the real reason for the move. At any rate, I had the pleasure of having two of my efforts kick off *Fame*'s debut on NBC.

Here's an interesting piece of editing trivia that dedicated fans might enjoy. Those of you that watched the show religiously might remember that during the first two seasons we would more than occasionally use an exterior of the High School of Performing Arts as an establishing shot before dissolving or cutting to an interior scene. That shot was actually of a famous building in downtown Los Angeles called the Bradbury Building that had been a filming location for many of Hollywood's early film noir productions, including *Double Indemnity* and the original *D.O.A.*, as

Debbie Allen dancing to "I Still Believe in Me" in the "Passing Grade" episode (Donna Lee Collection).

well as Roman Polanski's *Chinatown.* When we were first getting started, a second unit filmed several shots of the Bradbury Building to be kept in our library and used whenever needed. Ira Diamond, our art director, had dressed up the building with a School for the Arts sign over the entrance and a mockup of a New York subway entrance across the street. To add further atmosphere, an extra dressed as a New York policeman rode a horse through the shot. Actually, they shot it twice, with the policeman riding through right to left and then again left to right. The shot ended up being used so many times that it became a running gag, with each editor asking, "Which do you want, right to left or left to right?" Later, the problem was solved when an exterior of the school was built at the studio on one of our sound stages.

One morning Mel Swope called to say that the show needed a title sequence to introduce the kids at the beginning of each episode. He wanted me to put something together and told me that Michael Levine from NBC would be coming over to work with me on the project. I couldn't figure out why an NBC executive would be getting involved in something like this, but apparently Mel felt that I needed his help — or perhaps this was the exec's idea? Michael Levine arrived the following morning, and we settled in to discuss various concepts. Michael had brought along some storyboard illustrations that looked very complicated and most impractical. Obviously the inspiration for the title sequence originated from the song "Fame" that Irene Cara had made famous and that Erica Gimpel had sung in the pilot episode. After a lot of discussion, Michael and I agreed that a rapidly-edited montage of various school activities keyed to the rhythm of the music might be the right approach. And, of course, the soon-to-be-famous "You've got big dreams.... You want fame?" speech that Debbie Allen had delivered in the pilot episode had to be included.

As the supervising editor on the show that first season I would view the dailies every day and sit in with the producers on the screenings of all of the editor's first cuts, as well as editing every third episode. Since we were now several months into the post-production process, this gave me a pretty good knowledge of all of the material that was available, and I began pulling shots for us to consider. I asked Bob Mayer, our music editor, to cut the song down to a 60-second version for me to use, and I started putting something together. I had found another camera angle of the moment in the "I Can Do Anything Better Than You Can" number from "Tomorrow's Farewell" where dancers Stephanie Williams and Jasmine Guy were in the clear as they did their fabulous leap and split, and had MGM's optical department make me a freeze-frame of this action to use for the finish of the title sequence. Michael Levine came by to run my version and came up with a couple of good ideas that I incorporated into the piece. Bill and Mel loved what we had done, and apparently so did the members of the Television Academy, since the following year both Michael and I were nominated for an Emmy in recognition of our work. The title sequence remained basically the same throughout the show's entire six-season run, except for the obvious changes in close-ups as some actors left the series and new ones arrived. In fact, the very first time I directed anything on *Fame* was to shoot new close-ups for Valerie, Gene and Carol Mayo Jenkins at the beginning of the second season, when I was the associate producer.

Jasmine Guy and Stephanie Williams left the show sometime during the second season and went on to establish themselves as successful

Debbie (center) and the Fame Dancers with Jasmine Guy (right foreground) (Donna Lee Collection).

actresses. Stephanie co-starred on the TV soaps *The Young and the Rest-less* and *General Hospital* for a number of years, as well as appearing in such other favorites as *One Life to Live, Dynasty* and *Moesha.* Jasmine played Whitley Marion Gilbert on *A Different World* for six seasons, winning six consecutive Image Awards as Outstanding Lead Actress in a Comedy Series, before going on to guest star on numerous other television series. She is currently co-starring in *Dead Like Me* on the Sci Fi Channel.

    Fame debuted on NBC at 8 P.M. on January 7, 1982, followed by the premier episode of *Cheers* at 9 P.M. and the second season of *Hill Street Blues* at 10 P.M. *Daily Variety* gave us a lukewarm review, picking on Christopher Gore's story, which, admittedly, was no longer all his. The reviewer mentioned each of the performers in a perfunctory manner and even misidentified Gene as Gene Raymond Ray. In his final paragraph, the reviewer managed to prophetically analyze the problems facing us: "It's now a matter of building stories and viewer interest — and showing why the High School of Performing Arts differs from anything back in Paducah." The initial audience response was tremendous, with excellent viewer numbers; unfortunately, after the first airdate the numbers started to drop off. Our main competition was *Magnum P.I.* on CBS, and Mr. Tom Selleck and company were killing us. *Fame* debuted on the BBC on Thursday, June 16, 1982, and we heard reports that the show was extremely popular in Europe, particularly in England and Italy, but that wasn't going to help keep us on the air in the United States. Our initial order from the network was for the pilot and three episodes, and then in a piecemeal fashion they ordered an additional six episodes and finally six more. Brandon Tartikoff, the head of programming for NBC, liked the show a lot; but we all knew that business was business, and unless the numbers picked up we were definitely in big trouble.

In a recent newspaper article, TNT boss Michael Wright quoted Brandon Tartikoff's philosophy for running a successful network. "Create an environment where talent feels compelled to come to you first," said Tartikoff, "and create a commercially supportive environment to help them succeed." No one could say that Tartikoff wasn't supporting us; he even joined many of us on a panel that was sponsored by the Television Academy and was held one Saturday morning at UCLA in Westwood. The subject was *Fame*, and Brandon talked at great length about why he enjoyed the show and what it meant to him. The students responded with questions, the most popular being, "How do I get your job?" Brandon had graduated from Yale University and began his career at WLS-TV in Chicago. After a brief stint at ABC in New York in the mid–70s he moved to NBC as a program executive and then took over from Fred Silverman as head of the network in 1980. Brandon's health had always been fragile, having been diagnosed with Hodgkin's disease in the early '70s. It remained in remission until 1982, when it came back for a second time, but once again he beat it back. Brandon Tartikoff lost his battle with Hodgkin's disease in 1995 when it reoccurred for a third time. Tartikoff was responsible for many programming hits during his years at the helm of NBC, and he certainly wanted *Fame* to be one of those hits. Unfortunately, it wasn't meant to happen until after we left the network.

In the opening credits of every episode of *Fame* David De Silva receives credit as consulting producer, and Christopher Gore as story consultant, but neither man ever set foot on the MGM lot while the series was in production, nor participated in any way in creative discussions. What they did get was a nice fat check every week, which, according to my sources, was $15,000 per episode. De Silva explains his absence this

The original kids from *Fame* in Season One (Donna Lee Collection).

way: "I received a credit as consulting producer, and I did get the scripts every week, but I never really involved myself. It wasn't fair for me to not be there and have an opinion about anything going on there, so I just stayed away from it." What he was clever enough to do, however, was to retain the theatrical rights to the property. "My interest in the theater was always the most important," he declared. "And I always saw this as a stage musical as well. So I retained the stage rights to it, and that really was my interest, not to go to Hollywood and get involved in the television series." Although prohibited contractually from doing anything for five years, De Silva spent the time developing a theatrical musical version of *Fame* that would have its premiere in 1988, one year after the series ended production. De Silva, who now likes to refer to himself as "Father *Fame*," has had great success with *Fame—The Musical*, turning it into somewhat of a cottage industry, with productions being presented all over the world. De Silva likes to recall an amusing incident involving the movie's original title and his current nickname:

> The original title of *Fame* was *Hot Lunch*. In the middle of the making of the movie, Alan Parker and I got a legal note from MGM saying we had to

change the title because there was a pornographic movie called *Hot Lunch*, and the lead in the film was Al Parker. We didn't want to change it and we fought. We said, "No, no! Let's fight this, we like this title." Alan Parker said to me about two or three years ago when we were having lunch, "Had we not changed it, you would be 'Father *Hot Lunch*.'"

3

New Arrivals

As it turned out, I wasn't the only one who had worked with Bill Blinn in the past who was now joining the *Fame* experience; two others were Parke Perine and Donna Lee. The three of us had been together at Viacom with the Blinn/Thorpe production unit, and had probably worked collectively on at least half a dozen different projects.

Parke Perine, who was the associate producer on *Fame* the first season, originally became interested in theater in high school, appearing as an actor in various school productions. He then went to the University of Delaware to study law, where, Perine recalled,

> A friend asked me to try out for a part in a play, saying, "It will help you as you get up in front of a jury to be more theatrical." So I had one line in an historical play and I was awful. Then I did two or three more plays. And I was barely capable, but by the time I was a junior I was hooked and we did three more plays in my senior year. I did Og, the leprechaun in *Finnian's Rainbow*, and I was completely hooked. So from that point on, all I wanted to be was an actor.

Unfortunately, the Korean War interrupted his plans, and Perine spent the next three years in the Navy as the executive officer on an LST. Upon his discharge he entered the American Academy of Dramatic Arts in New York on the G.I. Bill. "The G.I. Bill not only paid my tuition," he declared, "but they paid me money on the side so that I could live in New York, so that's the way it worked out." His closest friends at the Academy were Bill Blinn, Michael Gleason and John Robinson and together they formed a foursome that has continued to this day. Of the four, only John Robinson, would choose not to pursue a career in show business, becoming a hospital administrator instead. Perine's favorite teacher at the academy was a guy named Michael Thoma who would much later perform on *Fame* as the drama teacher Mr. Crandall. Perine credits Michael Thoma, with helping him develop his skills as an actor. "I think because of him," he reflected, "I was a pretty good actor while I was there. Good enough to get jobs after I graduated."

Perine met his wife when they both appeared in *The World of Susie Wong* on Broadway and then went on tour with the National Company for nine months. After spending some time as a production stage manager at a theater in Southern California, he became an associate director for KCET, the Public Broadcasting outlet in Los Angeles, where he was Burt Brinckerhoff's associate director on the Emmy-nominated television adaptation of Bruce Jay Friedman's off–Broadway play *Steambath*. In 1973, Perine received a call from Bill Blinn asking, "How would you like to be an associate producer?" Blinn was at that time producing *The Rookies* for Aaron Spelling and ABC, and Perine became his associate producer. It was here that he tried his hand at writing for the first time, selling a spec script to the show. "I thought I'd found Heaven," he remembered. "You can sit at home, watch the kids grow up, write scripts and people will buy them." He continued with Blinn on several other shows as both a writer and associate producer, including *Starsky and Hutch*, *Eight Is Enough* and *The New Land*. Parke Perine became my associate producer when Jerry Thorpe and

Parke Perine (foreground) and me (center) at a WGA Awards Show.

Bill Blinn moved me up to producer on the short-lived ABC series starring Lou Gossett called *The Lazarus Syndrome*, and we've remained good friends ever since. We've worked together on several other shows, and Parke joined me on several Writers Guild Award Shows that I produced and directed. To this day we'll meet every other week or so for lunch, or, whenever possible, for dinner with our wives Katie and Flavia.

Donna Lee, a third generation valley girl, as she describes herself, came from a show business family whose father and grandfather were actor/stunt men, and her grandmother worked at Universal Studios as a seamstress. While involved in community theater she met and later went to work for Mike Farrell as his personal assistant. Farrell would go on to star as B. J. Hunnicut in the highly successful television version of *M*A*S*H* for eight years on CBS. After six years as Farrell's assistant, Donna Lee was ready for new challenges and accepted a position with one of Farrell's friends, Bill Blinn. She was his personal assistant at Viacom for five years and then went with him when he signed with MGM to take over as the executive producer of *Fame*. When asked how she felt about working at a major studio like MGM, Lee replied, "It was a fantasy come true. I spent the first three weeks — until the work got so busy that I didn't have time — walking around the lot and saying to myself, do you know who walked where I walked?" Donna and I shared a fondness for the studio's glorious days gone by. When I first came to MGM years ago I would often take my lunch and walk out across Overland Avenue to Lot Two where the standing sets from the *Andy Hardy* series, the old railroad station from *Goodbye Mr. Chips*, and the New York Street where Gene Kelly and Frank Sinatra went *On the Town* stood slowly decaying, waiting, I suppose, for Kirk Kirkorian to come along years later and tear them all down and sell the land to developers. All the same, here we were back at the same studio that once proudly proclaimed that it had "More Stars Than There Are in Heaven," making a television series with music and dancing! As Donna put it, "It was a fantasy come true, and there hasn't been anything like it since."

Donna was given the title of producer's coordinator, and, as she explained it, her duties covered a lot of ground:

> I was doing everything from okaying wardrobe, to going down to the set and okaying set dressings, to taking notes in dailies when Bill couldn't be there. Lee Curreri called me president of *Fame*, and somebody made a sign that said, "Donna Lee, Staff Psychologist for Fame," because whatever it was, they came to me.

Lee Curreri and Donna Lee at a *Fame* party in 1981 (Donna Lee Collection).

Donna's first priority was to get the cast members, newly arrived from the Big Apple, settled in:

> My first interaction with them was finding them all places to stay, because they were all New Yorkers. So I had to go through introductions via phone with them. Their guard was down and they were all very excited, so it was

really very nice. And as you know, they were all green and didn't have a clue as to what they were in for."

Bill Blinn remembers what it was like getting *Fame* on its feet:

> It was a little bit of a learning process for everybody because all of our performers, with one or two exceptions, knew absolutely nothing about film. If they'd done film it was the feature in New York and that was it. They never had to compress themselves to a seven-day schedule. The whole, tighter schedule of television was brand new to most of them. Erica Gimpel never did accommodate to it. Not in the *diva* sense, she just felt that it wasn't that achievable in the dramatic sense.

The production department at MGM told Blinn that there would be a schedule that he would have to hold to. It was assumed that on the first day of prep, when the episode's director would report to the studio to begin work, that there would be a completed script. This was true most of the time; but, unfortunately, sometimes, due to last minute casting changes, a director would have to begin prepping with a partially finished script. The script would then be sent out to Charles Koppelman and Martin Bandler's The Entertainment Company that had a stable of song writers, along with details describing what types of songs and where they would be needed for specific scenes in the script. Interestingly enough, this was identical to the process used to select songs for the Elvis Presley pictures I had worked on at MGM in the sixties. Bill Blinn describes what would happen next, "Let's say that was a Monday. By Wednesday we would have heard the four or five entries for each song and made our selections, taken the big songs that called for dance enhancement to Debbie and said, 'Okay Debbie, this is what's involved and these are the sets we have available; at the moment it takes place in the dance hall, the rehearsal hall, or the theater, or whatever you had available.' Blinn went on to describe, in admiring terms, how Debbie Allen worked:

> Debbie would then have approximately three and a half to four days to conceive and rehearse a dance number with 15 to 25 dancers, and to also be working with the director and the director of photography. She's now, let's say, in the fourth or fifth day of shooting, prepping for the production number, and we're dealing with getting next week's script done. I mean, it was a constant battle. We were always saying, "When do we land? Well, we're still building the runway."

Together, Blinn and Debbie Allen developed the formula that would become the basis for *Fame*'s success. As Blinn admitted:

> At some point, probably by accident, we discovered that no matter how good the musical number was, if it didn't relate to the story or advance the plot,

it was going to die. It was just an awful death. I mean, it's not an accident that so many musicals are set in show business. Yes, you can do a whole bunch of *West Side Story*s, you can do some wonderful things, but if you're under the gun a lot it helps if your people are performers in a theater; and putting that show on properly has a great deal to do with their emotional well-being. We missed a couple of times, but by and large we were always able to tie the musical numbers to the story that it was going through. I think that helped us a lot.

During the early eighties, at the time that *Fame* was being filmed, most series were written with an A and B plot line, and sometimes a runner — a story line that carried over from episode to episode. The A plot line was the principal story and usually concerned one or two of the main characters and a conflict that more often than not involved a new character or guest performer. The B plot line usually involved other members of the cast with an internal problem they needed to solve. The B plot line of "Passing Grade," the first episode I edited after the pilot, involved Danny Amatullo learning that Johnny Carson was in town and trying to meet him by taking a job as a busboy at Carson's favorite Italian restaurant. I have to admit that at first I underestimated Carlo Imperato's abilities as an actor, but he eventually convinced me that, given the right set of circumstances, he could pull it off. Although the main narrative was about Coco and Lydia Grant auditioning for an important role in a Broadway production, Danny's incompetent efforts as a busboy. and his description of cornering Johnny Carson in the men's room, were amusing, and Carlo skillfully played the scenes for maximum humor. "Passing Grade" aired as our second episode on January 14, 1982.

The following week's episode, "Tomorrow's Farewell," was a touching story, written by Bill Blinn and directed by Thomas Carter, that dealt with Leroy's brother Willard, a troubled ex-con who shows up at the school expecting Leroy to let him move in with him. The B plot line had members of the school board conducting evaluation interviews with each student. This is the show where Lydia sets out to prove to the board that the school doesn't need a gymnasium by putting a group of football players through an intense dance routine with her dance class. The "I Can Do Anything Better Than You Can" number was a show-stopper as choreographed by Debbie Allen and edited by Bud Hayes. There was also a wonderfully poignant montage with a distraught Leroy walking through the streets of New York, accompanied by the haunting tune "Come What May," as written by David Wolfert and Henry Gaffney, and performed by Gene Anthony Ray.

Glen Gordon Caron, a very imaginative writer who was just getting started in the business but would ultimately create three highly successful television shows — *Medium, Moonlighting* and *Now and Again* — wrote our next episode, "Alone in a Crowd," one of my favorites. It had a very complex scenario that explored Bruno's phobia about performing in public, some wonderfully funny scenes in Mr. Crandall's drama class, and Danny and Doris being trapped in an elevator by a power failure and using the time to gain an awareness of each other's true feelings. It also had one of the best scenes — a student audition with a singing and tapdancing accordion player who wasn't very good in either category. Lee Curreri introduced the title ballad, one the many compositions that he would write for the series.

Robert Scheerer brought his unique directing style to *Fame* with this episode, and would continue with the show through three seasons and a total of 17 episodes, receiving three Emmy Award nominations. Bob practically grew up in movies, starting as a dancer when he was thirteen with the *Jivin' Jacks and Jills,* a group of teenagers featured in a series of Universal musicals in the 1940s, mostly starring a young Donald O'Connor. He would go on to direct such stars as Danny Kaye, Andy Williams, Fred Astaire and Shirley MacLaine in various television specials, as well as directing numerous episodic television shows. Bob was a joy to work with, and the cast and the dance company loved him. The finale of "Alone in a Crowd" was a rousing production number, "We Got the Power," written by Barry Fasman and Steve Sperry, and filmed in a darkened ballroom illuminated by candlelight that showed off the talents of cinematographer William Spencer (winning him an Emmy Award), as well as displaying Mark Melnick's sharp editing technique.

I drew the editing assignment for the next episode, "To Soar and Never Falter," another insightful script by Bill Blinn that featured Bruno falling in love with a fellow classmate whose dancing career is threatened by the onset of multiple sclerosis. An old friend of mine, Harry Harris, an ex-film editor who had become a director in television in the late fifties, was assigned as director. Harry had directed just about every TV series that ever existed, including 64 episodes of *Gunsmoke*, 40 episodes of *The Waltons*. 32 episodes of *Falcon Crest* and 35 episodes of *7th Heaven*. All in all, he directed over 500 TV episodes and was still directing episodes of *7th Heaven* in 2005 while in his eighties. Harry and I had worked together a few years earlier on a series that Blinn/Thorpe produced for ABC called *The MacKenzies of Paradise Cove.* The series was filmed in Hawaii, and since Bill remained in Los Angeles to supervise the scripts, and Jerry Thorpe was directing every other episode, I, as the associate producer, inherited the producer's responsibilities on the alternate episodes. It was my good fortune that Harry was the alternating director and made my job that much easier over the next few months. When my wife Katie came over to Hawaii to spend a few weeks with me, Harry and his wife Patty joined us for dinner on several occasions. We became good friends and continued our friendship once we returned to the mainland. Although I spoke with Harry about granting me an interview, his poor health never allowed it to happen; sadly Harry would pass away in March of 2009.

Harry Harris' direction of "To Soar and Never Falter" was outstanding; he took Blinn's perceptive script and brought out the best in the ensemble cast, particularly with guest star Connie Needham's performance as Kathleen Murphy, the girl with M.S. About mid-way through the episode Bruno plays and sings "Be My Music," a song that Lee Curreri actually wrote, and in the episode supposedly has written for Kathy. Harry's staging beautifully captured the subtext of the moment, showing Bruno and Kathy falling in love. Harry Harris and Connie Needham knew each other from the series *Eight Is Enough*, another Bill Blinn project, in which Connie played one of Dick Van Patten's kids, and Harry directed her. In spite of the heavy dance requirements for Connie's character, she handled the chores easily, since she was a trained ballet dancer. The bittersweet finale where Kathy auditions for the Ran Taylor dance troop did give me a bit of a problem. But it wasn't with the dancing, which was excellent. The problem was that the main theme of the story, that Kathy Murphy was dedicated to letting nothing get in the way of her dance career (including her affection for Bruno), had gotten lost in the choreography of the number. We needed to be reminded of Bruno's feelings for her, and all I had was a loose shot of him playing the piano with the combo that's supplying the musical accompaniment. I came up with the idea of optically moving into a tight close up of Bruno and superimposing some shots of Kathy dancing in slow motion over him. It helped set up the ending where everyone crowded around Kathy congratulating her, and Bruno walks sadly away, unnoticed. Harry Harris' direction earned him an Emmy for Outstanding Directing in a Drama Series, and in his acceptance speech he graciously thanked me that night for my work on the episode. I happened to be sitting in the audience, but we'll talk about that later.

4

Reflections on a Group
of Talented Performers

The first time I laid eyes on Gene Anthony Ray, as he rehearsed a dance number on Stage 26 at MGM studios, I knew I was watching an amazing talent. Everyone was talking about the young black dancer who had created the role of Leroy Johnson in the motion picture. Gene was rehearsing the athletic-themed "I Can Do Anything Better Than You Can" number for the "Tomorrow's Farewell" episode, and Debbie Allen's choreography called for Gene and the rest of the dancers to do some extraordinarily physical steps in order to show the man from the Board of Education that they didn't need a gymnasium. The dance number was spectacular (I even used several cuts from it in the opening credits); but later, as I watched Gene perform in the dramatic sequences with the actor who played his ex-con older brother in the episode, I realized that here was a genuine talent who could act as well as he sang and danced, and do it all with a natural charm.

In Alan Parker's commentary for the DVD version of the movie *Fame*, he claims that Gene Anthony Ray was discovered dancing on a street corner in Harlem. However, Gene took exception to that, explaining that he was dancing in street festivals and winning every contest. "It got so that if they knew I was coming they'd drop out of the contest," he declared. Whichever version is correct, and I'd tend to believe Gene's, there's no disputing the fact that he almost didn't make the film. Parker had someone else in mind for the part of Leroy Johnson and only interviewed Gene in the final week before filming began. Just as in the film, Gene showed up for the audition in street clothes, telling the casting person that he had no need to use the dressing room to change into tights, as he hadn't brought any. He also had no need for the pianist to accompany him, as he'd brought

33

Gene Anthony Ray (center) with Carlo Imperato and Valerie Landsburg in a scene from "The Strike" (Donna Lee Collection).

a tape of Earth, Wind and Fire that he played on his own boom box. Impressed by Gene's extemporaneous dance routine, Parker and choreographer Louis Falco signed him on the spot. Gene was 17 when he auditioned for *Fame*, and like the character he was to portray for the next seven years, had never received any professional dance training. Just like the Leroy character, as those years went by under Debbie Allen's coaching and nurturing, Gene developed into an exceptionally accomplished dancer. Unfortunately, there was also an evil spirit that lurked inside Gene, and it was determined to destroy him.

According to David De Silva, Alan Parker had at one time considered Debbie Allen for the role of Coco in the film:

> It turned out that he really was considering using her, but then he finally felt that she wasn't as vulnerable and was a little too old for it. So she wound up with two lines in the movie. However, she will forever be identified with *Fame* the TV series. And you know, I've met her over the years at different times and she's a sweetheart. She's identified with the movie as well, but she really had just those two lines in the audition sequence.

Debbie Allen was born in Houston, Texas, and graduated from Howard University. She debuted on Broadway in the chorus of the musical *Purlie* in 1971, and then went on to a featured role in the musical version of *Raisin in the Sun*. By the time she auditioned for Alan Parker, Debbie had already been nominated for a Tony for her performance as Anita in the 1979 revival of *West Side Story*, and had won the coveted Drama Desk Award. But it was her portrayal of Lydia Grant, the High School of Performing Art's dance instructor in the television series that skyrocketed her to prominence. In addition to acting in almost every episode, she also took on the responsibilities of choreographing most of the big musical numbers for the first four seasons. Through the repeated use each week of her "Fame costs!" speech in the opening credits, she also became the unofficial spokesperson for the series' proclamation that anything is possible if you work hard for it. Debbie Allen was the living embodiment of that motto. Here is what Bill Blinn has to say about her:

> I would tell people that I was working with Debbie, and they'd say, "Oh, she's tough, she's tough, I don't want to work with her." She's not tough. If you have your shit together, she's not tough. She's there to support you and work with you. If you come in and you haven't done your homework and you are not prepared, she will be in your face. Well, good for her, that's the job! No, she's not tough; you just have to know what it's about, as she did.
>
> She was fiercely protective of the dancers. She was the mother to that dance group. The only time I ever saw her become more emotional than she wanted to be was when she was fighting to get a raise for her dancers in the second season. Telling me why they needed more of this and more of that and more of the other thing, and also we had to redo the floor of the rehearsal hall because it was too hard on their knees. I was to be her representative with MGM to plead her case, and about halfway through her pitch to me she started to cry. And then she just got enraged — not at me, but at herself for having become womanly when she was trying to be fierce and businesslike. Well, that's the balancing act that someone in her position goes through all her life.

Donna Lee remembers being with Debbie when she was auditioning dancers for the series:

> There was this little girl who was working her butt off, but you knew she was under eighteen. Yet she was trying really, really hard, and after the first combination, Debbie went over to her and put her arm around her and said, "How old are you, sweetie?" And the girl said "Eighteen." Debbie looked at her and said, "I'm going to ask you again. How old are you?" And she said "fourteen," and her voice started to quiver. Debbie shook her head and said, "You know we can't make this happen now." She was so sweet with

Debbie at auditions making those difficult decisions (Donna Lee Collection).

her and encouraging. She said, "This show is going to be a huge hit, and I want to see you back here in four years. Promise me that you'll come back?" So she left her with this hope.

I don't know whether it was a case of the writers using the actor's own personality traits as a basis for their character's attitudes in the show or perhaps the opposite, the actors channeling their own personalities into their characters, but whichever the case it was uncanny how much the two elements blended into one.

Like Bruno Martelli, Lee Curreri, who was a graduate of the Manhattan School of Music, made no secret of the fact that his main interest was his music and everything that dealt with keyboards and synthesizers. Donna Lee remembers her first conversation with Lee:

> I remember Lee Curreri, when I first called and introduced myself, he said, "Donna Lee — is that the Charley Parker tune?" I could always tell, not only a musician, but a hard-core jazz musician, when they brought that up. And then he started singing the song, which is, if you've ever heard that tune, pretty complicated. So we bonded with that right away. Lee's love has always been, always will be, his music. So this was a vessel for him to explore and expand on that. He didn't take the acting very seriously at all.

And, like the character he played, Lee loved the freedom of expression that came with composing and arranging music electronically. Over the first two seasons he would compose a number of songs and orchestral pieces for *Fame*. "I wrote seven songs for the show," he reported during an interview for the BBC *Fame Reunion Show*. "If people really wanted to do something on the show and they lobbied to do it and they spent a lot of time preparing for it, they could do it." Lee also wrote an original story idea called "Blood, Sweat and Circuits" that became episode 17 in the second season and had a computer as the main character. Christopher Beaumont, who was the executive story editor on the second and third season, worked with Lee on the script:

> I remember that we flew up to San Francisco because there was a computer company that Lee knew about up there that had developed this program. Now, in 2008 you can probably get it on any computer as a giveaway, but back then they were the only ones doing it in Silicon Valley, and we had to fly up there to get the background on it for the story.

Lee has always been much more than simply computer savvy; one has only to view his enormously complex website to see how enamored he is of computer graphics and electronic reverberation. However, in 1983 he hadn't totally sold his soul to the keepers of the internet highway, and actually made the computer the heavy in his story, hiding the school's new computer rather than let it be used to replace good old Mrs. Berg. Ultimately, Lee would leave the show early in the third season to successfully pursue his musical career as a composer and record producer.

Erica Gimpel, much like Coco Hernandez, constantly challenged authority and found it difficult to trust those in charge. Donna Lee bluntly described her this way:

> Erica was difficult to work with. Not that she thought she was better than everybody else or that she deserved better treatment, but she was all about the art, and nobody could convince her that we were selling toothpaste. Although we were all passionate about our jobs, there are compromises that just have to be made when you're making a full-blown musical in just seven days, and she couldn't get that.

Everyone involved recalled that there would be endless meetings with her on every episode that she was in; first with Bill Blinn, and then in the second season with Christopher Beaumont, who often found himself the target of Erica's difference of opinion. Beaumont reported:

> She would come in with four pages of questions on her character, and she was only in three or four pages in the script. I would remind her that it was a script written by guys with three Emmys on the show. I realized after about four or five of these meetings that she didn't mean to be openly hostile. Erica had an alcoholic parent, and having known people who had grown up in alcoholic families, I knew that they just don't trust anybody. It was an interesting lesson for me because my father wasn't an alcoholic, he was a workaholic. I didn't have to deal with any of those issues.

In meeting after meeting, some lasting one to two hours, Beaumont would go over her twelve, thirteen, fourteen lines, explaining why they were written as they were. "Wouldn't I say this?" she would ask. "Wouldn't I do that?" Having been a student at the High School of Performing Arts when she was first cast in the series, Erica would frequently argue that the school would do things in a different way. Beaumont would have to explain to her why the scene had to play as written for dramatic purposes. Declared Beaumont:

> But I think that it wasn't even about the scene, as much as she needed to go though this process to reassure herself that she was okay with it. She couldn't take Bill's word or my word because I don't think she believed that she could take anybody's word. It was hard for me to fathom because I didn't grow up with that, but eventually I realized that it really didn't have that much to do with the script. It had to do with the process that she had to go through.

In spite of all this, Beaumont still managed to maintain a philosophical outlook. "Actually, looking back on it," he said, "it was a great life lesson for me. I learned a lot about trust and people who don't grow up with it and how that transfers into your work. She just questioned everything."

If you took the description of Doris Schwartz — "impetuous, talented, assertive" — and applied it to Valerie Landsburg, you'd have a perfect match. Doris wanted to be an actress, a writer, a director or some combination of all three, and so did Valerie. Ultimately, she succeeded in proving that she was worthy of becoming all of the above, while at the same time making Doris one of the most beloved characters on the show. As it was, she still had to audition four times before she was finally signed for the role. According to Valerie, the director, Bob Kelljan was unsure of whether he wanted to hire her or not, and eventually it took a screen test to prove to him that she was capable of performing the role. Valerie was born in New York City and came from a show business family. Her father, Alan Landsburg, began as a documentary producer/director for David Wolper, eventually launching his own production company, where he executive produced such award-winning television specials as *Bill* and its sequel, *Bill on His Own*, both starring Mickey Rooney, and the *Kennedy* mini-series starring Martin Sheen. Valerie's mother, Sally Landsburg, is a psychologist and author. Valerie grew up in Southern California but returned to New York in 1980 to take over the role of Libby in Neil Simon's *I Ought to Be in Pictures*. She was still living in New York when she was cast in the pilot for *Fame*, which would bring her back to California to portray Doris Schwartz in the series. Although only 5' 3" Valerie still seems to virtually leap off the screen every time she appears, which is understandable for an actress who always "takes stage" whenever she is on. Later, when I was her director, I would find the need sometimes to give her the classic admonition that "less is more," but still she could break your heart, as she did in "Tomorrow's Farewell" as she struggled to put into words her reasons for wanting to be a student at the High School of Performing Arts. Valerie was 22 at the time she was first cast in the series, and, as it turned out, it would become harder and harder for her to continue playing a 16-year-old student as the show went from season to season. Valerie would later admit openly that she had become a "functioning alcoholic" who managed to conceal her condition from the powers that be, but not from her fellow cast members.

For Carlo Imperato, who won Bill Blinn's heart at his first interview, and went on to win everyone else's as well, playing Danny Amatullo, the tough kid from the Bronx, wasn't such a stretch inasmuch as he was born Anthony Richard Imperato in the Bronx. He first appeared on Broadway when he was 15 in Joseph Papp's production of *Runaways*. Carlo's perform-ance as Danny, who desperately wanted to become a famous comedian, could be both brash and vulnerable at the same time. Donna Lee described him as a puppy. "He was so adorable and sweet, one of the nicest guys you'd ever meet," she said admiringly. "He knew that this was a once-in-a-lifetime opportunity, and that he needed to toe the mark — and he tried, he never caused any problems." "I was in a world that I'd never seen before," Carlo reflected years later. "It really was a big family. Even when we had time off we were together, we depended on each other for moral support, for friendship, and it helped make the show more realistic." That being said, Carlo was never comfortable singing and dancing, even though he worked hard at it, and during his appearance on the BBC *Fame Reunion Show* many years later he seemed to express some bitterness about his expe-riences on the show. The characters of Danny and Doris complimented each other's personalities, and when the writers decided to make them a couple you found yourself pulling for them, hoping it would work out, even though in real life Carlo dated one of the dancers and later was briefly engaged to his co-star Nia Peeples. As the plots of the episodes descended from outrageous to ludicrous to appalling, Carlo has stated, "I wanted to get off of the show after the third season, but they wouldn't let me go." And so he would remain one of the few original cast members to labor on with the series right up to its final episode, valiantly portraying everything from Cyrano de Bergerac to Sherlock Holmes to Dr. Jekyll and Mr. Hyde.

When I first viewed the pilot, I remember admiring how well the actress playing Julie Miller had faked her fingering while supposedly play-ing the cello. Most actors can fake playing the piano with a few lessons, but the guitar, violin and cello are much harder to accomplish. The camera usually stays off the fingers as much as possible, and directors have even gone so far as to set up a shot so that an actual musician's arm and hand is doing the fingering. Imagine my surprise when I learned that Lori Singer was already an accomplished musician when she was cast in the pilot for *Fame*.

Lori was born in Corpus Christi, Texas; her father, Jacques, was a noted Canadian symphony conductor, and her mother Leslie a concert pianist. Lori was accepted at age 14 into the Juilliard School of the Arts in New York, where she studied the cello. The following year she made her debut as a soloist with the Western Washington Symphony. After gradu-ation Lori pursued a successful modeling career with the Elite Model

Agency, as well as studying acting. Lori's twin brother, Gregory, graduated from the Juilliard School of Music and became a concert violinist.
Another brother, actor Marc Singer, had already made a name for himself in Hollywood as the muscular lead in the adventure film *Beastmaster*,
and her cousin, director/producer Bryan Singer, would in a few years
become famous as the director of the *X-Men* and *Superman* franchises. In
spite of her cultured background, Lori was a bohemian at heart; she loved
going barefoot as much as she hated having to wear all of the makeup and
costumes. I'd guess that Lori's fellow cast members eventually knew it, but
most of the rest of us didn't learn until much later that Lori was already
married to attorney Richard Emery when she arrived in Southern California and reported for duty at the MGM Studios.

Of the other cast members, Albert Hague, who played music teacher
Benjamin Shorofsky, was completely cooperative and probably the best exam-
ple of art imitating life. Long before he achieved recognition as an actor,
Albert Hague was already a successful composer for stage and screen, with
Broadway productions like *Plain and Fancy* and the Tony Award–winning
Redhead, and the perennial holiday television special *How the Grinch Stole
Christmas*. Hague was born in Berlin and escaped from Nazi Germany to the
United States in 1939 with the intention of becoming a classical pianist. "I'm
living proof that America works," Hague wrote in an unpublished autobiography. "Here I was, an 18-year-old kid, all alone in a foreign country, not
speaking a word of English, without two pennies to rub together. Sixteen
years later, I celebrated the opening night of my first Broadway hit." He
studied music under a scholarship at the University of Cincinnati and also
at the Royal Conservatory of Santa Cecilia in Rome, but World War II interrupted his plans, and he ended up playing the piano in an Army Air Corps
special services band until his discharge in 1945. After the war he settled in
New York and found work as a piano player at neighborhood bars. His first
stage show, *Reluctant Lady*, had its premiere in Cincinnati in 1948, and in
1951 he debuted on Broadway as the composer of incidental music for the
original production of *The Madwoman of Chaillot*, starring Estelle Winwood
and Martita Hunt. It was during the production of *Reluctant Lady* that he
met his future wife, Renee Orin, an actress and a singer, whom he married
in 1951. In 1955 his Broadway musical about the Amish people, *Plain and
Fancy*, gave birth to the song "Young and Foolish," which became a hit recording for Tony Bennett. In 1959 Hague received his Tony Award for the score
of *Redhead*, which starred Gwen Verdon and was directed by Bob Fosse. The
murder-mystery musical received a total of six Tony Awards that season.

Albert Hague (right) and his wife Renee (second from right) with Katie and me at a *Fame* party in 1981.

Alan Parker has said that he was looking for "a real musician" to play the part of Mr. Shorofsky in the feature, and he found that in Albert, who was temporarily teaching at the High School of Performing Arts. Albert's special expertise was preparing young actors for the difficult process of auditioning. Albert's description of an audition: "A nervous artist who's not quite sure whom he's looking for who's interviewing a nervous artist who's not quite sure who he is." The relationship that developed in the series between Albert Hague's Mr. Shorofsky and Lee Curreri's Bruno closely mirrored their off-screen relationship. Both had an intense respect for each other's talents, and it clearly showed in their performances.

One of my favorites in the cast was Carol Mayo Jenkins. Perhaps because she was an adult and portraying English teacher Elizabeth Sherwood I could relate to her more readily than to the younger actors. Carol was one of the sweetest people I ever met, very talented and a joy to work with. Born in Knoxville, Tennessee, Carol had managed to cloak her southern accent by studying at the Central School of Speech and Drama in London. While in London she helped found the Drama Centre, considered to be one of the leading theatrical schools in England. After a series of Broadway appearances with such stars as Derek Jacobi, Jane Alexander and Henry Fonda, Carol was cast in the pilot for *Fame* and then came out to California to appear in the series. There was one change made between filming the pilot and the series, and that was to adjust Carol's hair color from dark red to light blond to soften her look, which in my opinion made her twice as attractive. Bill Blinn remembers how nervous Carol was when she first started filming:

> I remember Carol Mayo Jenkins just being terrified because she didn't have any concept of matching. You know, "When do I pick up the cup of coffee, put down the pencil?" That kind of stuff? And Bob Sheerer, to his everlasting credit, said, "Stop worrying about it, that's my job. That's the script supervisor's job, and we'll tell you when it doesn't work and we'll make it work. Do not concern yourself." And that helped her a great deal.

Carol's Ms. Sherwood ultimately appeared in 108 episodes between 1982 and 1987. She and Debbie became close friends, and I remember how much she enjoyed going against type and playing the wicked witch in our version of *The Wizard of Oz*, which we called "Not in Kansas Anymore." Carol even took out a full page ad in *Variety* in which she thanked everyone from the producers to the key grip, saying, "It was really lovely being green."

There's an interesting story that involves Carol that I don't believe I ever told her. For years, whenever I couldn't sleep, I would conjure up the image of a blackboard in my mind. I would then erase whatever thoughts were keeping me awake, draw a circle within a square and concentrate on that. Then I could go back to sleep. It was my version of counting sheep. This worked fine for years until I started working on *Fame*, for then, whenever I would bring up the blackboard, Carol Mayo Jenkins' character Elizabeth Sherwood would also arrive, along with some scene from her classroom, and the whole effect was ruined. I love Carol, but for years she ruined my sleep.

Carmine Caridi played Angelo Martelli in 14 episodes during the first and second seasons. According to Mark Seal's *Vanity Fair* article about the making of the original *The Godfather* film, Caridi was Paramount's initial choice to play the title roll. Upon learning that he had the part, Caridi outfitted himself in a brand new suit and returned to his old neighborhood for all of his friends and neighbors to congratulate him. Unfortunately, it wasn't too long before he was out in the street and director Francis Ford Coppola's original choice of Marlon Brando was signed for the role.

Feeling sorry for Caridi, Coppola wrote a part for him in the sequel, and eventually Carmine also appeared in *Godfather Part III*. Although he frequently displayed a disagreeable attitude toward some of the cast and crew on *Fame*, I have to say that he handled the role of Bruno's father beautifully, showing just the right amount of love, pride and sensitivity when it came to his son. Carmine left the show before I had a chance to work with him as a director, and I never saw him again except on television. I was therefore shocked in 2004 when I read about his having given a friend his copies of Academy Award screeners that ended up on the Internet. The Academy began an investigation when copies of several screeners, including *The Last Samurai*, *Something's Gotta Give* and *Mystic River*, appeared on the Internet, and special markings on the copies identified them as having originally been sent to Caridi. Since all Academy members are required to sign an agreement promising to prevent their videocassettes from being copied, the Academy instituted legal proceedings against Caridi and the man responsible for posting the screeners, Russell W. Sprague, Sr. Caridi was ultimately fined $600,000 and expelled from the Academy, and Sprague pleaded guilty to one count of copyright infringement, having previously admitted to making illegal copies of about 200 films. In a later interview in the *Los Angeles Times*, Caridi claimed that he had been unable to respond to the lawsuit because he couldn't afford an attorney:

> I gave the videos to someone who put it on the Internet without my knowledge. If I would've known that he was going to do that I would have never sent them to him. I feel the only thing I did wrong was dishonoring the pact I had with the academy by giving the screener to another person. I got my punishment from them — they kicked me out after 22 years.

Russell W. Sprague, Sr., was found dead in his jail cell four months later while still awaiting sentencing, having apparently succumbed to natural causes.

Caridi, who had played important roles in a number of films and television productions through the years, including a running part as Detective Vince Gotelli on *NYPD Blue* from 1994 to 1996, didn't work again after the DVD incident for several years until finally appearing in 2008 in actor John Lavachielli's low-budget feature film *Wednesday Again*. I suppose in a way he must be considered one of the early *Fame* tragedies.

There would be several other cast members who would join the show after the initial season, and I will talk about most of them in subsequent chapters, but there are two favorites of mine that I'd like you to meet now. I first met Ken Swofford, who joined the cast in season three as Quentin Morloch, the blustery vice-principal of the High School of Performing

Carol Mayo Jenkins as the wicked witch, with Lori Singer, in the "Not in Kansas Anymore" episode (Donna Lee Collection).

Arts, when he guest-starred in an episode of *The Lazarus Syndrome* that my then writing partner Bruce Belland and I had written. I next saw him on my first day as a director of the episode "Consequences." If I was nervous, it was to be expected, as this was, in fact, my first day as a director on any television series, and Ken immediately made an effort to make me

Ann Nelson (right) with Debbie Allen (Donna Lee Collection).

comfortable. I remembered Ken from his hundreds of television and movie appearances, and took an immediate liking to him and his no-bullshit manner. Red-headed, opinionated and always ready with a story about some other actor or director he had worked with, Ken was a lot of fun to sit with during the down time on the set. He'd made a career of playing explosive, loudmouthed, stuffy types, and now he was the perfect choice to become the students' bull-headed adversary, vice-principal Morloch. Ken was a true baseball fanatic, and one of the highlights of his life was going to a Cincinnati Reds baseball training camp one summer. He replayed the entire event for me, moment by moment (complete with photographs and memorabilia), when Katie and I visited with him and his wife years later. Ken had a lot to do with my getting my first directing assignment away from *Fame*, as he was good friends with Peter Fischer, the executive producer of *Murder, She Wrote*, and gave him a big build-up about me. I would repay the favor by casting Ken in two of the episodes of *Falcon Crest* that I directed. Tragedy would also strike Ken, who had problems with alcoholism, when he was involved in a dreadful automobile accident a few months after leaving *Fame*. Later on, after he reclaimed full and lasting sobriety, he would narrate a documentary on the dangers of drinking and driving for Mothers Against Drunk Driving. Ken retired from the business some years ago and is now living quietly with his wife in a beach community in Northern California.

And then there is Ann Nelson, one of the sweetest ladies I ever had the pleasure of knowing. Ann began with occasional appearances as Mrs. Berg during the first three seasons, becoming a regular cast member in Season Four. Ann, who began her acting career at the age of 61 after raising her family, was nothing like the ditsy school secretary she portrayed on *Fame*; in fact, a few years later I would write a script for an episode of another TV series, called *Bridges to Cross*, in which Ann played a homeless woman in Washington, DC, who turns out to be the long-lost daughter of a past president. I remember a wonderful party that she and her husband hosted at the Ivy at the Shore in Santa Monica for many of the cast members and some of the staff. Afterwards, Ann insisted that we all go across the street to the Santa Monica Pier to ride on the famous merry-go-round that had appeared in *The Sting*, with Paul Newman and Robert Redford. Ann, who appeared in a total of 45 episodes, would go on to appear in a number of movies and television shows after she left *Fame*, including playing the wacky grandmother Gramoo Sultenfuss in *My Girl*, with Dan Aykroyd and Jamie Lee Curtis. There's a wonderful anecdote about Ann that I'll save until later, as it also involves one of the new arrivals in the third season of *Fame*, Billy Hufsey. Ann, who was born in Los Angeles, died here in 1992 at the age of 76.

5

Gathering Clouds

As we neared the end of February 1982, we'd been on the air for seven weeks, and things were looking pretty good. Oh, NBC was still doling out the episode commitments to us like stingy neighbors with Halloween candy — or, as Bill Blinn called them, "kissing-your-sister pickups." Donna Lee remembered one incident, "We were in the screening room watching dailies, and Bill got a call from Brandon Tartikoff," she recalled, "and he hit the roof. He told him, 'This is insulting! We've been the first show to hold up against *Magnum P.I.* We haven't beaten them, but we held.'" Tartikoff explained to Blinn that his hands were tied, but that he was a big believer in the show and that he was doing everything he could. There was a promise that things would get better.

But a dark cloud was forming over the *Fame* production unit. The next episode to film was "Street Kid," written by Marc Rubin, who briefly held the position of story editor, and Bill Blinn. The central plot mechanism involved Doris deciding to go out on the street and pretend to be a prostitute in order to learn how to portray one in a school project. On her night out she meets Tracy, a real prostitute, and they become friends. Doris brings Tracy back to the school. Showing her around, Doris takes Tracy to several of her classes, including Miss Grant's dance class, where a dance number is performed by the class, featuring Debbie Allen and a young dancer named Michael DeLorenzo, who was actually replacing Gene Anthony Ray in the number. There had already been some indications of trouble with Gene showing up late for filming calls or not attending rehearsals for the dance numbers, and it came to a head on this episode. Ted Zachary, who was the Executive in Charge of Production at MGM at the time, recalls what it was like:

> You never knew when or if he was going to show up. I mean, that was the real tragedy, you'd have a big scene that you were doing, whether it was a

dramatic scene or a dance number, and I'd get a phone call from the set, "We've got a little problem, we've got Gene scheduled and he isn't here yet." And I remember one day somebody, whether it was Tony Amatullo, who was then our location manager, or somebody else, went to his house, and they ended up having to take the door off the hinges and found him unconscious. You always had to have an alternate plan with Gene Anthony Ray.

For Bill Blinn and Debbie Allen, this time the alternate plan was unavoidable — cut Gene entirely out of the episode and have Michael DeLorenzo dance with Debbie. It was a big break for Michael, who had also been a graduate of the High School of Performing Arts, had studied at the School of American Ballet, and had been a member of the *Fame* dance company since the very beginning; he did an excellent job. Unfortunately in Gene's case his problems would continue to worsen.

I will always remember an extremely emotional moment in "Street Kid" where Tracy attempts to sing "Blue Moon" as an audition piece, but can barely carry a tune and finishes in tears. As the editor of this episode, I found myself choking up every time I worked on this sequence. I guess as an ex-actor I related to the anguish of an audition gone bad, and Tracy's aching awareness that she just wasn't good enough to be a part of the school she wants so much to attend. But the real tragedy in this episode was that the actress who played Tracy so beautifully, Dominique Dunne, would die tragically at the hands of her boyfriend the following year.

Dominique, who was not quite twenty-three years old at the time of her death, was the daughter of novelist and *Vanity Fair* investigative journalist Dominick Dunne. Dominique made her acting debut in 1979 in a made-for-television movie, *Diary of a Teenage Hitchhiker*, and during the following three years appeared in three more TV movies and three television series. When she reported for work on *Fame* toward the end of 1981, she had recently completed filming on the feature *Poltergeist*, which, upon its release in June of 1982, would help to make her one of the hottest young actors in Hollywood. Shortly after completing work on *Poltergeist*, Dominique met John Thomas Sweeney at a party in the autumn of 1981 and later moved in with him. Sweeney, who was working at the time as a chef at the fashionable Los Angeles restaurant Ma Maison, was jealous of her friends and had a violent temper; their relationship was soon marked by physical abuse. As time went on, Sweeney's temper became more and more uncontrollable, and the abuse more violent, so much so that Dominique hardly needed makeup to play an abuse victim on an episode of *Hill Street Blues*. She eventually ended the relationship, but Sweeney continued to stalk her. In late September 1982 she was signed to play one of the leads in the science fiction mini-series *V: The Final Battle*, and on the night of October 30 she and fellow actor David Packer were at her house rehearsing for the next day's work when Sweeney showed up. In a rage, he dragged Dominique outside and strangled her into unconsciousness. She was taken to Cedars-Sinai Medical Center in a coma and died five days later. Sweeney was convicted of manslaughter and sentenced to six and a half years in prison. As it turned out, he served less than four years of his sentence before being released, having been given credit for time served during the trial.

Michael Thoma, who played Gregory Crandall, the school's drama teacher, had been friends with Bill Blinn and Parke Perine since they had all attended the Academy of Dramatic Arts in New York many years before. Blinn had first hired him to play Dick Van Patten's golfing buddy in *Eight Is Enough*, and when *Fame* came along, and Michael was by then the West Coast President of the Academy of Dramatic Arts and teaching drama at their Pasadena campus, Blinn thought he was just the guy to play Crandall. It was an inspired choice, as Thoma's performance was perhaps the most realistic and persuasive of all the adult cast members (with the possible exception of Albert Hague, who had also once been a teacher). One evening Blinn and his wife had Thoma over for dinner, and the next day Thoma called Blinn with some startling news. "He asked me who had cooked the dinner," Blinn recalled, "me or my wife. When I told him it was me he said, 'Well I want you to know that I had a heart attack and when my doctors looked into the heart attack they found out I also had cancer. So, you're not a very good cook.'" The heart attack proved to be relatively minor, but, unfortunately, the cancer wasn't. Thoma continued to work on the series, taking time off occasionally to begin treatment for his cancer. A month or so later he stopped by Blinn's office just to chat, something he did quite frequently, but this time he had a more somber message. He told Blinn, "I can be with you as a performer for about another four or five weeks, maybe a little longer, but after that I'm not too sure." Blinn was devastated, but knew that he had no choice but to write Michael Thoma out of the show. "So we wrote an episode," said Blinn. "I'll never forget this; we wrote an episode where his character was being phased out because of budget cuts, so that we could explain why next week we wouldn't be seeing him." Parke Perine was given the assignment. "Mike had been my favorite teacher at the Academy," he recalled, "and also a friend for all those years, and now he was dying. It was the easiest script I've ever written and also probably the most emotional." Perine's script for "A Special Place," which was to be the final episode of the first season, called for another visit from some of the unpopular members of the school board, who are there to decide which teacher would be the one to be let go. Robert Scheerer directed, and I was assigned to edit, and in an early portion of the episode a solo dance sequence with Debbie Allen presented some challenges for all of us. Debbie and Scheerer came up with the concept of having Debbie's reflection in a mirror begin to dance while her foreground image remained seated at a piano singing the title song, "A Special Place," that had been written by our regular composer William Goldstein, with lyrics by Susan Sheridan. The double image device required a split-screen effect, and Bob Scheerer asked me to be on the set with him when he shot the sequence. For the effect to work properly, it was important that the camera didn't move between set-ups. I had gone to the MGM optical department to get some advice on how to do this, and they had suggested putting a half-filled glass of water on the camera and making certain that the water remained still at all times. So I spent the entire time watching the glass of water and never saw Debbie's wonderful performance until I looked at it on my moviola and started editing it.

The finale took place in the school cafeteria, where the students and teachers stage a farewell party for Mr. Crandall. They all gather around him and sing "Starmaker" a song written by Academy Award winner Carol Bayer Sager and Bruce Roberts. The song had been used as a voice-over accompaniment to a montage in a previous episode, "The Strike," but was employed to far better advantage, and certainly with more poignancy, in this episode. When they shot the episode, Mike Thoma, who had been away from the show for four episodes having treatment for his cancer, looked pretty haggard. He had lost weight, but not his marvelous sense of humor. Yet, there was still more drama to be added to the moment. Blinn reflected:

> Somehow — and to this day I don't know how — somehow word got out to the kids and everyone else that Michael was, in fact, possibly terminal. So this farewell thing became real. That was the longest afternoon of shooting I ever saw in my life. And also Michael, on some level, realized that people were saying goodbye to him. And to his credit, he never once lost it.

For Bill Blinn, controlling his emotions wasn't that easy. "I walked on the set," he recalled, "and there were all the characters surrounding Mr. Crandall, who was in his place on stage, all holding hands, holding their hands up in the air and singing, and I just lost it and I turned around. I couldn't handle it, no way." Donna Lee, who had walked down to the set with Blinn, was standing next to him.

> There were people who thought Bill was unapproachable, snobbish and whatever. He was very shy and not very visible with his feelings. One of things I loved about him was when we would go to visit the set he would walk by my desk and say, "Come on, let's go see the magic makers." Because that's what he thought everybody on the set was, whether they were craft service or whatever, "the magic makers." And it was never truer than on that show. They were going to do the "Starmaker" number, and everybody knew that this was it. We went down and we were watching it and everybody was giving their tribute to Mr. Crandall, and Bill started to go and walked away from the set and I followed him. I found him way in the back behind some flats, and he was gone and so was I. And we hugged together and then he said, "Let's go, we're not doing anybody any good here." And then, when I saw the show on the air, it was such a beautiful thing, it was such a gift to everybody.

As the cast finished singing, the camera panned off the kids, looking up at Michael Thoma on the stage and up into the flies and freeze-framed on a group of lights. A title came up that read: "This episode of *Fame* is lovingly dedicated to the memory of Michael Thoma, our Mr. Crandall. He will be missed." Michael Thoma died at the age of 56 a few months later, on September 3, 1982.

As if all of this tragedy weren't enough, Donna Lee's sister Linda died of a brain tumor shortly thereafter. I had come to know Linda when we were all working at Blinn/Thorpe Productions, and she had been Jerry Thorpe's very able assistant. Linda had a wonderful sense of humor and a laugh that seemed to come from the soles of her feet, and all of us were very fond of her. A large group of us attended Linda's funeral, and Donna was so surprised to see all of us there that she exclaimed, "We're shooting today, who's running the show?" Lee Curreri, who was very fond of Donna, came to pay his respects, and after the funeral, he, Mike Farrell and some others gathered up the large collection of flowers and took them over to St. Joseph's Hospital in Burbank. According to Donna, "When Lee and Mike took the flowers back to the hospital, a woman looked up and recognized them and asked, 'Are you filming a TV show here?' And Lee answered, 'Yes, it's *Knot's Landing.'*"

Finally the sun did begin to peek through the clouds a bit. Brandon Tartikoff's promise that things would get better came to pass, and NBC gave us a firm pick-up of 23 episodes for the 1982–1983 season. "We were almost dead after the first season because our ratings were not spectacular," admitted Bill Blinn, "but the demographics in terms of young adults and teenagers were. And that's what got us the second season."

It was decided to celebrate with a wrap party for the cast and crew, and, as was the tradition at these events, we needed a gag reel to play at the party. One of our assistant film editors, Paul Rubell, who was assisting Mark Melnick at the time, got stuck with the task of creating it. Rubell remembers:

Paul Rubell (courtesy Paul Rubell).

> The other two assistants, being far more experienced than I, took a step backward when volunteers were asked for. That left me. My first question was, "What's a gag reel?" My second question was, "Where are all the gags?" I checked with the various editors, who informed me that nothing particularly funny had happened on film, so I began to panic. I started re-editing scenes from various episodes to try to make absurd juxtapositions, and I scoured the sound effects library for farts and belches. I decided to create a mock main title by freezing on unflattering frames of the stars and putting the actors' names over it, just like in the real credits. This involved sending film out to the optical department, so I charged it to whatever show I was working on at the time.

Paul Rubell became quite creative, trying anything and everything that he thought might be funny, including slowing down and speeding up the film, which, of course, entailed more work for the optical department. Finally, he was called into the office of the vice-president for television postproduction. As Rubell related:

> He showed me a stack of bills and asked me what they were for. When I told him they were for the gag reel he spluttered and asked me who had authorized the charges. I said no one had authorized it, but they said they wanted a gag reel and this is what it would take. He told me that I was out of control and that I was fired. He picked up the phone and called the executive producer, Bill Blinn, to inform him that I was no longer working for MGM. Bill told him to reinstate me and that he would pay the charges out of his discretionary account. The executive handed the phone to me, and Bill said five words: "It had better be funny."

Left to right: Mel Swope, Brandon Tartikoff, Werner Michel, Bill Blinn and Tom Tannenbaum at *Fame* wrap party (Donna Lee Collection).

Donna Lee (left) and Gene Anthony Ray (right) at *Fame* wrap party, with costumer Marilyn Matthews and MGM executive Ted Zachary in background (Donna Lee Collection).

The wrap party was held in the cafeteria set on Stage 26, the same stage where in 1939 Judy Garland had met the Munchkins and had first stepped onto the Yellow Brick Road in the *Wizard of Oz*. Donna Lee and Kim Kaufman, who was producer Mel Swope's assistant, helped coordinate the party, and it was a huge success. Tom Tannenbaum, then president of MGM TV, brought Brandon Tartikoff and Senior Executive of Bozell Advertising Werner Michel as his guests, and they happily posed for pictures with Bill Blinn and Mel Swope. Tom and I had gone to Beverly Hills High School together many years before, and seeing each other at the party gave us a chance to renew our friendship

"This was a big one and a nightmare for me," Donna Lee remembers. "Everyone and their brother from MGM wanted to be there because we were the flavor of the month. I remember that Eddie Murphy came, and he was in a red leather outfit with his entire entourage. Debbie had invited him." As for the infamous gag reel, was it funny? "It was," reported Paul Rubell, "or at least the drunken cast and crew thought so." Everyone danced and sang and tried to forget the sadness of the past and look to the promises of the future. It would be long after midnight before the last of the revelers would finally leave the party and the studio guard could turn off the lights and place the padlocks on the doors of Stage 26.

6

A New Hierarchy

After a relatively short hiatus, the production staff returned to MGM to begin preparing for the second season, only to find that while we were gone, MGM had gone through some major changes. Richard Reisberg, who had been president of Viacom Productions when Blinn/Thorpe was active there, had been approached by David Begelman, then CEO and president of MGM and its subsidiary United Artist, to take over as head of United Artist Television. Reisberg, who had studied law at New York's Fordham University at night and worked at all three networks in business affairs before joining Viacom, described it this way, "They decided that they wanted to start a television production company, and I agreed to do that. I got there, and within months after that, Begelman was gone, and they combined MGM and UA and I got to run both television companies." David Begelman had enjoyed a successful career as head of Columbia Pictures in the 1970s, but had later been involved in an infamous embezzlement scandal at the studio, as well as being accused of several other financial irregularities. After spending some time in disgrace, he managed to regain a position of stature ten years later at MGM. Unfortunately, he was unable to repeat his initial success at Columbia Pictures and was subsequently released by MGM before his four year contract had expired. By the mid–1990s, Begelman had declared bankruptcy, and on August 7, 1995, he checked himself into a suite at the Los Angeles Century Plaza Hotel and committed suicide.

Reisberg moved quickly to solidify his position at MGM/UA television by bringing in his two top lieutenants from Viacom. Recalls Reisberg:

> Jerry Gottlieb had left Viacom and went to Universal to run business affairs. When I went to United Artists I called him and said, "Why don't you come over to UA with me as executive vice president and we'll build it together?"

56

So he came over, and within several months of that they combined the two studios, and I brought Jerry with me to MGM. Shortly after that I decided that I was going to make a change in terms of how the production operation was going to be run, and, just in terms of reaching back, I brought Ted Zachary in to head up production.

I'd first met Ted Zachary in 1977 in Honolulu during the filming of *Stickin' Together*, the 90-minute movie-of-the-week pilot for the series *The MacKenzies of Paradise Cove*. Ted, who previously had lived in New Jersey and had spent his early years in the business working as an assistant director and production manager in New York City, had only recently moved his family to the coast to join Viacom. Although Ted was Executive in Charge of Production for Viacom, he was in Hawaii serving as production manager on the TV movie.

Richard Reisberg (courtesy Richard Reisberg).

I had also just joined Viacom and was still feeling my way around as the associate producer, and Ted made me feel right at home. Each evening after the company wrapped for the day, Ted and the first assistant director, Alan Werthheim, and I would go down to the Halekulani Hotel and sit on the veranda next to the House Without a Key to watch the sunset and enjoy a drink or two. The House Without a Key has been a famous setting ever since American

Ted Zachary (courtesy Ted Zachary).

author Earl Derr Biggers immortalized it in 1925 in his first Charlie Chan novel. Ted Zachary had a superb sense of humor and told jokes better than anyone I knew. He'd usually have me in stitches long before the musicians and the hula dancers had finished their set, and the hotel staff began lighting the tiki torches.

I didn't get to know Jerry Gottlieb quite as well as I knew Ted Zachary, but he was the guy who negotiated my contracts when I first joined Viacom, and again at MGM when I became the associate producer on *Fame*, and he was always fair with me. I worked with him again many years later when he was Head of Business Affairs with David Salzman Entertainment and *MAD TV*, and we used some of the cast as hosts for a *Creative Arts Emmy Awards* show that I executive produced. When I first saw Jerry at that time, I didn't recognize him. This guy walks up to me with this enormous salt and pepper grey beard and puts his arms around me, and I look at him for a moment, then realize, "Oh my God, it's Jerry Gottlieb!" We had several meetings in which Jerry participated, and he was very helpful in sorting out what turned out to be a complex situation. I'm sure that he would have had some interesting tales to tell, but, unhappily, Jerry Gottlieb died a few years ago, and I wasn't able to interview him for this book.

So for those of us who had worked together at Viacom, with this triumvirate in charge, it seemed like old home week as we settled down to begin work on the second season of *Fame*. There had been a number of changes that had taken place within the *Fame* unit as well. First and foremost was the departure of P.R. Paul, who had played Montgomery MacNeil during the first season. The MacNeil character in the film had been portrayed as openly gay, but that was not the case in the television show. When asked if that had been his choice or the network's, Bill Blinn replied:

> I don't think there was a choice made. At one time NBC was talking about story material, I think it was after we had reconfigured the pilot, but we hadn't started shooting episodes yet. One of the guys at NBC said something about we'll do a story about a gay dancer, and I said, "Tell me what the story is?" I mean, because in the dance troupe no one is going to go, "My God, John is gay!" What's your next headline? We'd have to manufacture something awful, and it wouldn't be a teacher coming down on him, it just wouldn't be a topic. I think at one time, P.R. Paul let us know that he didn't want to play him that way. We had a little mini-romance for him, and he was clearly so glad to see that. So it wasn't that we ever made a decision to stay away from it, it was just that we never found it fertile enough to go to. We couldn't do *That Certain Summer*.

Summer was a groundbreaking television movie that was one of the first films in 1972 to tackle the subject of homosexuality and earned three Emmy nominations (for writing, directing and producing). "We couldn't get that graphic at eight o'clock," Blinn continued. "So it was either going to be a topic that you do and you really do it or you don't do it, because if it's half-way then it's vanilla and silly business. So I think that was the decision." As it turned out, the character still presented a basic problem for the writers and the decision was made to drop MacNeil from the show. Blinn explained:

> P.R. Paul was marvelous. He couldn't have been nicer and [was] very professional, and he did anything I asked him to do. But P.R. was not a musical performer; he had some skills, but they were limited. If we put him next to Lee, or next to Valerie, or Debbie, or put him next to Gene, certainly he was not in the ballpark. So we just couldn't get the mileage out of the character — the marriage of the character and the performer was just limited.

In fact, there was only one episode in which Montgomery's character carried the story, and that was "Come One, Come All," in which his mother, played by guest star Gwen Verdon, takes over the supervision of a parent's night event — much to Montgomery's chagrin and the exasperation of everyone else. The only other episode in which Montgomery was at all featured in the dramatic through-line of the narrative was "The Crazies," where he and Doris agree to tell the truth for an entire day; but it was still Doris' actions that ultimately effected the furthering of the plot.

P.R. Paul left the show and after several years returned briefly to television in 2000 in the short-lived series *Falcone* on CBS. In the interim he had turned his interests away from acting and in a totally different direction when he and a partner opened a successful candy company that sells a very popular brand of fudge. I recently saw P.R., who now goes by his full name of Paul Ray Rosenbaum, being interviewed on a Los Angeles television newscast and describing how popular his fudge candy was with a number of Hollywood celebrities. It was nice to hear that he was doing okay.

More changes had taken place in the production staff, as our original unit production manager, Hap Weyman, had left the show, and Gene Law had been moved up from first assistant director to take his place. Armando Huerta had moved up from second AD to become one of the alternating first assistant directors with Denny Salvaryn. For those who

***Fame* cast for second season. Top row: Morgan Stevens, Lori Singer, Lee Curreri; middle row: Gene Anthony Ray, Carol Mayo Jenkins, Albert Haue, Erica Gimpel; bottom row: Valerie Landsburg, Debbie Allen, Carlo Imperato.**

aren't familiar with this terminology, the unit production manager's job is to supervise the budgeting and scheduling of each episode, and to represent the studio's interest by seeing that the filming stays on schedule and on budget. He is in charge of hiring certain production personnel, approving equipment rental costs, and authorizing all production costs that might exceed the original budget. His immediate superior is the producer, in our case that would be Mel Swope during the first two seasons, whose position is sometimes referred to as the line producer.

The first assistant director's job includes breaking down the script and setting up a shooting schedule, running the set and making sure that the crew is accomplishing the assigned work within the allotted time, and approving the daily call sheets that tell the cast and crew what scenes are to be done the following day and which cast members will be involved. He or she may also direct the atmosphere players that supply the background action in a scene. There are usually two first ADs on each series who alternate episodes, so that one can be preparing while the other is filming.

The second assistant director's responsibilities include, first of all, helping the first AD in running the set, creating the call sheets for the following day's work, making sure that the atmosphere people are available when needed, and helping to direct them in large crowd scenes.

There was also a change needed in the editorial department, since I had been promoted to associate producer, and that required someone to replace me. I had been impressed with Paul Rubell's work for quite some time, and I recommended to Bill Blinn that he take over as the third editor. Bill had also had his eye on Paul and thoroughly agreed, so Paul left the assistants' ranks to become a full-fledged film editor. It was the beginning of an illustrious career, for Paul would go on to be nominated for two Emmy Awards (for his editing on *My Name Is Bill W* and *Andersonville*), as well as two Academy Awards (for *The Insider* and *Collateral*). He would also win an American Cinema Editors Award for *Andersonville*, and be nominated for four additional ACE Awards, a BAFTA Award and two Satellite Awards. Paul would also co-edit such blockbuster films as *Miami Vice* and *Transformers*.

Upstairs in the producers' offices more changes had occurred. Parke Perine, who was giving up the associate producer's post, was moving into another office to work exclusively as a writer. With an order for 23 episodes, Bill Blinn needed a lot of scripts written, and he knew he could rely on Perine. Explained Perine:

Bill always had a theory that if he could find a writer that wrote the way he approved of, then he'd put him in a room and just let him think about it. I would sit there, I wasn't on salary, and I'd think about it, and think about it and I'd get an idea, and I'd go to him and I'd say, "I'd like to write this story," and he'd say, "Spell it out." And we'd go back and beat, beat, beat, beat, beat, like that, and he'd say, "Go write it," and that's that. God!! Nobody ever had it this good, nobody has!

Perine would write three episodes in Season Two and two more the following season to become the highest contributing writer during the first three seasons, with a total of seven scripts. Only Bill Blinn himself, who wrote eleven episodes, exceeded him.

So once again I was Bill Blinn's associate producer, and I moved upstairs into the producers' unit to share an office suite with the new story editor, Christopher Beaumont.

Chris Beaumont's father was Charles Beaumont, a well known writer of science fiction in the sixties who was perhaps best known for the 22 episodes he wrote for Rod Serling's *The Twilight Zone.* "My father was a

Christopher Beaumont.

writer and I grew up around writers," explained Beaumont. "I always wanted to be a writer, but my life was roadblocked because at age nineteen things changed dramatically and I needed to make some money." Chris' father died tragically at the age of 38 in 1967 at the Motion Picture Country Home of the effects of a mysterious brain disease. His mother died of cancer in 1971, leaving Chris with the responsibility of raising his two younger sisters and a six-year-old brother all by himself. His immediate challenge was to find a way to earn a living and still be there for his siblings. Beaumont recalled:

> A friend of the family knew a casting director and said that they cast a lot of commercials. So I went to a casting call, and a wonderful thing happened — I got the job. It wasn't really acting — it was a commercial — and I had three lines, and they were really casting a look that they were looking for. Years later, after I started producing, I realized my value — which was that I wasn't a great actor, I was a good actor, but I showed up on time, I knew my lines and I never gave anybody real trouble; and they hired me over and over again for twelve years. And it was great, it was the perfect job for me because I had three kids to raise, and I was doing it by myself and I couldn't really go to a straight job.

Chris Beaumont continued to make a living as an actor until his brother, the youngest of his siblings, reached the age of eighteen and went off to college, at which point he decided it was time to try his hand at something else. After spending a couple of years at a commercial production company directing promos for local TV stations all over the country, Beaumont took a job tending bar at a local bistro so that he could write spec scripts in his free time. "I tended bar for a year and a half at the Rive Gauche," Beaumont said, referring to the restaurant and bar in the San Fernando Valley. "Everybody from executives to carpenters and everything in between went there — high class, low class, people that would stay for hours and open up. It was a great bar. It was great fun and it gave me great material." Beaumont finally got one of his spec scripts to an agent, who in turn sent it to Jane Rosenthal at CBS. Rosenthal, who later co-founded Tribeca Productions with Robert De Niro, hired Beaumont to do a rewrite on a movie-of-the-week that CBS was developing. Then something interesting happened, as Beaumont explained:

> Bill Blinn was talking to Jane Rosenthal about something — to this day I don't know what they were talking about — but two days later I got a call from Blinn saying, "Hey, I was talking to Jane Rosenthal and she likes the work you're doing on the movie-of-the-week. You want to come in and talk about *Fame*?" I'd seen a couple of episodes, but I didn't watch it every week

so I hadn't studied it, I'd just seen it as a viewer. I remember calling a friend of mine, my VCR was broken and it was going to be on that night, a desperate call to him, "Please, tape it tonight because I've got to pitch in three days and I haven't seen the show in a month!" I remember freaking out over what the characters' names were. I did get some help from Donna Lee. I met Donna when I came in to pitch, and she gave me some scripts. I read all the scripts, but I wanted a visual feel of the show too, so my buddy taped the show and I went over and picked up the tape and watched it. I pitched some stories and Bill picked one.

Beaumont would write a *Fame* episode during the show's summer hiatus, and on the basis of that, Bill Blinn called him back into the office and offered him the story editor's post. "I had no idea what a story editor did," laughed Beaumont. "I was still tending bar during the day, moving my shift and trying to get other people to cover for me. Once Bill hired me as story editor and I knew that I was going to get a paycheck, that's when I gave them two hours notice." Chris Beaumont would remain *Fame*'s story editor for the next two years, supervising the writing of 47 episodes while writing four original episodes of his own.

Chris and I found that we were sharing a secretary who looked as if the studio had been built around her, and whose attitude reflected her longevity. In other words, she didn't give a shit about *Fame*; all she cared about was when she went to lunch and when she went home, and that wasn't going to work for us. The problem was how to get rid of her, short of slipping poison into her coffee cup, since the studio's secretarial department was very protective of their veterans. It took several weeks and some helpful intervention from Bill Blinn's assistant, Donna Lee, but we finally got a replacement that shared our enthusiasm for the show.

There were a couple of seasoned veterans who directed a number of episodes during the second and third seasons. Their names were Marc Daniels and William Claxton, and their credits were most impressive. Marc Daniels, who began his directing career in live television, directed 33 episodes of *I Love Lucy*, starting with the first episode of the first season, and then went on to direct almost 200 other television shows, including *Bonanza*, *Star Trek* and *Mission Impossible*. Bill Claxton began his career as a film editor in the early forties and then started directing B movies at Twentieth Century–Fox in 1948. Claxton directed over 100 episodes of *Bonanza* and *Little House on the Prairie*, as well as over fifty other television shows. Ted Zachary remembered Claxton fondly:

> Bill Claxton, who did *Bonanza* and all those great old westerns, was suddenly doing a show with a bunch of little high school kids — directing Gene

Anthony Ray and Lee Curreri and all these people dancing in the streets of MGM, and he was terrific. He was this feisty little guy who'd been dealing with Hoss Cartwright, and now he was dealing with high school kids. He reminded me of that actor Jimmy Gleason — this thin, wiry, Irish guy who took no guff from anyone.

Both Claxton and Daniels had worked for Bill Blinn on *Eight Is Enough*, and between them would direct over a dozen episodes of *Fame*. One of my favorite episodes that Bill Claxton directed was a script that Valerie Landsburg and I wrote for Season Three, but that's a story for later.

Some years after *Fame* ended and I had become a director, Bill Claxton and I ran into each other at Universal Studios. They were about to revive that old staple *Lassie*, and Bill and I were both there to meet with the producers. My first indication that this was not the usual interview was to find a half-dozen directors seated in the waiting room. Generally directors come in one at a time to a meeting, not in what we refer to as "a cattle call." Bill came out of the producer's office and, upon seeing me, walked over, grabbed my arm and whispered, "You're not going to want to do this." When the producer, who was so rude that he didn't even bother to turn down the sound on the television set that was playing in his office, explained the bizarre manner in which he visualized filming the series, I knew that Bill was right. In fact, I later called him to say that I'd turned down the offer. My wife and I remained friends with Bill and his wife until his death in 1996.

Five, Six, Seven, Eight

The first episode of the new season came and went without a hitch. Several of our dance company, including Michael DeLorenzo and Stephanie Williams, were featured in the episode and given dialogue to speak, their first names becoming established as the names of their characters. Soon Bronwyn Thomas, a talented ballet dancer and sister of *The Waltons'* Richard Thomas, would also step out of the ensemble and take on a featured role.

The associate producer's responsibilities were mainly in the post-production area, which included running the dailies each day with the other producers and consulting with them during the editing process. This meant that I spent a lot of my time in screening rooms. I remember one day, when we arrived to view our dailies, being surprised to see that several seats had been removed from one of the rows and a special wide seat constructed. Someone explained that this seat was to accommodate Luciano Pavarotti's enormous girth when he would come to this screening room to view his dailies on *Yes, Giorgio*, a romantic comedy that he was making for MGM. The film, directed by Franklin Schaffner (who had won an Oscar in 1971 for directing *Patton*), was soundly panned by the critics and the public alike, and became Pavarotti's only venture into feature films.

My primary responsibility as associate producer was to supervise the re-recording (or dubbing, as it was often called) of the soundtracks for each episode. After the final cut of each show was approved by the producers, Mel Swope and I would run the show with the composer, William Goldstein, and the sound and music editors to determine where background music was needed and sound effects and dialogue corrections would be required. A week later we would all gather in one of MGM's re-recording sound stages, where I would supervise, with the help of head mixer Aaron Rochin, the combining of the various music and sound effects tracks

The *Fame* dancers, with Stephanie Williams (second row, far right), Michael DeLorenzo (seated second from left) and Bronwyn Thomas (seated fourth from left) (Donna Lee Collection).

into a final mix. The next step was always the most unpleasant for me, as I would then have to run the final mix for our line producer, Mel Swope, who would inevitably give me endless notes on what he wanted corrected, most of which were minor, time-consuming changes that no one would notice in the final analysis. Nevertheless, I would then have to return to the re-recording stage and make these corrections, whether I agreed with them or not (*mine not to question why, mine but to do or die*). Although, later, others did question the unwarranted costs involved in making these changes, and I suspect that had a bearing on why Mel Swope was replaced after the second season. All things considered, we functioned pretty well, especially since we managed it with just one executive producer, one producer and one associate producer for the first three years of *Fame*'s existence and still managed to turn out an episode every seven days, with three musical numbers per episode. In later years there could be as many as seven producers, associate producers and executive producers on the show, and I'm not sure that it improved the quality of the show one iota. I'm constantly amazed by the proliferation of credits in today's marketplace, where one can see as many as a dozen or more producer credits on any given television show. I think that the most ludicrous credit I ever saw was the title "executive associate producer" that appeared in the end credits of a television movie a few years ago.

It didn't take long for another tragedy to befall the *Fame* production unit. Gene Law, who had been our first assistant director during Season One and had been promoted only recently to unit production manager for the new season, suffered a fatal heart attack one weekend. I had been talking to Gene the previous Friday at the Special Education School location we were using for our second episode, "Your Own Song," and he had seemed fine. We were all shocked to hear the news when we reported for work on Monday morning. Gene was a character, and we all loved him. He always wore outrageous clothes — bright colors and funny hats. As Bill Blinn explained, "Gene's trademark was funny outfits, outrageous Hawaiian shirts, stupid hats and quilted or patterned slacks. He always dressed silly to keep it loose on the set." Many of the cast members and the staff held a memorial service for Gene at Bill Blinn's house. We gathered outside by the pool, and Debbie Allen said a few words. When she was finished, she added, "Gene, this is for you," and jumped into the pool with her clothes on. Without a moment's hesitation everyone else jumped into the pool after her. It was a fitting tribute for a great guy.

A new production manager joined the show by the name of Ken Swor. Ken had been a high school teacher before he joined the Directors Guild, and he still displayed a certain scholarly demeanor. I remember Ken as a pipe-smoking, soft-spoken guy with a very dry sense of humor, who knew his business and ran the production department with efficiency. Ken would stay with us for two seasons and then move on to become the associate producer and then line producer of the second version of the TV series *The Twilight Zone.* Ken would continue working as a producer and production manager, alternating between films and television, until his death in 2004.

During Season One we'd utilized only two other guest stars beside Gwen Verdon, and they were Ray Walston and Art Carney in the "A Big Finish" episode, a charming story of two old vaudevillians living in the school's basement that was directed by the English character actor Robert Douglas, who had made a name for himself playing heavies in costume epochs such as *Ivanhoe* and *Prisoner of Zenda.* However, in Season Two there seemed to be a mob of guest stars who descended upon us, including Jimmy Osmond, Glynn Turman, Richard Simmons, Marge Champion, Tom Sullivan, Greg Evigan, Nancy Walker, Betty White and Brenda Vaccaro. We were still fighting for an audience, and the studio reasoned that inserting well-known personalities into the show might help bring up the numbers, so the budget was adjusted to accommodate the additional salaries, and Bill Blinn and his writers set out to create stories for them to appear in. Some of my favorites were "Your Own Song," written by Leah Markus, in which Jimmy Osmond was introduced as Troy Phillips, a mentally challenged student new to the school. Jimmy came back in "Love Is the Question," also by Leah Markus, in which Troy develops a crush on Lori Singer's Julie. Another favorite was "Solo Song," written by Linda Elstad, where performer Tom Sullivan guest starred as a blind substitute teacher who clashes with Lydia over preparations for a school performance. Sullivan wrote and performed two songs in this episode, which was ably directed by Mel Swope. A few months earlier Sullivan's autobiography, "If You Could See What I Hear," had been made into a TV movie, with Lori Singer's brother Mark playing Tom Sullivan.

At the beginning of the new season, Bill Blinn went back to New York to hold casting interviews. Rumor had it that at one of these sessions he saw and rejected a young woman who, in his opinion, just didn't meet his standards. Blinn admits that the story is true:

> I went back to New York for an open casting call on the second season when we were at the height of our teenage idolatry. I don't know how many people went through; a lot of them went through twice. They would go in another room, change jackets and come through again. At one of the auditions, there was a young woman who tried out named Madonna something, something, something. And I mean the woman has certainly proven herself, but I just said she's not for us. Maybe that's the mid-western in me, or maybe that's what she was, I have no idea.

Her full name was, of course, Madonna Louise Veronica Ciccone; she was the future "Material Girl," and Bill Blinn's been hearing about his decision ever since. "Yes," he smiled ruefully, "I did pass on Madonna."

My contract, when I signed on as associate producer, included a commitment for me to write an episode, and as soon as I could I came up with an idea and presented it to Bill Blinn. I had seen a program on one of the cable networks about some famous African American tap dancers of the thirties and forties, and it started me wondering what had happened to them. That led to a story, which I called "Star Quality," about a young boy who sneaks into the High School of Performing Arts to spy on the dance classes. He is already a very talented tap dancer whose father, once one of the tap dancing legends of the forties, now sits at home, a forgotten and bitter man. The boy has grown up hating tap dancing for what it has done to his father and wants to learn other forms of dance. Leroy tries to make the boy realize he should be proud of his heritage and of his talent, and eventually he and the boy make a pact to teach each other what they know. For the big production number at the end of the show, where Leroy shames the boy into joining him onstage for the finale, someone came up with the brilliant idea of re-creating the "Singin' in the Rain" number from the old Gene Kelly musical. The music department unearthed Conrad Salinger and Skip Martin's original arrangements, complete with Roger Eden's memorable "doodedoo do-doodedoo do" opening signature, and we pre-recorded the orchestral track on the very sound stage where the MGM orchestra had recorded the original back in 1952. I remember standing in the booth listening to the orchestra playing and feeling a chill run up my spine. With a little imagination I could almost envision standing there with Kelly, Stanley Donen and Arthur Freed when the original was first recorded. Although the Kelly version had been shot on the "East Side Street" on MGM's Lot Two, and ours took place on Stage 28 in the auditorium set of the High School of Performing Arts, we did include the famous lamp post and the umbrella for Gene Anthony Ray to use in homage to Gene Kelly. There was a big-city street scene on a painted backdrop at the rear of the stage, with the buildings outlined with flickering lights, and the rain effect was created by plastic streamers hanging from the rigging. Carlo Imperato played the policeman who watches Gene's dance with a distrustful eye, and Albert Hague's Mr. Shorofsky conducted the school orchestra in the pit below the stage.

For the subplot I came up with the idea of having an actor who makes his living doing television commercials invited to speak to the drama class. Coco dismissively announces that what he does doesn't constitute acting, and to prove himself, the actor movingly recites a passage from Shakespeare, forcing an embarrassed Coco to apologize. The selection of Arte Johnson as the actor was a brilliant casting decision — not mine, I hasten to add, but that of the director's, Gwen Arner, and casting director Meg Liberman. Johnson, who had made his name playing various silly characters on *Rowan & Martin's Laugh In*, fit the role perfectly and did a very commendable job of delivering the "What a piece of work is man!" soliloquy from *Hamlet*. Gwen Arner had directed a number of *The Waltons* episodes and had appeared as an actress in *Stickin' Together*, the Blinn/Thorpe pilot we had shot in Hawaii. She also had appeared in *A Question of Love*, a television movie that Bill Blinn wrote and Jerry Thorpe directed about a lesbian couple, played by Gena Rowlands and Jane Alexander, who become embroiled in a prolonged court battle with the father of Rowlands' children. I had the pleasure of being the associate producer on that one as well.

The fact that Albert Hague was an accomplished musician, composer and lecturer before he ever joined *Fame* was something that he never hesitated to let you know. However, Albert's far from insignificant ego never got in the way of his innate kindness. I remember one day during the second season, when I was on the looping stage recording some voice-overs with him, I happened to mention that my wife was visiting her family in Pennsylvania. Albert asked what my plans were for dinner, and when I replied that I had none, he immediately invited me to join his wife Renee and him for dinner at their Marina City condo in Marina del Rey. The twin-towered Marina City complex had its own private restaurant, and that's where Albert, Renee and I spent a delightful couple of hours together. It was that night that he told me the story of the unfortunate production of *Miss Moffat*, Emlyn Williams' musical adaptation of his play *The Corn Is Green* that Joshua Logan originally intended to stage, with Mary Martin in the title role. Williams had written some sample lyrics that Logan especially liked, and he asked Albert if he would be willing to write some songs using Williams' lyrics. According to Logan, Albert's answer was "Just give me the lyrics and get out of the way." When Mary Martin's husband became ill and she decided against doing the play, it was offered to Bette Davis, who had played the role in the 1945 movie. Davis' professional reputation at the time was somewhat tarnished by two previous disastrous stage productions that had failed to open. Despite serious reservations, she was signed to do the play, and a young actor named Dorian Harewood was cast as Morgan Evans. The rehearsal period was like a roller-coaster ride, with Davis brilliant one minute and lost in insecurities the next. The insecurities began to take on the form of physical ailments, with Davis retreating to her bed, complaining of severe back pain. As they drew closer to opening night, Albert and Emlyn Williams were writing new songs to accommodate changes in the play, and Bette Davis was growing more and more nervous. After a couple of fairly successful previews in Philadelphia, with everyone beginning to think they might have a hit, Davis suddenly announced that her health wouldn't allow her to continue. There was no

choice but to close the play and send everyone back to New York. At their
final meeting, with the entire cast present except for Bette Davis, several
cast members asked to perform one of the new songs that had never been
presented in front of an audience. It was the last time that any of the songs
were performed.

Albert Hague wrote some truly beautiful songs, a fact that I learned
first-hand when, some years later, after *Fame* had long since disappeared
into reruns, I directed a production of a new play, for which he had written the music, entitled *The Lady in Question*, based on the life of
writer/humorist Dorothy Parker. It was really a one woman piece; we had
an actress playing and singing Dorothy Parker, and four male dancers who
were her backup and also played all of the men in her life. Albert's songs,
with lyrics by the author of the libretto Tom O'Malley, weren't showstop-
pers, but they were melodic and pleasant to the ear and worked well within
the context of the play.

"Young and Foolish," the most popular song from Albert's hit musical *Plain and Fancy*, lent its name to a charming cabaret act that Albert
and his wife Renee Orin developed and appeared in all over the country,
including Carnegie Hall in New York. Albert would tell people that the
show, filled with comedy and his wonderful songs, and entitled *Still Young
and Foolish*, was "really about our lives." Albert Hague died of cancer at

The Lady in Question company. Author and lyricist Tom O'Malley (rear right center) stands beside me (rear left center), looking toward composer Albert Hague
on the end, who stands next to choreographer Lonnie Burr.

the age of 81 on November 12, 2001, at Daniel Freeman Medical Center in Marina del Rey. His wife Renee had died the previous year.

Because of his dancer's background, Bob Scheerer developed a rapport with Debbie Allen that showed to good advantage in episode after episode, but none more clearly than in "Not in Kansas Anymore," our version of *The Wizard of Oz.* Paul Rubell, the newest film editor on the staff, was the one who came up with the idea to do this show. Rubell remembers:

> The editors would often have lunch together at a big round table in the MGM commissary. One day, Bill Blinn sat down and was bemoaning the fact that he had one more episode to write but was blocked, fresh out of ideas. As he spoke, I glanced at a vintage 1939 poster of *The Wizard of Oz.* There was an uncomfortable silence, none of us knew what to say to Bill about his problem, and I blurted out that since we were an MGM show he should do an episode based on *The Wizard of Oz.* More silence, so I just started making it up; the kids could be rehearsing the musical number, one of the characters brought her dog to school, the dog breaks free, she runs after it, slips and falls, hits her head and she's Dorothy transported to Oz.

Bill Blinn loved Rubell's idea, and a script was quickly fashioned that was titled "Not in Kansas Anymore" in which Doris is the one who falls and hits her head and is transported back to the Land of Oz. Bob Scheerer and Debbie Allen came up with some wonderfully inventive stagings for several of the classic songs from the old feature, including "Over the Rainbow," "If I Only Had a Brain," "We're Off to See the Wizard" and "Ding Dong the Witch is Dead." Everyone agreed that the opening segment should be in black and white, just as in the film, and Bud Hayes, who was editing the show, and I worked closely with the MGM optical department to properly bleed the color out of the film and come up with a good transition from black and white to color when Doris opens the classroom door and steps out into the Land of Oz. Ira Diamond, our art director, redressed the school to become a magical setting, and our composer, William Goldstein, wrote some wonderful incidental music to set the mood (for which they would both receive Emmy nominations). It was probably the most difficult episode we'd worked on up to that point. I remember we had to keep everyone until after midnight one night to complete the filming of a tricky dance sequence and Bob Scheerer, who was generally one of the easiest-going guys in the world, practically tore my head off one time when I had to pressure him to complete his work with Bud Hayes on the editing so that we could turn the show over to the music and sound people on schedule. Bill Blinn remembers this episode affectionately:

> Probably my favorite episode was *The Wizard of Oz* episode "Not in Kansas Anymore." That was so much fun to do. Everyone was doing a different thing, the set was turned into something brand spanking new that it had never looked like before, and I also think you could see the kids respond to the new spin. You know, Gene got to be the Scarecrow, and Carlo got to be the Cowardly Lion, and Lee Curreri was the Tin Man. Debbie just had a ball, and her dancers just loved being the Munchkins.

Debbie indeed looked fabulous in her blond wig, Carol Mayo Jenkins had a ball all painted green as the evil witch, and Albert Hague, who played the Wizard, was hardly recognizable with his beard curled. But Carlo Imperato, in his lion costume, had a far different reaction than Blinn remembered. He spoke about it while being interviewed for the BBC reunion special in 2003:

> Why were we doing *The Wizard of Oz*? That was the biggest joke for me. A lot of people talk about it, and I'm sure it was very entertaining for an audience, but from an actor's point of view I just though that the show could have been more hard core. It could have really shown what was out there on the streets and what young people, young actors do.

Paul Rubell also had one regret: "I very much wanted to edit the episode, but it fell to another editor in the rotation. I did share a story credit with Bill, though, and I received a few residual checks."

I think one could say that "Not in Kansas Anymore" turned out to be one of the most popular episodes in the entire series. I remember that my young grandson, who must have been around five or six at the time, insisted on watching my tape copy of the show every time he came to visit. This went on for at least the next five years or so, and as much as I loved the episode, I did grow tired of viewing it after a time. On the morning of February 25, 1983, the morning after "Not in Kansas Anymore" aired on NBC, *Fame* was in 59th place in the Neilson ratings for the week. *Magnum P.I.* was cleaning our clock and not showing any signs of letting up.

8

Across the Pond

Fame had premiered on the BBC in the summer of 1982, and by the end of the year, with a strong following of 11 million regular viewers in the United Kingdom alone, the success of *Fame* in the European market seemed to be far outpacing what was happening in the United States. As if to support this phenomenon, an album of songs from the first season had been released in England and rose almost instantaneously to the top of the charts. Produced for RCA Records by Barry Fassman, one of the composers for Charles Koppleman's The Entertainment Company, the album had been recorded in 1982 at various studios around Los Angeles and contained ten songs, including "Starmaker" and "I Still Believe in Me," all sung by the original cast members. Over the next few years there would be a total of seven albums produced and released, with varying degrees of success.

To celebrate the Christmas holidays, everyone on the crew received a gift of a beautiful satin jacket with the *Fame* logo on the back and our names on the front. I couldn't decide whether to put Mike or Michael, so I ended up just putting my initials on the front. I was able to order another jacket for my wife, and Katie wore it proudly to work to show it off. Bob Scheerer gave everyone white porcelain coffee cups with the *Fame* logo and their first names on it. NBC sent over one of their satin jackets with the NBC logo on it, but I don't think I wore it more than a couple of times. I still have both jackets stuck in the back of a closet somewhere, and the coffee cup is in our kitchen cabinet (and although the *Fame* logo is faded somewhat, I still use it every now and then for a morning cup of coffee).

The *Fame* company took a three-week hiatus from filming over the Christmas holidays, but not everyone took a break. Those of us in post-production continued working, and some of the cast members also had another job to do. The initial album's enormous success couldn't be

75

My *Fame* memorabilia.

ignored, and MGM, in conjunction with the RCA and BBC record companies, decided to send the cast off on a three-city tour of the British Isles. So when *Fame* began its Christmas hiatus from filming, everyone who had appeared on the album, with the exception of Valerie Landsburg (who decided that she'd rather spend Christmas with her future husband's family), left for England, accompanied by the full dance company. Their first concert was in Brighton, and Donna Lee, who was functioning as the group's tour manager, remembers it well. "Our out-of-town tryout was Brighton, and that's when I got the first taste of how big we were," she declared. "Oh my gosh, you would have thought we were the Beatles. They had to set up barricades, and there were Bobbies everywhere." In the building where the group was performing in Brighton, the public could peek into the wardrobe and dressing room area from a parking structure across the street. The fans quickly figured out that they could spy on their idols as they were dressing. "So we were getting screams," recalled Donna Lee. "And Gene entertained everyone across the road with an impromptu dance. They were screaming, 'Leroy!!'" The group did twelve concerts in ten days in three different cities during the Christmas break. "'Whirlwind,' 'busy?'" declared Donna Lee. "That didn't even cover it." From Brighton, the tour moved to London and the Royal Albert Hall, where the cast was to perform on New Years Eve to a sell-out crowd. Between the afternoon and the evening performance a typical English meal was served that the cast found rather unappetizing, particularly Carlo Imperato. "I remember we were served some dinner, and the dressing was like meatloaf," recalls Donna Lee. "And Carlo, who was a doll, said, 'What the hell is this?' I said it's dressing, and Carlo shook his head, 'Not in Brooklyn!!'"

While they were in London the cast stayed at the Royal Garden Hotel on Kensington High Street. It seemed that the press couldn't get enough of "The Kids from Fame," and between performances they were deluged with requests for interviews. Everybody was pretty much exhausted by then, and Donna Lee was making tea with lemon and honey for everybody, especially Debbie Allen. Nobody wanted to get sick, as they were all looking forward to the New Year's Eve party that was being given for them by BBC and RCA Records. The cast album had sold over one million copies in England, and the record companies were celebrating by hosting this party. On December 30 Debbie, Gene, Carlo and Lee appeared at a hastily-called press conference. After the usual flurry of fan magazine-type questions, such as "What is your impression of England?" Gene Anthony Ray was asked if he was enjoying himself. Gene replied, "This is my first stage performance ever, and I can tell you it has been an experience and a half!" He was probably expressing the feelings of every one of his fellow cast members, with the exception of Debbie Allen, who had certainly already earned her stripes on Broadway.

However new the experience of performing in front of a live audience may have been for "The Kids from Fame," it didn't stop their adoring fans from giving them a standing ovation at the end of every performance. In fact, after the New Year's Eve show the adulation overflowed into the street outside the Royal Albert Hall, where a huge crowd had gathered, and the security people were concerned for everyone's safety. "The security people came in and gave us instructions on how to get from the Hall to the bus," remembers Donna Lee. "It was probably only fifteen or twenty feet, but we had to be instructed on what not to do. They said do not stop and shake hands, do not sign autographs, and keep moving because there was so little room to control the crowd. We flew as best we could in that fifteen feet, and it got so that there was a bottleneck." One of the secu-

Erica Gimpel, Carlo Imperato, Debbie Allena and Lee Curreri in London, with Big Ben in the background (Donna Lee Collection).

rity guards pushed dancer Marguerite Pomerhn Derricks to make her move faster, and she fell, hitting her knee on the step of the bus. As soon as they returned to their rooms at the hotel, Donna Lee examined Marguerite's knee and saw that it would need stitches. "It was bleeding like you can't imagine," she stated. "So I called down to the desk and said that we needed to take her to Emergency, and the desk said, 'You do not want to go into an Emergency Room in London on New Year's Eve. We will get you the House Doctor.'

Marguerite, who had trained at the National Ballet School of Canada, was sharing a room with fellow dancer Eartha Robinson, who, according to Donna Lee, seemed to be more upset than anyone else:

> God love her, she was going, "Oh my God, you'll never dance again! Oh my God, it's horrible ... it's horrible!" But that's how close they were. Any injury of any kind to a dancer is terrifying. Meanwhile, everybody's knocking at the door, asking, how is she? ... how is she? Every few minutes I'd pick up the phone and it would be the press, who had got wind of this. "One of the *Fame* dancers was injured. Will never dance again, bla, bla, bla." Finally the doctor comes, and he's in a tuxedo, and he's mad because we had to pull him away from a dinner party. He looked a little like that '30s character actor, Eric Blore. Eartha is just, she's borderline hysterical, and the doctor said, "All right, we are going to have to stitch her and I have to have quiet. Everybody out! Stop that knocking and take the phone off the hook, because I have to stitch her and I don't have a lot of anesthetic." I took Eartha by the shoulders and said, "You've got to stand outside the door and not let anyone knock. You stand there and you literally bar the door." So Eartha goes outside and stands by the door. I could hear her crying out there. The doctor did eight stitches, and Marguerite was a trooper. It was scary. We got her dressed, and meanwhile, everybody else has gone on to the party. We're the last ones to go, and some of the press knew that she hadn't appeared yet. I'd promised her we'd get her there by midnight, and we were walking out of the hotel, and the press is waiting, asking how she is. We told them it was nothing, just a little scratch, everything's fine. "Oh, will she dance tomorrow?" I remember saying, "Gentlemen, there are two things the Kids from *Fame* never miss. The first one is a performance and the second one is a party; now please excuse us." And off we went.

There were over three hundred partygoers at the New Year's Eve event, held in the main banquet room at the Kensington Close Hotel, including invited guests from the record business, members of the cast and crew, and a few celebrities as well. Boy George and members of his Culture Club band were there, as well as members of the British rockabilly band the Jets and the pop group Brotherhood of Man. The room was set up like a disco, with flashing lights and a D.J. playing hits of the day, including some of the songs from *Fame*. Everybody danced as if they hadn't already danced enough on stage, but then I personally have never seen a musician or a dancer that didn't love to jam after a performance; it's their way of getting the adrenalin in their system to slow down. Gene Anthony Ray had to pass on the dancing, as he had a pulled ligament and needed to save himself for the final performances the next day. After greeting 1983 with the chiming of Big Ben over the loudspeakers and the singing of "Auld Lang Syne," the cast returned to their hotel and packed for their early morning train ride to Birmingham, their final performance destination before returning home.

Terry Sanders, a documentarian who, in 1962 with his brother Dennis, won an Oscar for his short film *A Time Out of War*, had directed the filming of all of the concerts and backstage activity throughout the British tour, and now put together a one-hour special. It was edited, sweetened and laid down at a post-production house away from the MGM studios, so neither the *Fame* editors nor I had anything to do with the final product. This didn't make us unhappy at all, since the Christmas hiatus had put us behind on delivering shows to the network, and we didn't need any extra responsibilities. Sanders filmed host George Burns wandering around the school set and edited him into segments between various production numbers performed in England. The special, titled *The Kids from Fame in Concert*, aired on NBC in our regular time slot on March 3, 1983. John J. O'Connor, the reviewer for the *New York Times*, took some pretty big swipes at us:

> It would be nice to report that *The Kids from Fame* conclusively demonstrates that American audiences should take a cue from their British cousins. In fact, *Fame* is one of the better weekly series available on the current schedule ... but while these performers may be credible within the context of a scenario portraying them as fledgling actors and singers, they are way out of their depth in what is meant to be a slickly professional production. With the exception of the seasoned Ms. Allen ... the *Fame* kids generally seem amateurish in this instance.... Obviously the kids from *Fame* have connected solidly with their British fans, but this show is not likely to help the ratings of the regular series over here.

The Kids from Fame in Concert was our twentieth episode, which left only three more episodes before the end of the Second Season. Two would be written by Parke Perine and the other by Chris Beaumont. Perine's first, "...Help from My Friends," dealt with teenage suicide and had some interesting guest stars, including Lee Montgomery, who had befriended Ben the rat in the sequel to *Willard*, and Bill Blinn favorite Connie Needham, returning not as her character from last season's "To Soar and Never Falter," but as the potential suicide victim Kelly Hayden. Needham's Kelly Hayden character would be featured in both of the final two episodes. The director for this episode was an old acquaintance of Bill Blinn's from *The Rookies*, Georg Stanford Brown. Georg, who had also directed a chapter

Derrick Brice and Marguerite Derricks whooping it up at London's Stringfellows Club (Donna Lee Collection).

of *The Lazarus Syndrome* for me a few years before, was well suited for this particular episode since it was heavy on plot and light on music. In fact, a beautiful song written by our own Albert Hague and Allan Sherman, called "Light One Candle," was the one big musical moment in the show.

Chris Beaumont's "Ending on a High Note" was an intentionally lightweight episode about Leroy and Danny getting conned into coaching a church basketball team and almost missing an important school function. One interesting bit of trivia: Keith Coogan, who played Andy, was Jackie Coogan's grandson, and all of you movie buffs know that Jackie Coogan was Charlie Chaplin's companion in *The Kid*, Chaplin's first full-length feature film that he directed in 1921, right? No, then perhaps you'll remember Coogan as Uncle Fester on *The Addams Family*. Keith changed his last name from Mitchell to Coogan after he had played one of the kids in *The MacKenzies of Paradise Cove*. Oh, and speaking of Hawaii, Jack Bender, who directed this episode, now spends a great deal of his time in Hawaii as one of the producers, and frequent director, of ABC's hit series

Carol Mayo Jenkins, Morgan Stevens and Albert Hague (Donna Lee Collection).

Lost. Bender had also directed the *Fame* episode that finally acknowledged Mr. Crandall's death, "A Tough Act to Follow," which featured a subplot involving the new drama teacher, Mr. Reardon's, alienated relationship with his father.

Parke Perine wrote the final episode for the season, called "U.N.

Week," a study of narrow-mindedness that develops when another school, invited to participate in a special program at the High School of Performing Arts, behaves condescendingly toward our students. The subplot involved false rumors spreading throughout the school that Lydia and David Reardon, the school's new drama teacher, were having an affair. This was an opportunity to feature Morgan Stevens, who had arrived late in the second season to replace Michael Thoma as the drama teacher.

Morgan was born in Knoxville, Tennessee; he was extremely good looking in a boyish sort of way, tall with a shock of blond hair and a charming personality. Before he joined *Fame* he had played a recurring character in a number of episodes of *The Waltons* and had appeared in several other programs, such as *Quincy, ME* and *One Day at a Time*. The character he played on *Fame*, David Reardon, served as an excellent sounding board for his fellow teachers, as well as giving the writers an opportunity to exploit the non-musical aspects of the school. Morgan later went over to Universal and did a number of *Murder, She Wrote* episodes for producer Peter Fischer. Fischer then cast him in an episode of a new series he had co-created with Richard Levinson and William Link called *Blacke's Magic*, which, by coincidence, I was hired to direct. In "Death Goes to the Movies," Morgan played the innocently accused murder suspect with his usual style and brio, and then cooperated further by spending an additional day filming a second unit chase sequence for me that I needed to go out and complete after we had wrapped the episode. Morgan even tried his hand at writing an episode of *Fame*, and I will discuss that in a later chapter, but for now it's time to talk about one of our biggest triumphs.

9

And the Winner *Is*

It was an unbearably hot summer day in the middle of July, and we were filming in a dingy alleyway in downtown Los Angeles when Donna Lee joined us and handed each of us a piece of paper. It was a press release from MGM Television announcing that the Academy of Television Arts and Sciences had released its nominations for the 1981–1982 season, and *Fame* had received twelve Emmy nominations. I was astonished to see that I had personally picked up two nominations — one for designing the main title and the other for my editing of the "Passing Grade" episode. It was an exciting time for all of us as we celebrated with a victory lunch on the school cafeteria set, certain that this would guarantee NBC's picking us up for a third season. We were the show with the second largest number of nominations, second only to *Hill Street Blues*, having received nominations for Outstanding Drama Series, Cinematography, Art Direction, Costuming, Hairstyling, Main Title Design (a nomination I shared with Michael Levine), two nominations for Directing (Harry Harris and Bob Scheerer), and two for Editing (Mark Melnick and me). In addition, Debbie Allen had been nominated for Best Actress in a Drama Series and received a second nomination for her Choreography. Katie and I got a kick out of opening the engraved invitation from the Television Academy informing us that the awards were to be presented at the Pasadena Civic Auditorium on Sunday night, September 19. A few days later I received a sterling silver bookmark from Tiffany's as a congratulatory gift from NBC, and a basket of selected wines with a nice note from Richard Reisberg and MGM.

Earlier that summer, Bill Blinn, whose office was at the front of the MGM lot several blocks away from where the *Fame* sound stages were located, had also received a special gift, but it was one that he kept for only a short time. He recalled:

I remember the second year, the people at MGM, as a nice thing, said, "Listen, you're all the way up here, and the sound stages are all the way down there, so we're going to give you a golf cart to go from the office down there." I thought, "That's cool." The first day that the golf cart came I felt a little silly about it, but, well, it will save a little time, so I got into the golf cart and started down to the sound stage. It was brutally hot, ninety eight degrees — Culver City can get to be tough. I'm starting to pass the rehearsal hall where the dancers are inside with no air-conditioning. So if it's ninety-eight degrees outside, it's a hundred and three in there, and they're just dripping, pouring sweat, just exhausted and gasping for breath, and I'm in this little God-damned golf cart. And I said, "No! No, no, no! No golf cart, thank you very much."

On the morning of the Emmy Awards — I remember distinctly it was a Sunday — I awoke with a sharp pain in my right eye that felt like a sty had formed, but upon close inspection Katie reported that there was nothing there. As the time drew closer to leave for the Pasadena Civic the pain in my eye grew steadily worse. With the persistent throbbing I was experiencing, I was absolutely certain that my eye must have swollen to triple its usual size and that I looked grotesque. Once again Katie examined the eye and again assured me that she could find nothing out of the ordinary — my eye looked completely normal to her. However, the pain persisted, growing even worse, right up to the moment that they announced the names of the nominees for my category of Outstanding Film Editing for a Series. Then the most amazing thing happened. At the precise instant that the cast from *One Day at a Time*, Bonnie Franklin, Pat Harrington, Jr., and Valerie Bertinelli, opened the envelope and declared Andrew Chulack the winner for his editing of *Hill Street Blues*, the pain vanished. I thought that I had been quite blasé about the possibility of winning an Emmy, not even preparing a formal acceptance speech, but quite obviously subconscious anxiety had manifested itself into a psychosomatic — but very real — physical discomfort, and the instant the winner was announced the aberration disappeared. The presentation continued for another half hour or so without my feeling the slightest twinge of pain. I watched proudly as Harry Harris received his award for directing and gave a very graceful acceptance speech, in which he thanked a number of people, including me, and then as Debbie and the *Fame* dancers performed an electrifying number that brought the audience to its feet. After the awards concluded, the entire *Fame* family drove across town to the Century Plaza Hotel in Century City, where the Governors Ball was to be held in the hotel's Los Angeles Room. We drank a toast to our five winners; in addition to Harry

Harris, Bill Spencer had won for cinematography, Ira Diamond and Joseph Stone for art direction, Marilyn Matthews for costuming and Debbie Allen for choreography. Debbie would win again the following year for choreography, but in spite of being nominated three more times for best actress, that award would escape her. Tom Selleck came over to our table and graciously congratulated us on the high quality of our show. He jokingly added that he wished we were on at a different time since he was too busy watching his own show to see ours. Somebody at our table replied that we also wished he were on at a different time since *Magnum P.I.* was beating the hell out of us every week. Tom had been nominated that year for Best Actor in a Drama Series and hadn't won, but he would go on to receive the award two years later for his portrayal of Thomas Magnum, the marvelously caustic private detective. My disappointment at not winning an Emmy was lessened a few months later when I beat out several of the same *Hill Street Blues* editors to win the Eddie Award from the American Cinema Editors for my editing of "Passing Grade." I really hadn't expected to win, since I was up against the same group of *Hill Street Blues* editors as at the Emmy Awards, so I hadn't prepared any sort of acceptance speech. As it turned out, Robert Foxworth, who was presenting the award, gave me my opening when, before announcing my name, he remarked, "That's a surprise." Upon arriving at the podium I replied, "You think it's a surprise? How do you think I feel?" Bob later apologized, explaining that while he had been practicing his comments earlier in the day he had used my name as the winner and was therefore surprised to find my name in the envelope. Years later, when I directed Bob in *Falcon Crest*, he graciously signed a photograph taken of us that night and added an amusing comment.

Filming on the second season came to an end, and once again it was time for the traditional wrap party, only this time the mood wasn't quite so buoyant. We had all been waiting expectantly for NBC to announce its schedule for the upcoming season, and rumor had it that *Fame* was going to be picked up. Unfortunately, it was not meant to be.

Richard Reisberg had been in discussions with the network for some time, and this is how he remembered it: "Bill Blinn and I had several meetings with Brandon regarding the third season. Brandon was a big fan of the show, as was Grant Tinker." Tinker, once the head of MTM Enterprises, which he had formed in 1969 with his then wife Mary Tyler Moore, took over as chairman and CEO of NBC in 1981 when Fred Silverman left to form his own production company. Tinker would remain as head of

Accepting my ACE Award from Robert Foxworth. Note his amusing inscription.

NBC until 1986 and would earn the title of "the man who saved NBC." "What we were lobbying to do," said Reisberg, "what I was lobbying to do, was to put the show on at seven o'clock on Sunday night. It would be opposite *60 Minutes*, and it would be good counter-programming. This was when they had the family hour at seven o'clock on Sunday night, and

there were only certain kinds of shows that you could do." The concept
of the family hour, or family friendly programming, came about in 1974
when extensive criticism from the public regarding the continued expo-
sure of children to violence and sex in evening programs prompted the
networks to voluntarily adopt a policy that 8 to 9 P.M. Monday through
Saturday, and 7 to 9 P.M. on Sunday, would be devoted exclusively to family programming. Through the years the networks have gradually moved
away from this course of action, but in 1983 it was still in effect and *Fame*
would have been a perfect candidate for this time slot. Reisberg continued:

> I remember I went to New York to have a meeting with Brandon and with
> Grant, and it was done. It was going to be on, and it was going to be on at
> seven o'clock, and we were able to satisfy what the requirements were as far
> as family interests, educational and all those kind of goods things. It was
> literally the night before the schedule was announced that I got a call from
> Brandon, who said that that they were not going to put the show on. I said
> what are you talking about, I thought we had the order? And he said, "You
> did. We want to do it, but there's been a change. This is beyond Grant and
> me." I wasn't sure what their reasons for doing it, what the management or
> corporate or institutional pressures were, but that's basically what happened,
> and that's when NBC decided to put on *Dateline*, a news magazine, oppo-
> site *60 Minutes*, and they cancelled *Fame*.

Everyone had been hoping against hope that we would be coming
back in the fall, but three days after we wrapped filming we still didn't
have any idea what was happening, and nobody upstairs was saying anything. To be on the safe side we knew that we should all start looking for
another job, but first we had to say goodbye — and what better way than
with a party? The invitation for the wrap party read: "The High School
of Performing Arts invites you and your date to our Semester Break High
School Dance. Please wear our school colors of red, black and white. Be
there or be square." Once again the party was to be held on stage 26, and
the decorations included bunches of red, black and white balloons, crepe
paper streamers, red candles, and red and black tablecloths on every table.
Katie and I wore our *Fame* jackets, which were red and black, and I remember walking down the red carpet that led into the school set and thinking
that this would probably be the last time I would ever see this set. The
place was crowded, and people were already dancing in the cafeteria set to
a band called Captain Cardiac and the Coronaries. The caterers were serving hot dogs, hamburgers and potato salad, in keeping with the high school
theme, and a large bar had been set up in the school lobby. I definitely

needed a drink, so we headed over to the bar. The mood was somewhat subdued, everyone wanting to have a good time in spite of the reality that all of this could really be the end. This year's gag reel didn't seem as funny as last year's, even though all of the editors had worked on it, and Valerie Landsburg had put her two cents in as well. After the screening, Donna Lee made a special presentation to Bill Blinn and Mel Swope of two of the medals that had been used in "Not in Kansas Anymore." For Bill it was the medal for courage, for everyone respected him as our leader who had fought hard to maintain the quality of the show and make *Fame* as good as it could be.

It took us another six weeks or so to complete all of the post-production work on *Fame*, and then I was lucky enough to grab a quick assignment with Bill and Jerry Thorpe as associate producer/editor on a pilot they were making for CBS. Actually, it wasn't a complete pilot, since the network was trying to economize by having all of its producers only film certain scenes from the pilot script. Whether that worked against the project I can't say for sure, but the pilot didn't sell. By the middle of summer I was finished, and Katie and I decided to go for broke and take a trip to England. Since this would be my first time back since I had left as a child of three and a half (when my father decided he could do better as an actor in the United States and had brought my mother and me to New York), I decided we should do it up right and travel first class.

My friend Sven Libaek's wife was a travel agent, and I left all of the arrangements to her, and, by God, she did it up right, all right. We flew to England on British Airways in the first class cabin, stayed at that grand old lady the Ritz Hotel in London for a week, hired a car and drove for eleven days all over England, then took the overnight ferry from Liverpool to Dublin and toured Ireland by charter bus. Then we sailed home on the *QE2* to New York, stayed a few nights at the Plaza Hotel, caught a few shows and flew back to Los Angeles. You would have thought I had a job to come home to, but by then we had learned that NBC had officially cancelled *Fame*. We spent a delightful week sightseeing all over London and visiting with Neville Jason and his wife Gillian. Neville was an old friend of mine whom I had met when he had been evacuated from the Blitz during the war and came to live in Beverly Hills. Neville returned to London after the war and became a successful actor on stage and in film.

I'd asked Neville to see if he could arrange for me to visit Pinewood Studios, as I was interested in comparing a British film studio to one of

ours, and he suggested that I simply call up the MGM offices in London
and make the request. I did so, and at Neville's further suggestion, I
identified myself as one of the producers of *Fame*, conveniently leaving
out the associate part of my title. The young lady at the other end of the
phone couldn't have been more accommodating, graciously informing me
that a tour would be arranged for the following morning, and a car would
pick us up at our hotel. Since Katie preferred to go shopping with Gillian,
Neville joined me for the tour. When we walked out of the hotel to find
a liveried chauffeur with a Mercedes limousine waiting for us, I began to
worry that perhaps I had laid on the producer's title a bit too heavily.
Upon arriving at Pinewood to find a group of studio executives waiting
at the door to greet us, I was absolutely certain that I'd gone too far. Since
there was no turning back, we graciously accepted the official welcome and
started off on our guided tour of the studio, while I kept glancing over
my shoulder, looking for the messenger who would soon arrive to expose
my charade. Pinewood turned out to be a huge operation spread over 100
wooded acres, consisting of twelve sound stages, the huge 007 stage, an
extensive back lot, and various other buildings that housed the sound,
editing, wardrobe, props, and camera departments. The main offices were
housed in a former mansion called Heatherden Hall, once the home of a
multimillionaire named Lt. Col. Grant Morden.

After enjoying a pleasant lunch in the mansion's dining room and
being gifted with a published history of Pinewood Studios entitled *Movies
from the Mansion*, I assumed that now would be a safe time for us to thank
our hosts and beat a hasty retreat; but no, there was still one more surprise. I was informed that Alan Marshall wished to meet me. Mr. Marshall, the producer of the movie *Fame*, was, I was certain, about to correctly
expose me as a charlatan, and I tried my best to decline the invitation,
but to no avail. As it turned out, Alan Marshall, who had produced all of
Alan Parker's films from *Bugsy Malone* through *Shoot the Moon* and would
go on to produce three more with him (as well as many other successful
films), was a disarmingly down-to-earth Londoner, with a trim beard and
a warm smile. He cordially greeted Neville and me and immediately pulled
out a bottle of whiskey and several glasses, put his feet up on his desk and
began trading stories with me about *Fame* the movie vs. *Fame* the television series. He was obviously fond of several of the cast members from his
film, particularly Gene Anthony Ray and Debbie Allen, and was genuinely
curious as to how they were faring once having moved to Hollywood.
After several enjoyable hours and many refilled glasses, I had to beg our

leave, as it was nearing five o'clock and we had tickets to a revival of *The Prime of Miss Jean Brody* at the Barbizon that evening and needed to return to London. Once safely back in our limousine and on the road, Neville and I couldn't help but laugh as we compared notes on what had just happened. For months after I expected to hear a roar from Pinewood, along with a bill for lunch and the limousine, but apparently they never figured it out — or were just too civilized to make an issue of it.

10

We're Back in Business!

On our way to Southampton to board the *QE2* for our trip home we drove through West Sussex and into Brighton. I wanted to revisit one of the few places I could still remember from my childhood, and it was while we were spending the night in Brighton that we witnessed a most remarkable sight. Deciding to take a walk after dinner, we strolled along the streets and realized that we could see the televisions flickering in the living rooms of all of the homes as we passed by. It was eight o'clock on a Thursday evening, an episode of *Fame* was being televised, and it appeared as if every "telly," in every house in Brighton was tuned to our show. I'd known that we were enormously popular in Europe, but here was a clear example of just how popular, and it seemed hard to believe that the series could just disappear without a trace.

In point of fact, *Fame* had developed an impressive following of over 11 million viewers in the United Kingdom, and this fact motivated Richard Reisberg and MGM/UA Television to look into alternative distribution venues. "At the same time that we were dealing with NBC, to more or less cover our bet," explained Reisberg, "I started having some conversations with Larry Gershman at MGM about the possibility of trying to do the show first-run. I'd had some experience with first-run syndication at Viacom, but it really hadn't been done before with anything of this size." It would take several months for Larry Gershman to cobble together the first-run syndication deal with media buyers, advertisers and several European television networks, including the R.I.A. Television network in Italy. Even though MGM/UA Television had its own distribution organization, both domestic and international, a deal involving a cash guarantee was made with an outside distributor, Lexington Broadcast Service, to handle clearing the stations and securing the advertisers here in the United States. Reisberg added that "The deal was based on part barter and part cash."

Now here comes the complicated part, so I guess I had better try to explain just exactly what barter is. I'll try to keep it as simple as I can, so bear with me.

Normally, when a program finishes its run on a network and goes into re-runs in syndication it is sold regionally to various local stations or station groups for a specific amount of money for a specific number of play dates. On network television the Federal Communications Commission allows six minutes of commercial time per hour of programming, while in syndication that is increased to twelve minutes per hour, and the various stations can then sell that time to local advertisers. In the case of *Fame* the situation would be slightly different, primarily because the episodes would be brand new, and MGM's distributor would be asking for less money up front in order to keep a certain number of those commercial minutes, or units, to sell to media buyers. So that is what is called barter. Okay, got all of that? Good, then I'll let Richard Reisberg finish explaining the rest. "The combination of the distributor's guarantee plus what we projected we could get out of foreign sales would give us sufficient dollars to say this was worth rolling the dice." As a matter of courtesy, Reisberg had called Brandon Tartikoff at NBC some months earlier to inform him of MGM's plans to syndicate *Fame*. "I said, Brandon, there's a moment in time when we can still try to do something, but this is going to happen one way or the other." It appeared at that moment that there was nothing more that Tartikoff could do, but apparently that wasn't the case. "Maybe a month at the most before we would make the official announcement and do the whole thing," Reisberg recalled, "I got a call from Brandon saying, in effect, 'If I order the show, can you do it?' I told him, 'Brandon, the ship has sailed, this has gone too far to get it back, and I don't believe we can.'" Tartikoff asked Reisberg, "Is that final?" and then made Reisberg promise to "talk to whoever you need to" to see if anything could be done and then call him back. Reisberg admitted that he was actually ambivalent in his own mind about which way he'd rather go — accept a third season on NBC or take on the riskier challenges of syndicating *Fame* themselves. He bluntly observed:

> I mean, doing what we did was far more risky in terms of being able to get our dollars back, whereas the other way there was a guarantee put up of what we'd get. But guarantees are only as good as the people you're dealing with, and I wasn't so sure about some of the people — I mean, outside of MGM. I talked to the management du jour at that point in time. It kept changing at the higher levels at MGM/UA. There was Begelman, then there

was Frank Rosenthal, Frank Rothman, Frank Yablans — a lot of Franks, and I don't remember which Frank was there at the time. There was really sufficient commitments made with the distributor, the syndicator, with some advertisers, the ship had really sailed. It wasn't a game, it wasn't a bluff, and it wasn't any kind of business play. Even if I thought in my own mind that I could get NBC to buy us out of our commitments and do it, the more I thought about it, it would just be a pile of snakes. By the time you finished doing it, you could wind up with nothing. It would be too expensive for NBC, and by the time we finished delaying it, it would kill the opportunity to do it first-run.

Reisberg called Tartikoff back to tell him of MGM's decision and was asked to come over to Tartikoff's office at NBC. Remembered Reisberg:

> So I slogged out to Burbank. I had a fairly close relationship with Brandon. We were not close friends — we didn't hang out together, I don't mean it in that way — but I knew Brandon when he was manager of comedy before he rose at ABC and Freddie Silverman brought him to NBC. My relationship with him was as with most of the people I dealt with — it was a different time and place and we could have it — it was very direct and very straight. There really wasn't much gamesmanship. Sure, to try to sell a show you'd do what you did and all of that, but basically you could still do a handshake deal that was a good deal. He knew, but he had additional issues with MGM, and it just had to go this way.

And so the decision was made to go forward for a third season with MGM/UA Television syndicating new episodes of *Fame* to Europe and the United States. It would turn out to be the right choice, as *Fame* would continue for four more years in syndication and wrack up numerous awards and a healthy financial return for MGM/UA Television. In fact, for the 1983 Emmy Awards, *Fame* was nominated in nine categories, including Outstanding Drama Series, and Debbie Allen won her second Emmy for Outstanding Achievement in Choreography.

The third season brought a lot of changes to *Fame*. To start with, Mel Swope, who had been the line producer for the first two seasons, was replaced by newcomer Ken Ehrlich. Ted Zachary was the person responsible for introducing Ken Ehrlich to Bill Blinn. Recalled Zachary:

> Ken and I had never worked together. We had children at the same school, we took a computer class together, and we started playing golf together. I didn't know him before; Ken was originally from Chicago and we were from New York and New Jersey. I knew he had done the *Grammys*, I knew that he had done specials and some of those live music shows, and that he was looking for something else to do. I also knew that Bill Blinn was dissatisfied with Mel Swope and wanted to replace him, and there was nobody that he

had found. I just had the idea, even though Ken didn't have any experience in film — it was all live and tape but the fact is he was a musical guy, and we were doing a musical series.

Ken Ehrlich was born in Cleveland, Ohio, and moved to Chicago when he got out of college. "I'd been a P.R. guy for a few years," Ehrlich explained,

and then in 1968 I started producing a local show called the *Marty Faye Show*, which was a two-hour, late night show in black and white on a UHF station. Marty was this guy who knew everybody. He had been a disc jockey on a black jazz radio station, and so every Saturday night, Oscar Peterson, George Shearing, Carmen McCrae, Sarah Vaughn, they would all come over and they'd perform live in-between

Ken Ehrlich (courtesy Ken Ehrlich).

shows at their clubs. I was still doing P.R., that was my day job, but as a moonlighting thing I was bitten and knew that this was something I wanted to do.

Ehrlich then moved over to the Chicago Public Broadcasting station where he created and produced the *Soundstage* series. It was well received and was credited with being the forerunner of *Unplugged* and other live music shows. Remembers Ehrlich:

At the time there weren't a whole lot of outlets for this kind of thing, for people like Randy Newman and Tom Waits and Harry Chapin, Jim Croche, jazz artists who'd get two or three Downbeat jazz awards. So I did that for a few years and then moved out here in 1976 as a creative consultant on the *Tony Orlando and Dawn Rainbow Hour*, which lasted three months, and then that rainbow went right into the ocean. I did *The Midnight Special* for a year or so and a couple of other specials. I was primarily doing specials at this time.

In 1979 Ehrlich was approached by executive producer Pierre Cossette to join him as a producer of the *Grammy Awards*, the annual music award show put on by the National Academy of Recording Arts and Sciences. It would become an annual event for Ehrlich, as he eventually moved up to the executive producer position. He is still producing the show and has written a fascinating account of his experiences in a book called *At the Grammys! Behind the Scenes at Music's Biggest Night*. Ehrlich had been producing the Grammy Awards for two years when Ted Zachary decided to introduce him to Bill Blinn. Zachary remembers why he thought his idea would work: "Ken could apply whatever he knew from the *Grammys*, from the music specials, all of the people that he knew and he was also a musician himself; so I thought, 'They have to meet.'" Zachary picked Ehrlich up and drove him over to Bill Blinn's house, which, coincidentally, was on a hill in Encino that looked across a steep canyon to where Ehrlich's house sat on another hill. In later years, Blinn would tease Ehrlich about his view of Ehrlich's house by saying, "I see that you got up early to shave this morning." Of that first meeting, Zachary remembers:

> Bill was in the backyard, swimming laps in his pool. I introduced them and left them there. They chatted for a while, and the next day, I don't know whether they had lunch or what, but Bill called me up and said, "You know, I really like your friend, and I think that he would be an asset to the show." And, ultimately, in the next week or so, a deal was made and Ken was on the show. It was a great marriage, and Bill, Ken and I play golf most every Sunday to this day.

Ken Ehrlich describes his first impressions of meeting Bill Blinn:

> Obviously I knew about Bill's credits. I knew about *Roots*, I knew about *Brian's Song*, I knew about all the other shows that he had created. I was not prepared for the ... how can I describe it? He was the most unlikely, brilliant writer that I had ever met, although I haven't met that many. He was one of the guys, you know? He was quiet; he didn't volunteer a lot, and yet he was extremely warm. But there was this quiet strength that you felt around him, this quiet confidence. I just felt from the minute I met him that I wanted to do this show.

Bill Blinn also remembers meeting Ken Ehrlich:

> On the third season we released the producer. There was for me just a lack of creative chemistry with him. Good guy, nice man ... but. At any rate, Ted Zachary heard that we were looking around for somebody and asked me if I knew who Ken Ehrlich was, and I said no. He gave me his background, Ken and Ted were long-time friends, and his background was so full of music and musicians and composers and the whole thing, I was dumfounded. He's now the producer of the *Grammys* and the hardest worker I've ever known.

The fact that *Fame* was now being filmed for syndication meant that a number of other changes needed to occur in both the production and the post-production procedures. Recalls Ted Zachary:

We had to find a way to do the show for less because we couldn't get the kind of license fee for syndication that we were able to get from the network. So the first thing we experimented with was shooting the show on 16 mm. I remember doing some tests with the cameraman, I think it was Bill Spencer. We had this 16mm camera, and I remember walking on the set and there it was on top of the dolly. Bill Spencer looked at me and said, "I'm in the home movie business. Look at the size of this camera; it must be a joke." And next to it somewhere was the 35mm camera; so we shot the scene in 16 mm, and then we shot the same thing in 35 mm. And, of course, when you went to the screening room you could see the difference, but on a 17-inch TV set you'd never see the difference.

That idea didn't fly with either Bill Blinn or Ken Ehrlich, so the decision was made to stay with the 35 mm cameras and retain the quality look. The next thing they looked at was the music. Richard Reisberg recalls:

We had this deal with The Entertainment Company, Charles Koppelman and Martin Bandier's outfit, that was made before I got there. And I basically blew it up. The reason was that they got all the publishing rights for nothing, and when we were going to do the show in syndication I said, "This is crazy." I mean if you want the publishing rights to the show you're not going to do that without paying. And that's really what precipitated breaking up that deal.

Ken Ehrlich's knowledge of music, and his connections in the music industry, would have a major influence on the music in *Fame*. Says Erlich:

The reason that I think they wanted me to do the show — there were really two basic reasons. One, they felt that the music in the show could've been better. It was all being supplied by Koppelman's group, and there was an exclusive deal with Koppelman whereby any song that got on the show had to come through The Entertainment Company. They had a stable of writers, some of whom were pretty good, some of whom weren't. One of the suggestions that I made was to end the exclusive part of it, let them compete with other writers so that we would get a broader landscape of people writing, not just contract songwriters. We implemented that, and I think we ramped up the music quite a bit. It wasn't just sappy ballads and stuff from Broadway shows. I tried to make it much more contemporary and much more following what music was at the time. In the early eighties there was a whole new English beat coming in. There was *punk* that had just broken through. For its first two years this show was kind of stuck in ... it wasn't bad music, it just wasn't what appealed to the kids. And I started to get writers — I mean, I wasn't a magician, it was pretty easy. You know, call the Diane Lawrences and the Dave Steinbergs, the guys that had written for Madonna, and Tom Kelly. These were people that I thought would be great for the show. I said to them, "Look, I'm not paying you and you're not going to get rich on the show, but we're going to introduce it on network television." Nowadays it's the other way around, it's exactly the opposite. These guys fight for the chance; they know that television can break their music.

Ehrlich summed it up by saying, "It was a combination of my tape experience and my musical background." Because of his tape experience, Ehrlich also came up with another idea that directly affected not only me, but all three of the film editors who had been with the show since the very beginning. And for us, it wasn't good news.

11

Some Serious Changes

When we returned from England, and I heard the news that there was going to be a third season for *Fame*, I was delighted. I waited expectantly for the call to report to the studio and begin work, but it never came. Ken Ehrlich's other idea had managed to totally obliterate the post-production department and all of its participants. "The other reason they wanted me," says Ehrlich, "And I think equally compelling to Reisberg at the time, was that my whole career had been spent in tape, and here was a show that was now about to go into syndication." Ted Zachary saw the change as a blessing:

> We changed the way the show was edited. And I think we were one of the very first shows that did that. Instead of having the three teams of editors and all the various guys, we cut it down appreciably, and the shows were turned over much more quickly. So we saved a lot of money. We didn't even see our dailies in a screening room; we saw them on a cassette.

Ehrlich found these changes somewhat ironic:

> I'm not sure if I'll go to Hell or Heaven for this, but next door to the largest film processing plant in the world, the MGM lab, we set up two tape edit rooms. Well, that was a radical difference, and it wasn't universally received. There were people who said that this is going to go to shit, the show is over! The minute that piece of tape shows up, blah, blah, blah, blah! And the fact of the matter is, within two or three years every show on television was finishing on tape. All I know is that there were fewer days in post-production, and it was fifteen or twenty thousand dollars an episode cheaper by going this way.

Eventually I learned that I wouldn't be coming back, that I was going to be replaced as the associate producer by Scott Stambler, our former music editor during Season Two, and by Frank Merwald, whose background seemed to fit perfectly with the show's new requirements. Merwald recalled,

I read in the *L.A. Times* that *Fame* was coming back to television in syndication, and they were going to shoot on film and edit on video tape. A light went on and said this show is for me. I have a Bachelors in Radio and Television from the University of Detroit; I have a Masters in Film from USC; this will combine both of my degrees, and I love *Fame* anyway.

Merwald called MGM and spoke to a secretary in the *Fame* office, who told him, "You know we have a new producer, he's supposed to come in today, but I don't even know his name yet. Let me find out who it is and I'll call you back." When the secretary called back to tell Merwald that the producer was Ken Ehrlich, he immediately dispatched a résumé and cover letter to Ehrlich. The very next day he received a phone call from Ken Ehrlich saying he wanted to meet. "So I went over the very next day," Merwald continued. "We had a very nice conversation, and he said, 'You've got the job.' I said to him don't you want to at least check me out? And he said, 'I've already checked you out.' And that's how I got the gig, and it all happened within 48 hours." Frank Merwald would remain as one of the associate producers on *Fame* for the next four years, right up until the final episode in 1987. When asked which was his favorite season Frank replied, "I would say my favorite season, was Season Three with Bill Blinn. He was just such a prince to work for, and I thought I had died and gone to Heaven when I got that job."

I was feeling a little put out; hell, I was feeling downright depressed. I had been fired, or at least that's what I thought until I received a telephone call from Donna Lee with the exciting news that I had been given a directing assignment. The year before, Bruce Belland and I had written, and I had directed, a short film, a fantasy called *Those Were the Days* that told the story of a young, terribly shy college film student who was so fascinated with the early days of Hollywood that he wished he had been alive at that time. Through a series of strange events, the young man is granted his wish and becomes a character in an old silent movie. I had made the short with my own money to use as an audition piece as a director. Bill Blinn had seen, and was apparently impressed by, this short film and was now giving me the opportunity to try my hand at directing an episode of *Fame*. Although the company had already started filming the new season, I was scheduled to direct the seventh episode, which meant that I still had some time to kill before reporting to the studio to start my prep. By Directors Guild contract, a director of one-hour episodic television is given seven days to prepare before filming begins, and seven days to film the episode. Some of the duties to be performed during the prep period were casting of guest stars and bit roles, picking locations and approving of new sets, and, in the case of *Fame*, working with the choreographer, which was generally Debbie Allen, on the staging of the musical numbers. By the middle of the third season Debbie would become so adept at staging and filming the big dance production numbers that Bill Blinn gave her a shot at directing an entire episode. "When I first said, 'Do you want to direct one of these things?' she said yes immediately," Blinn recalls. "And then she said, "If you think I'm ready.' And I said, 'Not if I think you're ready, do you think you're ready?' Obviously she could, and she just got better and better." By the fourth season Debbie Allen was doing quadruple duty — besides choreographing and playing Lydia Grant in just about every episode, she added co-producer responsibilities to her list in addition to directing several more episodes. Having already won two Emmys for her choreography, she would earn a third and fourth nomination, as well as four nominations as Outstanding Lead Actress in a Drama Series.

Ted Zachary, being more concerned with fiscal responsibilities than creativity, had a slightly different point of view:

> As an actress and a choreographer, this was an area that you couldn't really get into because she was so good at it, and those dances that she did were terrific. But then somebody invariably creates the monster and says you should direct one of these things. It's a lot different when you're saying action and you're saying I need more time, and maybe you need an extra day, or you need something else, and she became a little bit unreasonable. I think it was the first show she did, or the second show — suddenly there was a crane outside in the street, there was all kinds of other stuff, and she suddenly became a big-time director. I remember she sent me a memo about why we had to do this and that, and I sent her a memo back about the fact that she had been given this incredible opportunity, only we had to do the show for x dollars, and everybody that preceded her did the show for those dollars and so should she. She said, "Well, I'm glad that we're communicating with each other." And after that we had a very nice relationship. She was a little wary of me because she knew that I wasn't afraid to say something to her, but I always respected her talent because she *was* that show.

'Richard Reisberg remembers another event that occurred while the studio was retooling *Fame* for syndication. As he tells it, an agent representing one of the cast members contacted him and requested an increase in his client's salary. Recalls Reisberg:

> I said to him, "You don't really understand the concept here. When you get cancelled, that's called failure, and you don't get more money for failing. And the fact that we're doing the show is relevant to your client because we're putting out the money to do this. So it's real simple. I'm not going to ask your client to take a reduction in what their episodic fee is, and you're

not going to ask me for an increase, because if we can't agree on that then they're not going to be in the show. So you've got about an hour to call me back and let me know. You can call Bill Blinn if you want, but it's not going to make any difference. "Bill knew what we were doing. Bill was never in the dark about any issues with the cast, so that was not going to be a problem.

Interesting story, don't you think? As you can see, even in a family relationship like ours you had to observe the rules, and sometimes, like spinach, they could be hard to swallow.

The third season began with a two-part story, written by Bill Blinn and directed by Bill Claxton, called "Gonna Learn How to Fly" that set into motion some of the major changes that were established in an attempt to create new life in the story lines and new interest in the series. Ken Swofford, as Quentin Morloch, the new vice-principal, arrives at the school and proceeds to make it clear to students and faculty alike that he intends to hold everyone to the full letter of the law, no matter what the consequences. Bruno's father, played by Carmine Caridi, is written out of the series by means of his off-screen death, and Bruno is forced to leave the school and take a job as a waiter at Caruso's Coffee House, which gives him a greater opportunity to play his music. Two new students, Christopher Donlon and Holly Laird, portrayed by Billy Hufsey and Cynthia Gibb, are introduced, and Dave Shelley becomes Don Caruso, the owner of Caruso's Coffee House.

Billy Hufsey was born in Brook Park, Ohio, and started out to be an athlete until an injury put an end to that ambition. He then studied music and dance, and that path led him to *Fame* and the role of Chris Donlon, the dance major whose overpowering self-confidence came across as a giant ego and made it hard for him to earn the respect of his fellow students—a situation that seemed to replicate itself in real life. There was no denying, however, Billy's talents as a singer and musician who could play piano, drums, guitar and several versions of the sax, as well as a trumpet. After performing on *Fame* through its final season, Billy would go on to co-star in *Days of Our Lives* from 1988 to 1991. After that he returned to his music, putting together a nightclub act and taking it on the road. Having seen a video of Billy's nightclub act, I have to say he gives the audience their money's worth, and they seem to love it.

The Ann Nelson/Billy Hufsey story that I referred to earlier is actually a two-part story and a bit risqué at that, but it's so good you'll have to forgive me for sharing it. According to Donna Lee, the story actually began during the second season when NBC's Standards and Practices sent a note to the *Fame* offices complaining that some of the male dancers weren't wearing a dance belt. "So guess who got the lovely job," declared Donna, "of going to wardrobe and making sure that dance belts were mandatory all around?" Then in the third season, with the rule still in force, Billy Hufsey arrived. Recalled Donna:

> Sure enough, I got called down to the set because Billy Hufsey refused to comply. He was putting up a big stink, insisting that the belt was very uncomfortable because he was "much too big to wear one." His exact quote was, "I'm 9 inches, for God' sake! It hurts to wear one of those things!"

Donna managed to talk Billy into returning to his dressing room with the wardrobe assistant and giving it another try. A few minutes later the wardrobe assistant came out of Billy's trailer, struggling to conceal his laughter. When wearing a dance belt, the object of male anatomy in question should always point north, and Billy was trying to point it south. The problem was solved.

Now for the second part of the story. At Bronwyn Thomas' wedding reception, Donna Lee was seated next to Ann Nelson when Billy Hufsey walked in with his date for the evening. Reported Donna:

> He was strutting with his usual full-of-himself strut. Ann leaned over and said, "It's too bad that boy doesn't have a higher opinion of himself." I replied, "Yes, it is a shame, isn't it?" Then Ann added, "Well, who can blame him? He has a 9-inch dick, you know." I almost fell off my chair!

Bless dear old Ann Nelson.

Cynthia Gibb was born in Bennington, Vermont. Her early dance training led her into modeling and a contract with the Eileen Ford Agency in New York. Having seen her on the cover of *Vogue*, director Woody Allen cast her in *Stardust Memories*. After appearing in an off–Broadway show and the daytime soap, *Search for Tomorrow*, she joined the cast of *Fame* as drama major Holly Laird. I always thought that Cindy was terribly sweet, but even though she could dance and sing as well as anyone, she didn't seem to have the sparkle — the star quality, if you will — that the original cast members projected with their awesome energy. However, my appraisal must obviously have been wrong, because Cindy would go on to star in a number of television movies during the breaks between seasons, including *Youngblood*, *Modern Girls* and *Salvador*, in which she played Jean Donovan, one of the four nuns murdered by an El Salvadorian death squad.

Bill Blinn had grown unhappy with the way some of the cast was starting to behave:

> I felt that Lee and Valerie were just giving up. It was just the old cliché that those young people, Lee and Erica and Valerie and, oddly enough, Albert to some degree, had absolutely formed a family. And one time, I think it was the third season, Albert found out that one of the kids was smoking grass in the dressing room. It wasn't just one — it was probably all of them. I went to read them the riot act, and I did it very badly because I wasn't stern and I wasn't the bad cop. I probably did it as I would have to my own children; my voice was trembling, I felt a little betrayed. I even said, "This is not how you're supposed to behave." I just couldn't help it. So we started bringing in some new people. And it started to change somewhat. They all liked and got along well with Cindy Gibb, but they were less at ease with Billy Hufsey, who was a good singer and a good dancer and a good bunch of things — but Billy was never as good as he thought he was.

Unfortunately, smoking grass wasn't the only drug on the set. Lee Curreri admitted as much in a television interview. "There was pot," he reported, "and there were things to keep people awake on the set — I mean nothing obviously sponsored by the show." Carlo Imperato also spoke about drugs:

> In that era cocaine was such a big thing. There were a lot of people getting high at inappropriate times, but when you had a 5:30 A.M. call you needed to be on the set and you needed to be clear eyed and have your stuff together. I always tried to be on time. Drugs were accepted back then; you weren't put down for doing it, which people should have been.

Most of us knew that Gene Anthony Ray was using coke, and it was beginning to affect his performance. Bill Blinn, still hoping to talk some sense into a young man for whom he had great affection, remembers his frustration.

> That was the thing — everybody fell in love with Gene, even while he was screwing you up and not showing up for production numbers and all that stuff. Gene had been late for something, and I mean really late — we didn't even know where he was for a day, that kind of thing. I said to Ken Ehrlich, "Let's suspend him for a week or two." And he came in, and I was going to be tough, but Ken was more, "Let's work with him." So Gene came in and sat down, and he looked back and forth between us, and he said, "Ken, I'm not going to talk to Bill because he doesn't trust me at all, so I'll just talk to you."

There was no question that Gene had an irresistible sense of humor. "Gene was a puzzle," noted Blinn.

> He was so talented and so bright and so effervescent. One of my big regrets about the show, and I heard it from any number of people who said that

Gene did an absolutely spot on, brilliant imitation of me — and he would never do it for me. He also did a sweet impression of Tina Turner. He had all the tools there.

Ken Ehrlich could see that there was no easy solution with Gene. As Ehrlich observed:

> It was difficult because he was so ingratiating. There was never a time when he didn't say, "I'm sorry, I'll never do this again," and, "This is the last time and I'm going to be better. I want this more than anything in my life. You don't know where I came from and I'm not going back there." I mean, all of that, and it took me probably a little while to figure out that it was just a riff. That was it. The guy didn't mean a word of it. I mean, he may have meant it, but he couldn't stand behind the words. So, I don't know; I mean, during the time that I was there I don't think he got any better. I remember I took a couple of trips to his house to wake him up and get him out of bed, and there were times that Debbie just covered for him and the number changed, but most of the time I remember him, whatever condition, showing up and hitting the marks and being brilliant.

For the moment, everything continued on as it had been; but it would merely be a matter of time before things would grow worse, much worse.

The problem with Gene had already become so critical by the second season that it had inspired Chris Beaumont and Bill Blinn to write an episode dramatizing the situation called "Feelings." Blinn recalled:

> The premise was that the Gene Anthony Ray character, Leroy, had missed a rehearsal. There was this huge, big production number that he was to be starring in, and it meant a great deal to the school that the production came off because it was going be performed in front of the Board of Regents. I got to thinking, and just a couple of days before we were going to shoot the number I said to Debbie, "You realize that in real life you would kick that kid's ass out of here." So we ended up with her saying to Leroy, "If you can't show up for rehearsals, you don't need to show up for the show. You're done, you're history, and you're gone. Michael's doing the show. Period. Out." They banter back and forth, and Gene's character gets pissed off and stalks off. So they start the production number on stage. Michael DeLorenzo is in it, and he's doing it very, very well, and then they cut to the wings where Debbie is watching the production number. This was where Bob Scheerer corrected me because what I initially had was somebody asking where Leroy was, and Debbie going downstairs to the dressing room where you can still hear the music playing and the production number going on upstairs — very faintly, like a college band in a stadium as you are walking to the parking lot — and she walks in and sees Gene in there doing the number all by himself. Bob's suggestion was that somebody ask Debbie, "Where's Leroy?" and Debbie says, "I don't know" Then her attention goes back to what's happening onstage with the production number. Back to the backstage area and the camera moves down the stairs and moves through the

hallway and comes around the door to the rehearsal hall. We've also started a rainstorm, so the rain was pouring down over the windows, the light was variegated and undulating, and he's doing the dance number all by himself against the muted sound of the production number. And that was infinitely more powerful and more real. When it all comes together you realize it doesn't have to be words, that you have a thousand tools by which to tell a story.

As a story, "Feelings" accomplished something, but in real life the problem continued to exist, and no one told Gene Anthony Ray "You're history." Perhaps if they had, things might have turned out differently for him; but, then again, perhaps it was already too late.

Bill Blinn understood what was driving Gene on his path of self-destruction:

> Gene was into drugs because his family was into drugs. His mother and grandmother both dealt, it was just a part of his life. His mother did time in prison for weapons possession, and I mean serious possession; it wasn't just a 22 pistol. Gene was gay and playing this mischievous heterosexual; it wasn't the first time that had happened, but it's hard when you're in a racial minority and a sexual minority. You're portraying a role, and you're *really* portraying a role, if you will — I mean a whole different attitude. It took its toll.

Donna Lee remembers an incident that took place with Gene's mother, "I remember at a meeting with his mother, we're sitting on the sofa in Bill's office, and she opened her purse and there's a pearl-handled, nickel plated revolver in her purse." Donna also tried to reason with Gene:

> I took him out to dinner once, to Le Sere [a very fancy restaurant in the San Fernando Valley], on Bill's credit card at Bill's instructions, to try and talk some sense into him. And I just did everything I could. I said, you know, "You're just forgetting the first and foremost issue here, and that is our love for you. And when you love somebody you're so concerned when they are putting themselves in harm's way." And I tried, I just gave him the best I could. And you know, he was ... he seemed like he was responding at the time. But nothing; I think he got better for a week or two. I do remember going to Jerry Gottlieb at one time and saying somebody has to do something, or we're going to knock on that door one day and we're going to find him dead.

Nobody cared for Gene more than Debbie Allen. She truly loved him, and she worked with all her heart to try to turn Gene around. "Gene was this amazing ball of energy and fire, that was sweet and sour at the same time," is how she described him. Gene would eventually clean up his act, but only after his health forced him to do it, and not while we were together on *Fame*. "We brought in, at Debbie's request and with her help, a drug counselor," remembers Bill Blinn. "A black guy, and I remember his first name — who could forget his first name — it was 'Hiawatha.' He seemed to help Gene, he worked very hard with him; but, I mean, Gene's background was what it was." And Gene held his future in his own hands.

12

And Some New Directors

Once it was certain that there would be a third season, plans were drawn up for a second concert tour. This time the kids would go to Israel, and this time Valerie Landsburg would join them to perform before sold-out crowds. As Valerie related it in 2004 to Mike Cohen of London's *Jewish Telegraph*, the trip had an enormous effect on her. "It was a big thing for me, being the Jewish member of the cast," she declared. " I was a second generation U.S. Jew who had no inclination to ever go to Israel, but when I got there it was such a profound experience that had I not been in a relationship nor had my career I would have stayed." Valerie, who didn't speak the language, had one of the troop's bodyguards teach her phonetically how to introduce her solo, "Beautiful Dreamer," in Hebrew. "They went crazy for it," she recalled. The taped broadcast of the concert became the fourth episode to air during the third season, but, unfortunately, since the studio had hired a local television director and crew to tape the concert, the lighting and camerawork were of poor quality, and the direction lacked imagination. *The Kids from "Fame" in Israel* came and went with hardly a splash.

Debbie Allen's creativity continued to flourish, as she now took on the new task of directing in addition to her other responsibilities as actress, dancer and choreographer. In "Lisa's Song," Debbie's first directorial effort, written by Karen Davis, she inherited a rather soporific ghost story in which Valerie Landsburg ends up singing a duet with a phantom. In spite of all this, Debbie still managed to give it her usual classy treatment. Over the next three years Debbie would direct a total of 11 episodes and eventually add a producing credit to her portfolio. Bill Blinn described her evolution in these words, "Debbie had much that she didn't know, but she had every pore open to learn as much as she did by the end of the first season." Debbie Allen and Bill Blinn made a formidable creative team, as Chris Beaumont recalls.

I didn't have that many dealings with Debbie directly because Debbie dealt with Bill. So, my dealings with Debbie were almost always when I would be in the room with Bill in a meeting, and Debbie would have a problem, and she'd come in. It was a great education for me to watch, because they had a good relationship and respected each other. And they were honest with each other. So whether it was switching Debbie's production number or Debbie coming in to lobby one more time for the "Deer Dance," which was a dance that Debbie wanted to do and had pitched to Bill a number of times. It was a very artistic dance, but it was a ballet, and I think Bill was afraid that the energy level might come down. It was fun to watch the two of them go back and forth about it.

Blinn finally did give in to Debbie, and the dance was filmed as a production number on the auditorium stage. I remember seeing the dancers in brown leotards, wearing fabric deer antlers attached to their heads. I had to agree with Chris Beaumont when he said that the dance "was beautiful, it was absolutely beautiful, but it wasn't...." At which point he broke into a laugh, adding, "She had wanted to do something different, and she succeeded in doing something different."

Continued Beaumont:

> It was a great education, because she was a strong-willed woman who had opinions. She wasn't afraid to ask for what she wanted. I never saw them yell at each other, never insult each other. She was very respectful of Bill, and it was a great education for me to see two people with some power use it in a healthy way as they'd come to a compromise.

Debbie was both Mother Hen and Mother Superior to the kids in her dance company; she adored them, and the feeling was mutual. Many of the dancers had come from New York to do the pilot and stayed on for season after season, some to the very last episode. Some of the original dancers, like Eartha Robinson (who frequently assisted Debbie in choreographing *Fame* and other events), Michael Rooney and Marguerite Pomhern-Derricks, would later become accomplished choreographers in their own right. Marguerite would return in 1997 to choreograph the pilot of *Fame L.A.*, MGM's attempt to recreate the magic of the original show. Having choreographed over 30 films and television shows, Marguerite has also won three Emmy Awards and an American Choreography Award. She is the coach for the United States team on the NBC reality series *Superstars of Dance*, and is also the choreographer of MGM's new feature version of *Fame*, in which Debbie Allen plays the role of the school principal. Others, like Joni Palmer, Kim Layton and Cameron English, would pursue their acting and dancing careers, with Cameron winning a featured role in the film version of *A Chorus Line*. Rocker Verastique, another of the original dancers, returned to Broadway, appearing in a number of musicals, including the revivals of *Carousel* and *Chicago*. He is now a member of the faculty of Ballet Austin in Austin, Texas. Serge Rodnunsky, who began as a dancer with the American Ballet Theater, working with such notables as Agnes DeMille, George Balanchine and Mikail Baryshnikov, and was with *Fame* for three seasons, has gone on to build a career for himself as a filmmaker — writing, directing and producing seventeen independent feature films for his own company.

Then there was Darryl Tribble and Derrick Brice, two of the most wonderful dancers and happy individuals you'd ever want to know. They added luster to every dance number they were in, and they were in almost all of them during the first four years. Off the stage, however, life wasn't so easy for either of them. There was an unhappy incident involving Darryl that occurred during the filming of one of my shows that Donna Lee reminded me of. As she recalled:

> We had filmed the master shot of the production number, and then we went to lunch. Darryl and another friend went off the lot on their lunch hour, and they got a *DWB*, as we called it, which meant *driving while black*. They were in a rental car, and the car had been reported stolen, so I get a phone call from Darryl, who was in Culver City jail, saying he'd been arrested. He needed something like fifteen hundred dollars bail. I called Bill, and, as usual, Bill said to take care of it, so I called Jerry Gottlieb, who was head of finance, and got the $1,500.

Donna Lee and Ken Ehrlich then went down to the Culver City Jail to bail Darryl out, and they had to do it quickly, since Darryl was one of the featured dancers in the production number and I had already filmed the master shot. If he wasn't there when we filmed the closer angles, we would have a matching problem. Continued Donna:

> We're sitting there waiting for Darryl, and we get all the details, and there's been a big mix-up. Of course he hadn't stolen the car. So we're sitting there, and I said to Ken, "Do you suppose if we tell them we're his parents they'll believe that? I've never seen Ken laughing so hard.

I'm sure it wasn't as funny to Darryl, but the future held even darker times for both him and Derrick Brice; both of them would die of AIDS within a few years of leaving the show. The AIDS epidemic officially began on June 5, 1981. A study, conducted by the Centers for Disease Control and Prevention in 2008, confirmed that H.I.V., the virus that causes AIDS, has its greatest effect among gay and bisexual men of all races (53 percent of all new infections), and among African-American men and women. Just their luck, Darryl and Derrick were both gay and black. Derrick died first, in 1987, and Darryl died in 1991. Bill Blinn recalled attending Darryl's funeral at the Old North Church at Forest Lawn Memorial in Burbank, California, where Eartha Robinson danced a tribute to him. I often think of both of these young men and wonder what they might have accomplished in their lives if not for that damned disease.

One day, while I was still impatiently awaiting the start of my first directing assignment, I received a phone call from Mel Swope offering me an editing position on a new series he was producing for Universal Television called *Miami Vice*. It would have meant a full season of work, but I'd have had to give up the directing assignment on *Fame*, so it took me only a moment to make my decision and turn Mel down. Of course, the show became one of the biggest hits of all time, and who knows what might have happened for me, but I still never regretted making that decision. A short time later, Jerry Thorpe called, offering me the associate producer/editor position on a television movie that he was about to start filming. I was surprised to find out that it would be a Blinn/Thorpe production, and even more surprised and delighted to learn that the script had been written by Chris Beaumont. It turned out that the movie, called *Happy Endings*, was based on Chris' experiences while raising his brother and sisters. An old family friend, Rubin Carson, had written a magazine article about Chris and his family responsibilities, and Jerry Thorpe and Bill Blinn's agent, Leonard Hanser, had sold the idea to NBC as a backdoor pilot. A back-door pilot means that in addition to the commitment for the TV movie, the network also commits to a certain number of episodic scripts to be written, which in this case was six. I was very happy for Chris, who, in addition to writing the movie, would also write two of the episodes and be one of the producers, along with Blinn and Thorpe. As usual, during pilot season the networks never give you enough time to do the job properly, and that was to be the case with *Happy Endings*. Thorpe indicated to me that there would be an accelerated post-production schedule that would require two editors. I immediately thought of Bud Hayes, who had recently been laid off from *Fame* and was available. I explained to Thorpe that Bud would have to start the movie without me, because my directing assignment on *Fame* conflicted with *Happy Endings'* schedule. As it turned out, both Jerry and I started filming on exactly the same day, but since I had only a seven-day shooting schedule, I would be able to join Bud by the middle of the second week. Thorpe wasn't too happy with this arrangement, but there really wasn't much he could do about it.

My relationship with Jerry Thorpe had always been a bit strained, even from the very beginning when I had first edited the pilot movie for the *Harry O* series, starring David Jansen, for him. I had initially made a big hit with him when I did some creative editing on a sequence he'd had some trouble with on the set. Thorpe loved what I had done and started bringing people up to my cutting room every day during his lunch break to have me run the sequence for them. I was pleased when the *Los Angeles Times* reviewed the film and singled out the editing as a major contributing factor to its success. *Harry O* went on the ABC schedule and ran for three very successful seasons. Jerry Thorpe asked me to edit his next project, this one a pilot for NBC about a hospital and its staff called *The Healers*, and also to become the associate producer on his other highly successful series, *Kung Fu*. Unfortunately, the star of *Kung Fu*, David Carradine, was starting to misbehave on the set, causing production delays, so the studio decided that Jerry should spend more time watching over his recalcitrant actor and have someone else direct *The Healers*. Jerry would remain the executive producer, but, much to his dismay, they brought in Tom Gries to take over the directing reins. Tom, who had created the television series *Rat Patrol*, for which I had coincidentally written one of the early episodes, had just finished directing a very successful mini-series based on Leon Uris' book *QB VII*, and I found him to be a charming and delightful man who knew exactly what he wanted on the set and was a pleasure to work with. During the making of *The Healers*, Thorpe's attitude toward me seemed to alter, as if he somehow resented my collaboration with Tom Gries. One day he informed me that he'd changed his mind and that I wouldn't be assuming the duties of associate producer on *Kung Fu* as planned. When I asked him why, he told me that he'd been asking around, and a great many people at the studio didn't like me. It was a devastating thing for me to hear, particularly since it was the Warner lot, where I had worked for so many years and where I believed that I had made many good friends. When I finished the film, I turned down Thorpe's offer to become one of the editors on *Harry O* and left the studio. I would work again with Jerry Thorpe many times after that, but from that day forward I was always on my guard with him.

Having already worked on *Fame* for two years, I knew every one of the cast and crew, and they all made me feel welcome on the set. Still, it was both exhilarating and daunting to find myself directing a television

With Debbie Allen on the set of "Consequences."

episode for the very first time. The seven days of prep had given me a chance to familiarize myself with the script, which was called "Consequences" and was written by Billy Field. I was happy to see that the story had some dramatic moments, particularly between Leroy, Danny and Chris Donlan. The main theme of the story was maintaining personal integrity and responsibility, and the challenge came when Danny discovers that Chris has cheated on a test that Miss Sherwood has ordered Leroy to create. I had decided to open the episode as spectacularly as I could, and since a camera crane was now assigned to the company, I designed an opening shot of Leroy arriving in the school lobby and dancing his way down the hall until he runs into Miss Sherwood in front of the dance class. A crane can usually elevate a camera up to fifteen or twenty feet into the air, so I started my shot at the very top of the elevation, then boomed down to meet Leroy and track backward ahead of him down the hall. It was a tricky shot, but the grips — the guys who had to control the lowering of the boom and the speed that the crane moved in front of Leroy — did a fantastic job, and we got the shot in just a couple of takes. The rest of the day went smoothly, and by the time we wrapped I felt like I'd been doing it all my life.

The next afternoon, Bill, Chris and Donna came down to the set. They had just come from the screening room where they had run my dailies, along with Jerry Thorpe's dailies for the first day of shooting on Chris' movie, and since they were all smiling I assumed that they were happy with my work so far. They congratulated me on my work, and Chris added, when the others were out of hearing, that he thought my dailies were better than Thorpe's. I enjoyed the compliment, but I thought to myself, "Don't tell Jerry Thorpe that." As it turned out, the network was unhappy with some of Jerry's first-day dailies, particularly a sequence filmed at Los Angeles International Airport, and they wanted it to be re-shot. Somewhere along the way, something was said to Jerry about my directing the retakes when I finished shooting my episode, and you can imagine how well that went over. I continued directing "Consequences," happily unaware of all of this. When I reported to *Happy Endings* the following week and went to see Jerry on the location, I could sense a distinct chill between us. He asked me my opinion of the disputed sequence, and I truthfully told him that I thought there was nothing wrong and there was no reason to re-shoot it. I edited the sequence, and we ran it for the network; nothing further was ever said, but Jerry Thorpe hardly spoke to me for the rest of the time we were together on the film. I didn't really give a damn, as I had already been told that I would be given another directing assignment in a few weeks, and I had signed for representation with a new agent, so things were looking up. Unfortunately, for Chris and Bill, *Happy Endings* never became a series, and I don't think I ever saw Jerry Thorpe again.

13

A Family Crisis

"Break Dance," the episode that followed "Consequences," was important for a number of reasons. It would be Erica Gimpel's last appearance on *Fame* until returning for a guest appearance in 1985 and then the final episode in 1987. In an interview in 2003, Erica attempted to explain her reasons for leaving, "I really wanted to go and be an actress in New York; that was a dream of mine. For me on a personal level I just had to go and check in with myself and reground myself. And that's what I did." And so, still seeking answers, Erica left the series. As a final tribute, she would reprise the song "I Still Believe in Me" in a simple setting, with Lee Curreri accompanying her on the piano, and beautifully photographed in one long single take.

Another important element of "Break Dance" was its director, Michael Peters, who had won a Tony Award the previous year for choreographing the Broadway musical *Dreamgirls*, and had just finished choreographing Michael Jackson's hit video *Thriller*. I only met Michael Peters briefly when he came on the set of "Consequences" with Bill Blinn to have a look around, but he impressed me as someone who already knew his way around a film set (and I hadn't even seen *Thriller* yet, which wouldn't be released until a few months later and would draw rave reviews for his work). Michael Peters' successful career would sadly be cut short by AIDS, and he would die in 1994, but not before he would win two Emmy Awards and an American Choreography Award.

The script for "Break Dance" was significant in two ways: it introduced a new style of dancing into the show, and it was written by Michael McGreevey, who would go on to become one of the show's producers, write nine more episodes and remain with *Fame* until the very end.

McGreevey, who is the son of writer John McGreevey, began his career as a dancer. He recalled:

Michael McGreevey.

As a five year old, I watched old Astaire and Rogers movies and went to my mother and said I want to do that. So I went to a dance school, and it happened to be bought by Gower and Marge Champion. And Gower Champion was then given his first job choreographing production numbers in a feature film for RKO, which ended up being the last feature film at RKO, called *The Girl Most Likely*, with Jane Powell. He needed a number with kids, and he went to his own dance studio. And because I had red hair and freckles — maybe not because I was a very good dancer — I got cast.

The following year McGreevey tried his hand at acting in an Alan Ladd movie called *The Man in the Net*, and soon after that in a Robert Ryan western, *Day of the Outlaw*. "I started working as a kid actor and sort of learned how to act by working with really great actors," recalled McGreevey. "I had a very good career up to my mid-twenties as an actor, but always felt that I wanted to go to the other side of the camera at a certain point, so I went to UCLA Film School and got my degree in film there." While continuing his acting, McGreevey started trying his hand at writing, and while appearing on an episode of *The Waltons*, a series that his father was writing, he decided to use the connection to see if he could sell a script. "My dad had been writing *The Waltons*, and Earl Hamner was a good family friend," recalled McGreevey. "I asked Earl if I could submit ideas to him, and finally, after about twelve ideas over a period of time, I got my first assignment in television writing a *Waltons* episode, and ended up writing about seven of them." McGreevey next wrote a TV movie with his father based on the JFK assassination called *Ruby and Oswald*, which they sold to Valerie Landsburg's father, Alan Landsburg, and CBS. From that point on McGreevey concentrated on his writing and over the next five years would write over a dozen scripts for various television programs. In 1983 a chance meeting with an old friend eventually led him to *Fame*. Recalled McGreevey:

> While I was doing *Palmerstown*, I ran into an old friend, Chris Beaumont, whose father had been a writer, and Chris had been an actor like me, and we reminisced. He said, "You're doing *Palmerstown*, and I think that's so cool." And I said, "Yeah, but we just got cancelled. What are you doing?" And he said, "I'm doing *Fame*" Oh my God, I should do that," I said. "Who's producing it?"

McGreevey had met Bill Blinn several times before when he was an actor and had great respect for him:

> "I'd had a connection with Bill because my friend Kurt Russell was doing *The New Land*, which was a series based on a movie about Swedish immigrants that Bill was doing. We went in, and I tried to tell him how he should do his show, without any background as a writer at that point, and he very graciously said, "Those are good ideas, but you have to develop them before you can sell them." *Fame* was my kind of show, and I thought that what Bill and Chris were doing story-wise was wonderful. I thought the show was innovative in its editing and its pace and how they were using production numbers, and I really loved the show.

McGreevey pitched one idea to Blinn and Beaumont that they liked, but after turning in his treatment the idea was shelved. "I remember being disappointed," he continued, "but I got a call from Bill or Chris saying, 'Call if you have any other ideas,' and I had the open door, which you always hope for as a freelancer." One night, when he was half asleep and half watching television, McGreevey suddenly became aware of some very unusual dancing on the screen.

> I turned up the volume and I came to find out that it was a form of street dancing called break dancing, and that it came straight out of gang culture. Well, immediately the next morning, because I figured that they'd get a lot of calls, I called Bill and asked him if he knew anything about break dancing. When he said that he didn't, I told him, "Well, you're going to hear a lot about it; you're going to get a lot of calls today." To my surprise, I went

in the next day, I'd put together a story and pitched it to Chris and Bill, and nobody had come up with it. So finally I was off and running, and I did my first *Fame* script.

The story involved Danny Amatulo being terrorized by a street gang and being forced to find the best dancer who could help the gang win a dance contest that was to be held with a rival gang. In McGreevy's original draft, that would, of course, have been Leroy, but Gene Anthony Ray was up to his old tricks of being late for work or not showing up, and once again Michael DeLorenzo stepped in to replace him. Once again McGreevey was disappointed:

> I was really excited because they had this director/choreographer, Michael Peters, who was the Michael Jackson guy, the hottest thing in the business. They had brought in a break dancing expert, and it was all falling into place beautifully. I was really excited for the possibilities. At the last minute, Chris called me and said, "Mike, I apologize for this, but Bill and I have to do a fast rewrite on the script." And they did, they had to adjust it, but the good thing that came out of that is that it gave a young man, whom I later became friends with, and who I thought was a terrific talent, too, Michael DeLorenzo, his opportunity.

DeLorenzo would build on that opportunity throughout his remaining years on *Fame* and afterward, in dozens of various television shows, including his starring role as Detective Eddie Torres on *New York Undercover*.

The next episode, "Secrets," was written by Parke Perine and directed by Victor French, both of whom would later work for Michael Landon on *Highway to Heaven*. Victor was primarily an actor who began directing while appearing on *Gunsmoke* in the early '70s and ultimately doubled as an actor and director on several other television series. He would actually return to *Fame* later in the season to portray Christopher Donlon's father in "The Home Front." This episode, "Secrets," allowed one of our supporting players to come to the fore, David Greenlee, who had been playing Dwight Mendenhall, the hall monitor, since the beginning of the second season. Dwight began as the officious little twerp that you loved to hate, but evolved over time into a character with more sympathetic tendencies. For a couple of episodes he even had a love interest, played by the future voice of Bart Simpson, Nancy Cartwright. "One of my favorite characters, I just have to say, was Dwight Mendenhall," admitted Michael McGreevey. "I don't think he was a great actor, but he was perfect, and it was fun to write that character because every school had the fink, the hall monitor who was full of power." In "Secrets," Dwight arrived at the school one day with several severe visible bruises, and, upon investigation, it turned out that he had been the victim of a bully. The subplot concerned rumored drug trafficking at the school, so once again *Fame* found itself dealing with far more serious subjects than just music and dance, something it would continue to do all through its run on television. David Greenlee would go on to co-star on the television series *Beauty and the Beast* in the highly unusual role of Mouse, and then build a successful career for himself as a voice actor in animation.

On December 27, 1983, at the Santa Monica Civic Auditorium, the cast from *Fame* and the *Fame* dancers once again performed before a live capacity audience. This time it was Ken Ehrlich holding the producing reins, while an experienced hand at directing live concerts, Walter C. Miller, controlled the cameras. Ken Ehrlich remembers how he came to be involved:

> They had done Europe very successfully. So when I made my deal with Jerry Gottlieb I said that I wanted to be involved, that I wanted to do at least a couple of concert shows too. "Oh that's great, you're great for that. These will be your shows, and we'll give you a little extra for that.

Fame Looks at Music '83 was a look back at the music of that year. Cynthia Gibb and Billy Hufsey joined regulars Debbie Allen, Valerie Landsburg, Gene Anthony Ray and Carlo Imperato in performing, before a star-studded audience, songs by Prince, the Eurythmics, Billy Joel, Lionel Ritchie and a tribute to Michael Jackson. Since Erica Gimpel had left the show, the movie's original Coco, Irene Cara, joined the cast to perform the title song, as well as two songs that she had written. The show was a smash and could probably have been aired as a special instead of merely as one of the season's episodes on January 28, 1984.

14

Another Assignment
and a Mistake

The next few episodes brought guest actors back into the fold, including Donna McKechnie, the Tony Award — winning actress from *Chorus Line*, who joined the cast in a reoccurring role as Holly's mother, and Lew Ayres, Oscar nominee and the movies' original Dr. Kildare, who played an unusual love interest for Valerie Landsburg's Doris. Melissa Manchester made her dramatic television debut as a substitute teacher who gave up a career as a singer because of stage fright. Chris Beaumont wrote the script for "Home Again" based on a story idea of Manchester's, and in which the Grammy Award–winner sang two of her hits, "City Lights" and "Better Days."

Then Morgan Stevens came up with an idea for an episode that featured the late comedian George Kirby as a down and out former nightclub comic, now homeless and suffering from alcoholism. Chris Beaumont remembers working with Morgan on the script:

> Morgan had a commitment, good writing through research. However, he took it to an extreme, I remember, because the story revolved about a homeless person, so he went down to the Hope Mission in Skid Row, and somebody, if I remember correctly, somebody came after him with a screwdriver or something, and he had to fight his way out of there. I mean, it got dangerous, as it does down there. I think that he did it for all the right reasons; he wanted to get into the head space of what he was writing about. I remember saying to him, be careful. Not that I'd had all that much experience with that part of town; however, I knew it could be dangerous. But Gung-Ho, he was going to go find out what it was like, and I remember he came back a couple of days later and said, "I maybe should've listened to you. It got dangerous down there." And then he wrote a draft, and it was my job to do the rewrite. There were several scripts that were written by actors, Bill [Blinn] was very generous in giving Valerie and Morgan and several others a chance to write, and I'd hope that they would also say that they learned

120

a lesson that it's not as easy as it looks. Morgan did a fine job for someone who had never written a script before, but they all got rewritten.

I've been trying to remember the genesis for "Signs," the teleplay I wrote with Valerie Landsburg, and I seem to recall that I read or saw something about a theater project that was operated by and for hearing-impaired actors. It sparked an idea for a story for *Fame*, but only in the most general sense; I didn't really have any details worked out. Then one day, this must have been at a looping session during the second season, I mentioned something about it to Valerie, just in passing, and she said that she knew one of the actresses at the theater. When I mentioned that I was thinking of incorporating the subject into a script for *Fame*, Valerie became very excited and announced, "That's great. I'll write it with you." I more or less laughed that off and thought nothing more about it — until early in the third season when I received another phone call from Bill Blinn. "Congratulations," he said. "I've got good news and bad news. Good news, you have another writing assignment. Bad news, you get to write it with Valerie." She had apparently burst into Blinn's office with the announcement that she and I had this terrific story idea, and that Bill should put us to work on it immediately. Maybe it was because Valerie's father was a successful producer, or maybe it was just her nature, but Valerie came equipped with a strong sense of entitlement. If she wanted something, nothing could stand in the way of her getting it. So Valerie and I set out to come up with the "terrific story idea" that she had already sold Blinn on hiring us to write. Of course, we had no idea what it was at that point, except that it should include one of the cast members and a hearing-impaired person, preferably of the opposite sex. I would go down to the set and sit with Valerie between set-ups to toss story ideas about, and eventually we came up with enough beats to make up a complete story. Somewhere along the way I had researched the fact that an injury could cause temporary deafness, and Valerie and I decided to make Chris Donlan our victim. Valerie knew a little sign language because she had a friend who was in the Los Angeles chapter of the National Theatre of the Deaf. I think that I suggested to Valerie that she write up the story in the form of an outline, and I would do the same, then we would combine our ideas. When I saw Valerie's outline I knew that I was in trouble — it was terribly flimsy, with hardly any developing of the story beyond what we had initially discussed. Since we had a firm commitment for story and teleplay, there was no point in going to Bill Blinn until I had fleshed out the idea properly. I went over the concept with Chris Beaumont, who arranged for Valerie's friend from the Theatre of the Deaf to come in and talk to us. I then wrote up a revised treatment and sent it to Blinn, who okayed it. Since Valerie was so busy acting, I suggested that I take a run at the first draft, and then she could later add her thoughts to it. As it turned out, there was a bit of a push to get the script out, so I had to really concentrate on it.

Katie and I had planned a weekend visit with my son in Santa Barbara, and we were staying at a small bed and breakfast near the marina that was really lovely, at least I think it was. After a breakfast with Katie and my son, I closed myself off in our hotel room and started to write, and I didn't come out until it was time for dinner, so I didn't get to enjoy much of the hotel's beauty. The next day was the same thing, but by the end of the weekend I had a complete first draft. I gave it to Valerie on Monday morning, and she went through it, making a few corrections here and there, but not changing anything of any consequence. As was the usual procedure, Bill or Chris, I can't remember which one, took a pass at the script and cleaned it up a bit, and the next thing I knew, "Signs" was on the shooting schedule. I rather liked the story that we had come up with because it gave us a chance to get away from our school environment and explore fresh ground, both literally and dramatically. Billy Hufsey did a credible job of portraying the fear and uncertainty his character felt when his hearing began to go, and later his resistance to leaving the growing relationship that he had developed with a deaf student at the new school. Valerie's friend Jackie Kinner played Theresa, Chris' new girlfriend, and we filmed at an actual school for the hearing impaired and used a number of the students as extras. The only problem for me was that Bill Blinn offered me the chance to direct the episode, and I turned it down. It was a foolish mistake, but at the time I was afraid that I would have problems with Valerie challenging my direction, saying, "That's not the way I wrote it!" I should have realized that Valerie was too professional to do that. Bill Claxton did a terrific job of directing, and sometime later the script for "Signs" actually won an award. The California Governor's Committee for Employment of the Handicapped nominated our script for "Increasing Public Awareness and Changing Attitudes Toward Persons with Disabilities." A nice thought, but I doubt that our script achieved that lofty goal. Valerie and her fiancé, James McVay, and Katie and I shared a table at the Beverly Hilton Hotel's grand ballroom. Jim was a talented musician who we had met previously when Valerie had invited Katie and me to the Sidewalk Café in Venice Beach, where he and his band played every weekend and Valerie would join in as their vocalist.

The dinner was the usual banquet food, some form of chicken and vegetables, and the other guests at our table were complete strangers to us. We passed the time with small talk until the ceremonies began, and then suddenly we heard our names being announced as the winners in our category. I was shocked, and I think Valerie was too, although she covered it well and was the first one on her feet and heading toward the podium with her acceptance speech. I can't remember what either of us said, but I'm sure that Valerie's was far more coherent than mine. I returned to our table still in shock and clutching the wood and imitation brass plaque, to receive congratulatory hugs from Katie. My plaque for "Signs" still hangs on my office wall, along with the Emmy nominations from the first season of *Fame* and several other awards.

Because of my rather foolish decision not to direct "Signs," I was given the next episode in rotation, a script written by our producer, Ken Ehrlich, called "Heritage." The idea grew out of a discussion between Ehrlich and Bill Blinn over different music styles. "I said as long as I know the performer I'm fine," Blinn recalls telling Ehrlich. "You like people I've never heard of in my life, and he replied, 'Well, you're not in our demographic. You don't know what Klezmer music is.' I had no idea what Klezmer was." According to Wikipedia, *Klezmer* is a Hasidic musical tradition developed around the 15th century. Originally, klezmer referred to musical instruments, and was later extended to refer to musicians themselves. The repertoire is largely dance songs for weddings and other celebrations, the lyrics, terminology and song titles are typically in Yiddish. From that background sprang the idea for "Heritage," where Doris appears to reject her heritage when she initially resists performing at a Holocaust Survivors Benefit. Ken Ehrlich had fond memories of his writing experience:

> I just loved writing for *Fame*. And you know why? I don't want to say it was easy, but why it was really fun to do was because Bill had defined the characters so wonderfully and not as clichés; they had heart. I believe all he ever asked of writers, he never said it this way, but to me it was like, "Here's this tree that I grew, and the branch going out this way is a story. So now all you need to do if you want to write successfully for this show is just take the bough over here and just add something that hasn't been there before, but make it part of the tree."

Chris Beaumont recalled how Ken Ehrlich first approached Bill Blinn with his idea for "Heritage":

> I remember Ken saying that he had an idea for a show, and he was cute
> about it. He said, "I'm not going to tell you anything now about it, I'm
> going to schedule a pitch session." So Bill played along and said, "Great.
> I've got time at two o'clock tomorrow, don't be late. Beaumont, you be
> here." So we were in Bill's office at two o'clock, and Donna Lee came in and
> announced that the writer was here for the pitch. He came in, and he was
> wearing a tweed jacket, some costume to look like a writer, and he came in
> and he pitched the Jewish part of the story.

Most likely the idea for the other half of the story came from Bill Blinn
or Chris Beaumont, as it involved Lydia being hired to teach a dance class
to a basketball team. They cast a bunch of real basketball players, including Rick Barry, Jerry Chambers, Happy Hairston and Debbie's husband
and former guard for the L.A. Lakers and Clippers, Norm Nixon. To say
these guys were ill at ease would be putting it mildly. Only Bob Seagren,
the 1968 Olympic Gold Medalist for the pole vault, who had been cast as
the team's coach, had any prior acting experience; but eventually I got
them to loosen up and say their lines like normal people. It was a bit of
a challenge for me, but that was nothing compared to the challenge when
Debbie decided to feature Norm Nixon in a fast-moving dance number
that involved the entire dance company and was to be shot on location at
a park in downtown Los Angeles. Norm had never danced before in his
life, and even though I'm sure that Debbie worked with him at home, he
wasn't up to the intricate moves that were called for, so a photo double/
dancer was hired. Although this dancer handled most of the complex routine in the wider angles, Norm still had to match some of the dance moves
in his close shots, and that took some fancy editing to make it work. I
remember it was freezing cold that day, and the March winds were blow-
ing, helping all of us to believe that we really were in New York's Central
Park instead of in McArthur Park in Los Angeles, the park that Jimmy
Webb and Richard Harris had immortalized in the song of the same name.

   Thanks to Debbie's supervision of the dance, and the film crew's hard
work, I was able to get the day's work done, including several dialogue
scenes, just as the sun was setting over the distant palm trees that we had
tried so vigilantly to keep out of every set-up. No palm trees in New York
City, you know.

   The other half of the episode involved Valerie Landsburg, Albert
Hague and a wonderful character actor named Milton Seltzer, playing a
Holocaust survivor, and, of course, a Klezmer band. It also featured a
lovely actress, Madlyn Rhue, playing Doris' mother. I had first met Madlyn back in the early sixties at Warner Bros. when she played Rosalind Rus-

I'm sure that Norm Nixon isn't telling Debbie and me, "And here's where I do my pirouette."

sell's married daughter in *A Majority of One*, with future *Fame* director Ray Danton as her husband. I remember I went down to the set one day to watch them filming a scene between Madlyn and Rosalind Russell. The director, Mervyn LeRoy, was standing in the middle of the set watching a rehearsal through a camera viewfinder. The viewfinder, an optical device attached to the camera and normally used by the camera operator as a monitor, is designed to match the characteristics of the camera's lens. In those days directors often took it off the camera to find the right spot to shoot their scene. Now, Mervyn LeRoy was a famous filmmaker; After all, he'd directed such classics as *Little Caesar*, with Edward G. Robinson and *They Won't Forget*, in which he introduced Lana Turner to movie audiences, and he'd produced *The Wizard of Oz*, but on this day he seemed a little unsure of himself. LeRoy asked Russell and Madlyn to run the scene as he began to circle them one step at a time, watching the action through the viewfinder. Each time they came to the end of the scene, LeRoy would simply say, "Once again," and continue circling. This went on until he had completed the circle and was back where he started. LeRoy lowered the viewfinder and turned to Harry Stradling Sr., his cameraman, and said, "Put the camera here." Stradling then informed him that they had already filmed the scene from that position. Without missing a beat, LeRoy put the viewfinder back to his eye, and saying, "Once again," he began to circle Madlyn and Russell once again. At which point I left the set.

I have great admiration for the way Madlyn continued to handle a very successful career, in spite of being diagnosed with multiple sclerosis in 1977. She played Mrs. Schwartz in eight episodes, starting with "Street Kid" in 1982 and ending with "Dreams" in 1985, by which time she was confined to a wheelchair. When we shot "Heritage," Madlyn was using a cane and still able to stand for a limited amount of time, so I was able to stage one of her scenes with Valerie with the two of them standing at the kitchen sink washing dishes. Madlyn never complained; in fact, she was one of the most joyous people I ever met. She continued acting in her wheelchair until 1997, when she retired to the Motion Picture and Television Country Home retirement center in Woodland Hills, California. She passed away there from complications from her multiple sclerosis in December of 2003 at the age of 68. I think a quote of hers that appears in her biography sums up her feelings about her life quite eloquently: "We each have two lives. The one we learn by and the one we live by after that."

In one of the Holocaust Survivors Benefit sequences, Valerie Landsburg sang and Lee Curreri played the piano in a duet with the Klezmer band — a rousing folk tune-inspired song called "Let Your Feelings Show." While Debbie Allen would conceive and choreograph most of the big production numbers, the staging and designing of the camera moves for the songs was left to the creativity of the directors. My ability to read music had been reduced over the years to a reliance on the childhood paradigm "Every Good Boy Does Fine" in order to picture the keys on a piano. From there I could decipher the notes on the sheet music just enough to plot the points in the song where I would move my camera or have the performer change positions. By the time I'd arrived at "Heritage" I was getting pretty good at it, and even had the extras, a group of elderly men and women from a nearby Jewish retirement home, join in with hand clapping and dancing. In spite of everything, I have to say that "Heritage" still rated higher on my list of favorite episodes than some of the shows that I would be assigned to direct in the coming years. I also remember that Debbie was pregnant with Vivian, her first child, and we had to be careful how we photographed her, as she was beginning to show just a little. This was Lee Curreri's final episode; he left without further mention, and his disappearance from the show was never explained.

Armando Huerta, who had been with the show since the very beginning as a second assistant director, and had been promoted to first a.d. in the second season, had been working with me as my first assistant on "Consequences" as well as during the prep for "Heritage." One day he showed up at the office wearing a patch over one eye, explaining that he was having eye problems; but it seemed to me that there was more to it than that. When I asked Donna Lee about it she remembered the situation quite clearly:

> He was having perception problems. I think somebody said that he tripped on the set and he shouldn't have. I remember when my sister Linda, when the cancer started to go to her brain, she stuck her head in the door frame to say hello and cracked her head because her perception was off. He had done the same thing. I had to have this conversation with him, saying you can't come back until we get a doctor's diagnosis, and that was the beginning of the end. He never did come back.

An assistant director's job isn't easy, but Armando had a special talent for making it look like anyone could do it. He had been very supportive when I first moved up to director, and when he left I greatly missed his being there. His had been a very short career in a business he quite obviously loved — a mere six years. Armando died on September 6, 1984. He was only 33 years old.

15

We Have to
Say Goodbye

The final episode of the third season, "The Home Front," was filmed against a background of uncertainty and gloom; it was, in fact, the end of an era for *Fame*. Bill Blinn, the man most responsible for the success of the series and the guiding light for all of us, was leaving. I had been hearing rumors for some time that Bill was going to be leaving the show, but nothing had been said officially. The first real indication I received that there was any truth to the rumors came about because of a totally separate project that Bill Blinn and I were involved in. Some months before, I'd seen a local program on CBS with Steve Edwards called *Two on the Town* that documented a non-profit community training course that was held each summer at the Marine Corps Base at Camp Pendleton in San Diego County. The course took young men ages 12 to 17 and ran them through an accelerated and modified Boot Camp. A popular film at the time was *The Bad News Bears*, and it seemed to me that this subject had many of the same elements in it and was a natural for a feature film. When I mentioned it the following day to Bill Blinn, he liked the idea and agreed to produce the project with me, so I began the process of tracking down the rights. It took me quite some time to accomplish this, but eventually we had the rights and had signed a writer by the name of David Chisholm to work with me on developing a story we called "Devil Pups," which was the name of the youth program and was based on the label "Devil Dogs" that was given to World War I marines by German soldiers.

We had already held a couple of meetings with potential buyers, and could see that we had a solid project that would sell somewhere very soon, when I received a phone call from my agent with upsetting news. He had just heard from Bill Blinn's agent, Leonard Hanser, that, without any explanation or apology, he was pulling Bill Blinn out of his arrangement with me. Bill, who had intended to tell me before Hanser made it official, was genuinely embarrassed by the whole affair, but that's how I first learned that there was a renegotiation going on between Bill and MGM over his contract, and that Hanser was worried that our arrangement could conflict with the negotiations. David Chisholm and I decided to press on by ourselves, and eventually the project ended up at Disney Studios. Over the next few years, as I continued directing *Fame*, as well as episodes of some of television's most successful series (such as *Murder, She Wrote, Dallas*, and *Falcon Crest*), we entered into what is mockingly referred to in our business as "Development Hell"—but that's another story that I've already covered in great detail in my first book.

The fact was that ever since MGM had moved *Fame* into first-run syndication, they had been reexamining the budgets to find ways of cutting costs, and Bill Blinn's salary kept jumping out at them. He was undoubtedly one of the highest paid executive producers in television at the time, with a per episode salary reportedly in the neighborhood of $75,000. Blinn's agent, Leonard Hanser, seeing the handwriting on the wall, had started negotiating with Lorimar for them to take on Blinn's services. Richard Reisberg, who was having his own problems with MGM at the time, remembers the way it went down:

> My relationship with MGM at that point was somewhat tenuous, to be kind. You read about this, you pick up a trade paper, and it says that so and so is going to get it, and I was the so and so they were writing about. Leonard, God love him, he called me and he said, "I'm in conversations with Lorimar." I told him Bill is what makes *Fame* run. I think it's important for what the show is, what it does, and I want you to be able to do the deal. We talked about it for a bit, and Leonard, who had a penchant for the direct, said to me, "You know, we're not even sure that you're going to be there. How is it working between you and Yablans?" I said, "Not terrific; I can't tell you in all candor that I'm going to be here, but this is beyond that." And he said, "Not where I see it." I don't know if it would have made any difference, but I couldn't tell him that I was going to be here and Bill wasn't going to sign into the unknown, or Leonard wouldn't let him.

By the time I began filming "Heritage," the deal was already signed, sealed and delivered; Bill Blinn would be leaving MGM to go over to Lorimar. One afternoon, when the "Heritage" company broke for lunch, everybody gathered in front of the set for the exterior of the High School of Performing Arts on Stage 28 for a group photo. There must have been over 150 people in the photo, including Ken Ehrlich, Debbie Allen, Chris

Beaumont and me, and most of the cast and crew — everyone but Bill Blinn. The group that knelt in front held a banner aloft that proclaimed, "We Love Bill Blinn!"

As a final mark of respect, the school auditorium was renamed the "William Blinn Auditorium." I don't know how Bill felt about this tribute, but my guess would be that he was terribly embarrassed by all of this fuss. He would spend the next few years at Lorimar, where he would first produce *Bridges to Cross*, with Suzanne Pleshette, Eva Gabor and Jose Ferrer, and then reactivate his partnership with Jerry Thorpe to write and produce two more series, *Our House* and *Aaron's Way*. For many of the *Fame* family this would be the end of their professional relationship with Bill; but, luckily for me, that would not be the case. As if in an unspoken tribute to Bill Blinn's contributions to *Fame*, he and the show would be nominated for the third time for Outstanding Dramatic Series at the 1984 Emmy Awards (the *Fame* cast and crew received a total of eleven nominations that year). Howard Brock, one of the new tape editors, would win an Emmy for Outstanding Video Tape Editing for a Series for his work on "Gonna Learn How to Fly, Part II." In 1985, *Fame*'s Emmy count would drop considerably to only two nominations and one award, with Howard Brock's partner, Jim McElroy, winning an Editing Emmy, and Debbie

Our farewell tribute.

Allen being nominated once again for Best Actress and Choreography. In 1986, *Fame* would receive no Emmy nominations at all.

Richard Reisberg would also leave MGM, being replaced by Larry Gershman, the man who had put together the syndication deal and who had, in fact, worked with Reisberg, Jerry Gottlieb and Ted Zachary a few years earlier at Viacom. It was not a happy parting, but Reisberg still retains fond memories of his experience with the series:

> *Fame* for me was my safe harbor. What I would do when I'd had a really bad day, I would go over to the set and just hang out. I mean, it wasn't about creativity — you guys did the show, and my job was to do what I did. There were a few shows that I was lucky enough to be involved with, and when people talk to me about things that I've done and things that I remembered best, *Fame* was just a very special show in a very special time. It was a great, warm feeling.

Chris Beaumont was literally in the room when MGM and Bill Blinn began their negotiations:

> I was with William Morris when I started the show. But then when Bill and I did the pilot about my family and we had some other projects going, I left William Morris and went with Leonard Hanser. I got a little bit of info from Leonard about what was going on; obviously, I didn't know everything. As I understood it, Bill's salary had gotten quite high for that time, and the new guy that came into MGM/UA TV wanted to make a deal with R.A.I., the Italian television company, and he was saying, "Do we really need this guy at $75,000 an episode?" It was a lot of money, and he was looking to cut costs. I don't know the figures, but whatever deal they offered Bill was unacceptable to Leonard and Bill, and there was a stand-off. Bill said, "If that's the deal, then I'm leaving." There was a lot of consternation for me personally, because they offered me the executive producer position.

With Bill Blinn leaving the show, Beaumont found himself in an awkward situation. Continued Beaumont:

> Ken Ehrlich and I were going to executive produce. Bill let me know that he was going to go with Lorimar, and he was going to do other shows. To tell you the truth, after two years I thought that it was a mistake on MGM's part; I didn't think that I was ready to executive produce a show, and I was nervous about it. And looking back, I felt horrible about Ken because he was calling me saying, "It could be you and me doing the show." I understand from his point of view he was ready to executive produce the show, and I really wasn't. I felt that I had more to learn. I had been tending bar two years before, and now I didn't want to shoot myself in the foot and pass up an opportunity; but Bill let me know that he wasn't going to stop working, and that he liked working with me. So I remember I had a very difficult decision to make. And I went into Reisberg's office and I said, "It's lovely that you've offered this to me, it's a wonderful vote of confidence, but I don't

want the job." I turned down a lot of money, and at the time I didn't sleep for about six nights in a row. I look back on it now and I'm absolutely certain that I did the right thing. I'm sorry, because I think I messed up Ken's plans, but he's done okay. If he'd been on that show for two more years, who knows — somebody else might have gotten the *Grammy*s and he would have had a whole different life. I've run into him a couple of times, and he doesn't seem to hold a grudge. But it was a difficult time, what with Ken calling me at home and saying, "Please stay and do this." I liked them both, but as a writer my allegiance was to myself, and I thought, "Golly, I had so much more to learn from Bill."

So now the focus was shifting, as virtually an entire new creative team was being formed to head up the new season. Michael McGreevey, who had already written an episode of *Fame* (as well as a script for Blinn and Beaumont's unrealized series based on their movie *Happy Endings*), was approached to become a story editor on the show. "I think it was Chris that informed me that there was something going on with Bill, that he was not going to be back, and that probably they were looking at the head writer/story editor position for me," recalled McGreevey. "I said, 'What about you?' and he said he'd had a meeting with MGM, with the powers that be." Beaumont filled McGreevey in on his decision to leave the show and wished him luck. Said McGreevey:

> That's the point that I got a call from the Landon people saying, "Michael wants you to do *Highway to Heaven*; would you be interested?" And then the *Cagney and Lacey* people called, and I went in and had a meeting with them. Then the next thing I knew I got a call from MGM saying, "Would you be interested in coming onto *Fame* as a story editor?" So I had these three situations. And the Landon one — I think my feeling was that as much as I loved working with him, it was that I would always just be this guy in the background. I wanted to produce and direct, and I knew that wasn't going to happen on a Michael Landon show. *Cagney and Lacey*, at that point, was beginning the second season, and it was a hot show, and I saw good possibilities in that; but my real affinity was for this high school dance and music show because that's my background. So I went in and met with John Levoff, who was the MGM executive covering *Fame*. He was a fan of mine, and he said, "We want you on the show, but the direction is changing." That was the second time I'd heard that there was a desire to take the show in a different direction, that somebody had expressed the opinion that the show had gotten too dramatic and too serious minded, and that they wanted it more light-hearted and more fun.

John Levoff told McGreevey that MGM had hired two new show runners, and that they needed people with a background in drama to help them because they came directly from comedy. When McGreevey expressed a desire to become a part of *Fame*, Levoff told him that he would set up a meeting for him with the new executive producers, Donald Reiker and Patricia Jones, who, coincidentally, happened to be husband and wife. It turned out that Reiker and Jones wanted to first read some of McGreevey's writings before meeting with him, but eventually he received a phone call asking him to report to the *Fame* executive offices the following afternoon. Recalls McGreevey:

> I went in and I had a very cordial meeting with them. In the room was someone they had just hired that morning, this weird little guy all dressed in black. And I thought, "Boy, I'd never be friends with him." He did do one thing that endeared me to him — he recognized me as an actor and actually knew my credits.

The "weird little guy" just happened to be Ira Steven Behr, who at all times assumed the Goth look, wearing black clothes and dark glasses indoors as his trademark. The following year he and McGreevey would both grow beards, but Behr's would be much fuller and much blacker. Behr, born in the Bronx, had studied Mass Communications and Theater at Lehman College in New York City, and then came to California to pursue a career in writing comedies for television and film. In the few short years since his arrival, Behr's credits were mostly dramatic scripts for shows such as *Maverick* (his first credit) and *Jessica Novak* (a short-lived series that had a brief run in 1981, starring Helen Shaver as a television news correspondent, for which Behr served as story editor). Behr would gain greater celebrity in coming years with his involvement in several manifestations of *Star Trek*, including *Star Trek: The Next Generation* and especially as executive producer on *Star Trek: Deep Space Nine*. In 2005, as one of the executive producers of the Sci-Fi series *The 4400*, he would share an Emmy nomination for Outstanding Miniseries. As it would turn out, Ira Steven Behr and Michael McGreevey would not only become friends, but partners for the remaining three years that *Fame* continued on television.

16

The New Producers

Every television series can suffer from what is known as the third season slump, when it becomes harder for the writers to come up with fresh stories, and the actors start to grow lazy in their performances. For *Fame* that actually happened in the fourth season, and the irony was that a whole new creative team had just joined the show. To be fair, not all the blame was theirs. MGM TV had decreed a new direction for *Fame*—less heavy dramatic stories and more comedy. "Lighten it up," were the orders for executive producers Donald Reiker and his wife Patricia Jones.

As it happened, Donald Reiker, like Bill Blinn, was also a product of the American Academy of Dramatic Arts, having studied there for two years before spending the next decade as an actor. He and his wife, Patricia Jones, sold their first script to *The Bob Newhart Show* in 1976. Entitled "Some of My Best Friends Are...," the plot revolved around a friendly homosexual, played by Howard Hesseman, who temporarily joins psychologist Bob Newhart's therapy group. For the next ten years, Reiker and Jones remained exclusively sit-com writers on series such as *Alice*, *Chico and the Man* and *The Tony Randall Show*. Reiker returned briefly to acting with a small role in his friend Gary David Goldberg's *Family Ties* (Reiker and Jones had written a script for Goldberg's TV series *The Last Resort* in 1979). Then in 1982 Reiker and Jones became writer/producers on the short-lived comedy TV series *Report to Murphy*, which was canceled due to low ratings after six episodes. However, it gave them an intro to EMI Television, and a short time later the duo would write and produce their first TV movie, *Packin' It In*, for EMI Television and CBS. A rural comedy/farce about a back-to-nature, paranoid survivalist that starred Richard Benjamin and his wife Paula Prentiss, the movie received mixed reviews. In 1984 Reiker and Jones joined MGM TV as the new executive producers of *Fame*, with Ken Ehlich continuing as supervising producer and Debbie Allen now also receiving a producer credit. With MGM's stated desire to put more comedy into *Fame*, Reiker and Jones, with their sit-com background, seemed to be the perfect choice to take over the show. The only problem was that *Fame* wasn't a comedy and never could be. (I would have liked to have included Reiker's and Jones' personal recollections of their time on *Fame*, but Donald Reiker, after first agreeing to be interviewed, later changed his mind and declined the invitation.)

Michael McGreevey reported for duty, still not sure what he was in for. "MGM wanted Reiker and Jones because they were going to bring comedy and fun to the show," he recalled. "Which they did; they did make it comedic. I was a little at a loss because that was not my background at the time, but I think I was there to temper that, and so was Ira Behr." Behr was actually hired earlier to help the Reikers write the first three scripts and make the transition from the half-hour comedy to the one-hour dramatic format.

Another new member of the staff was Carol Gary, a friend of the Reikers who had been hired as a creative story consultant. Gary's background was also in sit-coms; she had been one of the writer/producers of a very clever comedy called *Buffalo Bill* that starred Dabney Coleman and Geena Davis on NBC for two seasons, and had been twice nominated for Emmys as Outstanding Comedy Series. Shortly after the *Fame* season started, Michael McGreevey was assigned to work with Carol Gary on developing story ideas. Remembered McGreevey:

> I was thrown into a room with Carol the very first day to break a story, and every one of her comments were punch lines. She was saying, "Don't we need a punch line?" And I said, "No, we don't need a punch line." "Well, wouldn't it be funnier?" I guess I hadn't gotten the idea that we were supposed to be so funny. Finally, at the end of the day she said to me, "I really don't know what I'm doing. I think I've been trying to make the show funny." And I said, "I think you have been, but you're going to have to learn the show." I liked Carol a lot, and she's a very talented writer — she wrote beautiful dialogue.

Ken Erlich was not happy. Apart from not getting the executive producer post, he wasn't impressed with Reiker and Jones, and this would have a detrimental effect on their relationship, as he, perhaps unfairly, compared them to Bill Blinn. "That was a rotten year," Erlich flatly declared. "That was my last year and that was rough; I don't think they ever got the show. Granted, you'd had the Pope there the year before. God was there. But what they did to that show ... they questioned everything, they changed everything." Season Four had started off fairly traditionally, with auditions once again being held and once again several future stars being passed over. Erlich recalled:

> Melissa Etheridge and Paula Abdul both auditioned for the show that year. We held open auditions, and I thought the two of them were terrific. I thought Melissa was amazing. I didn't know she was gay at the time, but it didn't make any difference. And had we found out it would have been an incredible story line in 1984. I remember having a conversation with the Reikers, but I was definitely out-voted, and to this day, Melissa, both publicly and privately, to me will say, "The best thing that ever happened to me was not getting on that show." I thought Melissa would have been great.

One can presume that Erlich can take the credit for introducing the first hip-hop number on *Fame* when new arrival Jesse Borrego is introduced in "Czech-Mate," singing "We've Got a Good Thing Going" on location in New York.

Erlich wasn't the only one that was unhappy; several cast members were responding negatively to the new scripts. Michael McGreevey remembers it this way:

> What started to become apparent to me was that Valerie, Ken, Carole Mayo Jenkins, Debbie Allen — all were responding to these initial scripts, and they were all very upset that the Bill Blinn vision was not just being adjusted, but that it was being destroyed. And I really can't say that I didn't agree with them; I did. Ira and I tried that first year to instill good dramatic ideas into the pieces. Reiker and Jones, right or wrong, their background was that you would hand them something that you had written, and they would stay late at night and you would come back in the morning and get the new pages. And — Don knows this, as I've said it to his face — they would have gutted the scene as far as my sensibilities were concerned. There wasn't the same drama that was originally intended in the scene. So what my focus became, really, was just to make sure that the stories worked. Because if I tried to do anything else I either got re-written or shut down.

I first met Reiker and Jones in the old *Fame* offices at MGM studios shortly after they had taken over their positions as executive producers. Bill Claxton had been signed to direct the first two episodes of the new season on location in New York, and I had been signed to direct the third episode back at the studio. This was to be my introduction to my new bosses. It was a pleasant enough meeting, although I did get the sense that the Reikers were a trifle unsure of themselves. Donald asked me a lot of questions about the cast and crew and my experiences on previous seasons. I was to direct a script that Reiker, Jones and Ira Steven Behr had co-written called "Spontaneous Combustion." I clearly remember that I didn't like the script very much, it wasn't up to the standards of the previous three seasons. The main plot point dealt with an edict that the kids couldn't dance in the hallways or the cafeteria, which causes a rebellion in the school, led by Leroy. There's an ironic moment in the script, given Gene Anthony Ray's ongoing problems, when Leroy tries to explain to Vice Principal Morloch why he needs to dance to express himself and is utters the line, "I don't drink or do drugs."

That summer had been a particularly hard time for Gene — half of his family, including his mother, his grandmother and three sets of aunts and uncles, were arrested in a drug raid in Harlem. Gene's mother, Jean, was charged with dealing cocaine and heroin; and his grandmother, 66-year-old Viola, had six ounces of cocaine and a loaded .38 caliber pistol in her purse when she was arrested. Gene's mother was convicted and sentenced to fifteen years in prison, and although Gene wasn't implicated in the drug dealings, he was very close to his mother, and the incident served to put more pressure on him. Chris Beaumont had his own appraisal of Gene:

> There was such an incredible dichotomy for this guy to be touched by the gods in terms of his talent. He had an interesting voice, not a perfect voice, but an interesting voice, full of feeling. I tell the story to this day about how difficult it was to discipline him, because he would show up on the day of the production number, having been to none of the rehearsals, and Debbie would show it to him once.... I was there for it once when he finally — Michael DeLorenzo had been practicing all week because they figured they'd have to shoot it with Michael. They finally tracked down Gene on the day of the production number. And he came in, she showed it to him once, and they had to shoot it in half an hour, and Gene did it absolutely perfectly.

I also remember that this assignment was my introduction to Janet Jackson, who played Cleo Hewitt. Jackson, along with Nia Peeples and Jesse Borrego, were the new additions to the cast for the fourth season. I was very impressed with both Nia and Jesse, and they would develop into terrific performers over the next few seasons, but Janet Jackson was another matter entirely. "I brought Janet Jackson on board," admits Ken Erlich. "But, here's the thing, I have to say she never auditioned and I knew they protected her." Erlich described late night phone calls he received from Gary Scott, the series' music producer and occasional composer, reporting that he was having difficulty recording Janet Jackson. "I was getting phone calls from the recording studio at eleven o'clock at night," Erlich recalled, "saying, 'I don't think we're going to get this track.'"

Janet Jackson had a strange personality as well. Michael McGreevey was constantly frustrated by the way that Jackson deliberately ignored him.

Each time he greeted her she would turn her head the other way and walk on. Although his partner Ira Behr kept telling him to ignore the insult, it finally got to be too much. One day, when she snubbed him once too often, he followed her down the street repeatedly shouting hello at her. It did no good; Janet Jackson calculatingly ignored him and walked away, leaving him standing there in frustration.

The Jacksons had lived down the street from us in Encino when my kids were growing up. Janet was just a baby at the time, and Michael was still performing with the Jackson 5. We'd heard stories about odd goings on at the family compound and about their father and manager, Joe Jackson's, overbearing behavior. It would appear that Janet Jackson grew up rebelling at being controlled by others. According to the *Los Angeles Times* 9/19/08 review of *Rock Witchu*, Jackson's first concert tour in seven years, control has been the catchword of her career — her 1986 breakout album was even titled *Control*—which might perhaps explain her attitude during her *Fame* interlude. Playing a character that was not at all like her, being told when and where to show up and how to perform, she probably felt a considerable lack of control over what was happening.

I had my own dose of frustration with the late King of Pop's sister. In "Spontaneous Combustion," Janet Jackson literally sleepwalked her way through the few scenes that she was in. At one point I remember that we were set up in the hallway in front of some of the lockers, and I wasn't getting what I wanted from Janet. I tried giving her a piece of direction, but all I got in response was a blank stare. I tried a different tack and got the same reaction. Finally, in total frustration, I said to her, "If you can hear me, just blink your eyes so that I know I'm getting through to you." Back came the blank stare once more, and I knew that it was hopeless. As I remember it, Janet Jackson appeared in only one episode that I directed during the fourth season; however, that one experience was certainly more than enough for me.

The script for "Spontaneous Combustion" also introduced me to an obnoxious character that was new in the series named Cassidy. I never knew what to do with him because I could never figure out where his character was coming from. I suppose that he was the producers' idea of an acid-rock musician, because the actor portraying him, Sam Slovick, who was himself a musician, wore his hair heavily greased and standing straight up on end, but his motivations were totally unfathomable. In the end, the writers, having had the same problem with his character, wrote him out after six episodes. Cassidy's long-suffering father was played by Ernie Lively,

The author in the not-so-comfortable director's chair.

who I would later direct in a number of episodes of *Falcon Crest*, and whose daughter, Blake Lively, has appeared in both of the *Sisterhood of the Traveling Pants* films, as well as costarring in the *Gossip Girl* TV series.

On top of everything else Debbie Allen seemed equally uninspired by "Spontaneous Combustion's" story line about a Board of Education prohibition against dancing in the hallways, and came up with some very weak choreography for Gene Anthony Ray's solo number at the end of the episode. Essentially it consisted of Gene dancing defiantly back and forth between two close and menacing rows of lockers that ultimately pressed in on him in a symbolic finish to the number. This meant that for the entire number I was locked into a highly restrictive framing pattern with virtually no opportunity to move my camera except to change the size of the image. In desperation, I tried everything from dramatic light changes to tilting my camera into odd angles, and even some optical wipes, but it really didn't help that much. All in all, "Spontaneous Combustion" was not one of my favorite experiences on *Fame*, nor one of my better efforts. However, I must have done something right because Reiker and Jones asked me back several times that season and again the following year.

For the next episode, "I Never Danced for My Father," the writers decided to get rid of Caruso's Coffee Shop and introduce a new hangout for the students (and with it a new character) — a bowling alley called Lou's Lanes, owned by Lou Mackie (played by Dick Miller, that wonderful character actor and veteran of twenty years of Roger Corman's "B" movies). Miller, who was a native of the Bronx, actually worked in the psychiatric department at Queens General Hospital and at Bellevue Mental Clinic before deciding to move to Hollywood and try his hand at acting. He played an Indian in 1955 in *Apache Woman*, his first movie for director Roger Corman, and over the next thirteen years he appeared in twenty-one more films for Corman. In 1979 Miller was still a regular member of the Roger Corman stock company, appearing in the Corman-produced film *Rock 'n' Roll High School* (directed by Alan Arkush). By the time he made his first appearance on *Fame* in 1984, Dick Miller had racked up a phenomenal list of over one hundred films and television appearances, having also found time to have understudied Jack Cassidy in the Broadway musical *It's a Bird ... It's a Plane ... It's Superman*. Miller would continue to ply his Bronx charm as Lou Mackie through the next three seasons until the final *Fame* episode in 1987. He is still active in films to this day.

Earlier that summer, while the cast was in New York filming location sequences, they took time out to perform a live concert at Jones Beach on Long Island. They called it "The Heart of Rock 'n' Roll," and once again Ken Erlich, who was clearly back in his element, wrote and produced the show, with Debbie Allen choreographing and staging the concert, and Walter C. Miller directing the cameras. It became the fifth episode of the new season, airing on October 28, 1984. The concert was basically a tribute to the music of the fifties and sixties, and, with over twenty-four numbers, gave everyone a moment to shine in the spotlight. Janet Jackson did three numbers, including the classic "Chapel of Love" and another song that she co-wrote with her brother Marlon and John Barnes. Billy Hufsey attempted a tribute to Elvis Presley, and there was an extended acknowledgment to the music of the Beatles, featuring Gene Anthony Ray, Carlo Imperato and the wonderful family of singers that backed up most of the *Fame* musical numbers — Luther, Oren, Julia and Maxine Waters, known collectively as "The Waters." The Jones Beach concert was actually divided into two parts, with "The Heart of Rock 'n' Roll II" airing the following January. Some of the concert's two dozen rock 'n' roll favorites also featured Nia, Jesse and Valerie, in addition to Gene, Carlo and Janet. Unfortunately, although the live performances by the *Fame* kids were still enormously popular, the idea of rebroadcasting these concerts as part of the series had become somewhat passé, and their only real value was one of dollars and cents by amortizing the overall cost of each episode. They served to fill out the delivery quota, and the combined cost of these two episodes was less than that budgeted for two filmed episodes. There would be no more live concerts after the Jones Beach event, and because of that, Ken Erlich found himself further marginalized. Referring to Reiker and Jones, Erlich admitted, "I really wanted to do more, and after Bill left I actually wanted to do something the next year with them, but that wasn't going to happen." Erlich would continue to exert his influence over the music used on the show, and, in fact, a great many more licensing deals would be made with major talents for the use of their hit recordings. He would finish out the season by directing an episode and receiving story credit on another. Upon returning to his producing post on the *Grammys*, Ehrlich would ultimately assume the executive producer's position, and as of 2009 has been successfully presenting one of the top award shows on television for 30 consecutive years — quite a record, I would say. On July 7, 2009, Ehrlich would produce the Michael Jackson Memorial at the Staples Center in downtown Los Angeles. It was an event that, according to the *Los Angeles Times*, was viewed by over one billion people world-wide.

17

A Downhill Slide

The next episode, "Blizzard," written by Paul and Sharon Boorstin, and directed once again by Bill Claxton, managed to return to the style of the previous seasons with several stories framed around a major snowstorm and the inherent problems it causes the students and teachers. It was dedicated to the memory of Armando Huerta, the young assistant director who had died a few weeks before the season began. However, the episode that followed began a series of farfetched story lines with even more farfetched titles. "The Monster That Devoured Las Vegas" was based on an old show business superstition of never whistling in a dressing room. Ira Behr's script modified the superstition to have Mr. Morloch commit the blunder in the auditorium, and the episode marked the introduction of director Allan Arkush to the series. Arkush was a good choice for the revised *Fame* format, having begun his career working in the trailer department of Roger Corman's New World Pictures. After serving as assistant director and second unit director on Ron Howard's *Grand Theft Auto*, and co-directing and co-editing (with Joe Dante) the low-budget comedy *Hollywood Boulevard*, Arkush wrote and directed the cult film *Rock 'n' Roll High School*, and followed that up with one of the strangest movies ever made, *Heartbeeps*, with Andy Kaufman and Benadette Peters as lovesick robots. Arkush would direct a total of nine *Fame* episodes for the Reikers over the next two years, shows with such titles as "The Ballad of Ray Claxton," "Bronco Bob Rides Again" and "Holmes Sweet Holmes." After directing numerous television episodes in the ensuing years and winning an Emmy Award for his direction of *The Temptations*, the television movie about the legendary Motown vocal group, Arkush today is one of the executive producers and a frequent director of the once hot, but now cooling NBC Universal Television series *Heroes*.

This episode also introduced the character of High School of Performing Arts student Miltie Horowitz, played by Robert Romanus, the younger brother of actor Richard Romanus who would guest star later in Season Four with Joan Baez in "Tomorrow's Children of the Sixties." Robert Romanus, who had co-starred in the rock 'n' roll classic *Fast Times at Ridgemont High* and numerous television series before arriving at *Fame*, would reappear periodically as Miltie throughout the final three seasons, right up until the final episode.

Episode number eight, "The Return of Doctor Scorpio," introduced British actor and composer Anthony Newley to *Fame* in the role of Trevor Kane, a Shakespearean actor and alumnus of the school who had become famous playing a Dr. Who–type character on a popular science fiction television show. Kane, whose popularity had slipped since his TV show ended, was returning to the school to guest in a school production in hopes of bolstering his career. Michael McGreevey, who would write a later episode that brought back the Trevor Kane character, felt that Newley was the wrong choice for the role. "The idea was," stated McGreevey, "that Kane had been classically trained as an actor. Anthony Newley was Broadway. Patrick McGoohan was one of the people we had originally tried to get, but, unfortunately, MGM didn't have the money to hire him." Newley had been acting since childhood, appearing as the Artful Dodger in David Lean's 1948 version of *Oliver Twist*. He would later join up with Leslie Bricusse to collaborate on two Tony Award–winning musicals and several hit songs, including "What Kind of Fool Am I?," "The Candy Man" and the title song from the James Bond film *Goldfinger*. Newley's acting career peaked during the late sixties, around the time that his marriage to Joan Collins ended, and by the time he arrived at *Fame* he had been acting in television for several years. Newley would return as Trevor Kane later in the season in McGreevey's episode "Take My Wife ... Please." Although as a successful singer he was number one in the pop charts twice, Newley didn't sing in either episode. He died of cancer in 1999.

Another famous singer who guest starred on Fame (in the "Tomorrow's Children of the Sixties" episode was Joan Baez. "Actually, that one came out of Patricia Jones," noted Michael McGreevey:

> She said we ought to do a story that means something. We all sat around and tried to figure out the story, and Donald said, "I remember back in school sitting in the classroom and they did the duck and cover drill, and then I sat back up and I was so distracted my thoughts started to go, and I looked out this window from the classroom and I envisioned a mushroom cloud." I think we later put his speech into the piece. And [Reiker] said, "I

thought, why am I sitting here? You know, what's the purpose? Why am I here?"

Reiker and Jones would write the script, and Debbie Allen would direct the episode that dealt with a feud between Miss Sherwood and Mr. Morloch involving an attempt on his part to introduce an R.O.T.C. program into the school and cancel a student production of *Hair* intended to benefit the nuclear freeze movement. Two songs from *Hair*, written by Galt Mac-Dermot, James Rado and Gerome Ragni. "Aquarius" and "Let the Sunshine In" are performed by the entire cast, and Joan Baez sings Bob Dylan's "Blowin' in the Wind." Once again, a number of songs from the sixties are heard on the soundtrack, including Aretha Franklin singing Otis Redding's "Respect," and Redding doing another of his hits, "On the Dock of the Bay." Michael McGreevey remembers this show with a touch of pride:

> We had to be careful because supposedly MGM didn't want too many serious things. But I remember that show turned out very well. It was, well, Bill would have looked at that and said, "That one works pretty good. That one's okay." So occasionally we did do serious themes.

As if to make up for what I went through on the previous episode, my next assignment was an absolute dream. Written by Carol Gary, "Parent's Week" was probably the best script and had the best cast of any of the shows I did on *Fame*, and it, too, had a serious theme. As the title suggests, the focal point of the plot revolved around various students and their parents as they visited during the annual parent's week at the school. There were three separate stories; the first involved Danny's heartrending reaction to his parents' separation; the second was Nicole's response to the pressure from her mother to enter the New York Science Fair, and the effect that it had on her relationship with Jesse; and the third and least important involved the oddball character Cassidy and Morloch's attempt to have Christopher befriend him to impress his parents. Danny's story was by far the most interesting and most emotionally charged, with several poignant scenes between Danny and his parents, splendidly played by Louis Giambalvo and Betty Karlen, and one terrific moment when Danny loses it and dashes down a school corridor, ending with him smashing his fist through the glass window of a locked classroom door. I shot that moment using an unusual camera mount known as a Steadicam, a body-mounted movable camera rig that permits the camera operator to film a tracking shot while walking without the usual shaking and jostling of a handheld camera. The Steadicam was invented in the early seventies by a camera operator named Garrett Brown, who received both an Oscar and an Emmy for his invention. It was first used by cinematographer Haskell Wexler in Hal Ashby's Bound for Glory, and people still talk about his famous shot that introduces the dust bowl squatters' camp with a spectacular crane shot that then moves smoothly through the camp, following one of its inhabitants. My shot wasn't anywhere near as spectacular, but it captured the moment beautifully as it followed Danny down one hallway and into another and ended in a close-up of his face. I would use the Steadicam whenever possible to photograph musical numbers, particularly when one of our kids was performing solo. In fact, I used it again to good advantage in "Parent's Week" when Carlo and Valerie sang "It Didn't Work Out That Way" while seated together at a piano.

In the old days, motion picture cameras could be large and unwieldy, mounted on even larger wheeled carriages called a camera dolly that required moving on metal tracks. Crew members known as grips would take a great deal of time to arrange these tracks so that they would be totally level and allow the camera to move smoothly without running over any bumps. Subsequently, long tracking shots, though enjoyed by directors, were frowned upon by the studio production departments. Once the industry converted from the bulky Mitchell camera to the much lighter Panavision camera that was used to photograph *Fame*, it required smaller and more maneuverable camera dollies. Our Panavision camera was generally mounted on a crab dolly, which got its name from the fact that the dolly could move forward or sideways without the need to rely on tracks. A dolly grip would handle the movement of the dolly, and Owen Marsh, our camera operator, would control the movement of the camera with two sets of steering wheels that would allow him to tilt and pan the camera. Owen joined the show in the first season with our first director of photography, William Spencer, and stayed until our original first assistant cameraman, Jack Regis, replaced him. Owen was born and raised in the film industry; his father was a cinematographer, his mother was a studio musician, and his two aunts, Mildred and Mae Marsh, were both actresses. He was a terrific asset and helped many of the directors, including me, out of countless tight spots. Now retired, he lives with his wife in Oregon.

I remember Jack Regis as a quiet, dark haired young man with glasses who probably wasn't as young as he looked. Jack was what the British called a focus puller, the assistant cameraman who measured the distance between the actor and the lens of the camera, and would then adjust the focus during a shot. I used to hate it when I would print a take and Jack would then ask for another one because the scene had gone out of focus. As frustrating as it was, I would always agree; whenever Jack Regis asked for another take it would almost always be because the actors missed their marks, and very seldom because it had been his mistake, and besides, it was better to find out at the time than to discover the mistake in dailies the following day when it would be much harder to correct. Jack kept a tape player in the camera room where the camera crew could watch the dailies each day. According to Frank Merwald, Jack gave the tape player to him when *Fame* finished filming, and Frank has kept it in running order to this day. Jack would later become the camera operator on *Dr. Quinn, Medicine Woman* for the final three years of that series' run, and then retire to Palm Springs, California, where he passed away a few years ago.

The Nicole segment of "Parent's Week" had another terrific actress, Jennifer Rhodes, playing Nia Peeple's mother, and their scenes together showed me that Nia was an extremely capable player with the potential to develop into a first-class actress. Nia, which is a contraction of Virenia, grew up in West Covina, California, and went to UCLA on a music scholarship. Before auditioning and winning the role of Nicole Chapman in *Fame*, Nia had played small roles in several television shows, including *T.J. Hooker* and *Hardcastle and McCormick*. She joined the cast in 1984 and was quickly paired with fellow newcomer Jesse Borrego as a romantic duo, while in real life she and Carlo Imperato briefly became an item. At the halfway point of the final season Nia asked for and was granted a release from her contract, but the manner in which she exited the show was both dramatic and controversial, and I will discuss that in a subsequent chapter. After Nia left *Fame* she starred in a few films over the next couple of years and then concentrated on television appearances. Since 2007 she has been playing the role of Karen Taylor on the CBS daytime serial *The Young and the Restless.*

Jesse Borrego, who performed a terrific song and dance number in "Parent's Week," with two of my favorite members of the original dance company, Darryl Tribble and Derrick Brice backing him, impressed me from the get-go. Jesse could dance, sing and act his way around most of the cast, and on top of that he had the body of a young athlete and kept himself in great shape, a fact that was obviously appreciated by the female members of the cast. He won his role as Jesse Velasquez on *Fame* by attending an open casting session in Hollywood after having appeared in several stage productions in his home town of San Antonio, Texas, and studying acting at the California Institute of the Arts. "It was at places like Su Teatro and the Guadalupe Cultural Center in San Antonio that I really built my chops," he is quoted as saying. Like Carmine Caridi's previous experience with *The Godfather*, Jesse Borrego's career-making opportunity for instant stardom slipped through his fingers when scheduling conflicts in *Fame*'s final season de-nied him the chance to play Ritchie Valens' older brother in the biopic *La Bamba*. Ironically, Esai Morales, the actor who would ultimately win the role, appeared opposite Jesse in a fourth season episode of *Fame* called "Savage Streets."

Directing Nia Peeples in "Parent's Week."

Shortly after we finished filming on "Parent's Week," Valerie and James McVay were married. Val's proud father, Alan Landsburg, hosted a grand affair at a country club in the hills of Encino just off the 405 Freeway, and just about every member of the cast and crew was invited, including those who were no longer with us on *Fame*. Bill Blinn, Chris Beaumont, Bob Scheerer, Parke Perine, and Katie and I enjoyed ourselves immensely, and joined in toasting the happy couple, who are still happily married twenty-five years later. But at this happy time, as I was to later discover, for Valerie things were not as rosy as they appeared.

18

Things Get Crazy

After the good work on "Parent's Week," the scripts tended to once again shift from the sublime to the ridiculous. Michael McGreevey recalls the protracted story session on the next episode:

> I remember there was a show called — it was a Cyrano rip off — "Danny De Bergerac." When we ripped off something, we were obvious about it. I remember that particular battle, I kept saying to myself we're going in the wrong direction. It wasn't Danny De Bergerac, it was the reverse, it was Jesse who was playing Cyrano. And I think I said it early on in the evening — this is my experience on my first year of *Fame* — at 7:30 in the evening I said, "Shouldn't Danny be Cyrano?" And Donald Reiker said, "No, no, no, no, it's all wrong, boys." And at 12:30 that morning Donald Reiker leaped off the couch and said, "Danny should be Cyrano!" To wit, I answered, "I said that five hours ago!" That pretty much sums up my first year on *Fame*. I was always being not listened to. But that does give an example of what would happen. I was there, and I would get the story structure to the point where, even though they were doing comedy within the story, the stories themselves at least started to have good dramatic structure.

Donald Reiker tried his hand at directing for the first time on the next episode, "Team Work." The Ira Behr script was a step in the right direction, since it dealt with professional jealousy, as Christopher, gaining some recognition for his part in a comedy teaming with Danny, attempts to sabotage his partner's career. All in all, it was a success, and Reiker would give himself another directing assignment later in the season.

The next episode, as its title proclaimed, brought Erica Gimpel back temporarily in "Coco Returns." It also had, as a special guest star, Milton Berle playing a well known director who comes out of retirement to direct a school production, a device that *Fame* used too many times over the course of the six seasons. Berle, who began in movies as a child actor, and at one time was the highest paid performer on television (with his 30-year contract with NBC earning him the nickname of "Mr. Television," was one of the first television personalities inducted into the Television Hall of Fame in 1984, the year before he appeared as Nathan Adler on *Fame*. I was told that he demanded and was given a portable dressing room right on the stage, the only time that was ever done during the filming of the series. Berle's appearance, Debbie Allen's direction and the pleasure of seeing Erica Gimpel back on familiar turf and performing two numbers helped to make this a popular episode.

I drew the next assignment with a light piece of fluff called "Wishes," written by Michael McGreevey. Michael had the idea of taking the old saying "Be careful what you wish for, as you just might get it" and making it the theme for the episode. He divided his script into three parts: the first being Leroy's appearances on a TV game show in a desperate attempt to raise money for his rent, the second being Ms. Sherwood's taking temporary charge of the school while Mr. Morloch attends a school administrators conference, and the third dealing with Doris' infatuation with, and her effort to date, a good-looking student who doesn't even know she's alive. Of course, none of this works out the way our characters want it to, and the playing out of the three stories, particularly Leroy as a contestant on a wild and wooly game show, is actually quite a bit of fun. We cast a one-time stand-up comedian named Stuart Pankin as the game show host, and he pumped a lot of fun and energy into his sequences. Stuart had worked previously for an old friend of mine, John Moffitt, on the very funny cable series *Not Necessarily the News*, and his sense of comedy timing was impeccable, helping to make the game show sequences the best part of "Wishes." The idea was that Leroy kept answering the game show host's questions correctly, albeit mostly by guessing, but winning nothing but roomfuls of merchandise instead of the money he desperately needed to pay off his demanding landlord. This was the first time I became aware of the term "product placement," when our set decorator, Joe Stone, took me to a warehouse in Culver City that was filled to the rafters with all kinds of commercial products. Everything from dining room and living room sets to barbeque sauce, television sets and candy bars — all supplied free of charge by the manufacturers to be placed prominently in view in various television programs, thereby giving them free advertising. I suppose I shouldn't have, but when offered, I took home a couple of bottles of a tasty barbecue sauce that we fell in love with. But were never able to find in any market — so much for the power of advertising.

Nia Peeples and Cynthia Gibb played supporting roles in Valerie

Landsburg's frustrated love story, and we cast a good looking young actor named Yves Andre Martin to play the sought after young man who turns out to be a bit of a disappointment for Doris. Valerie, Nia and Cindy did a wonderful song, "Geometry," that I shot in the school cafeteria with lots of sweeping camera moves as the three girls moved around the room. Debbie Allen's choreography had a cute bit with a cut-away to a very tall girl dancing with a very short boy. We wrapped up the episode with Leroy still trying to raise money by holding an auction of all of his winnings, and an appropriately named song, "Shopping from A to Z," that gave Nia, Cindy, Billy Hufsey and Carlo Imperato a chance to show their stuff. One of the song's composers was Toni Basil, who I had first met when she was David Winter's assistant choreographer on *Tickle Me*, the first Elvis Presley movie that I worked on. Toni has since choreographed many films and television specials, including *American Graffiti*, *Legally Blonde*, *Legally Blonde 2: Red, White and Blonde* and *The House Bunny*.

I have to admit that while I was working with Valerie on *Wishes* I had no idea how desperately miserable she was. I don't recall ever smelling alcohol on her breath, but Valerie has publicly admitted that, although she has been clean and sober for many years, at that point she was drinking pretty heavily, even resorting to carrying a bottle in her purse at all times. "I was a very, very high functioning alcoholic," she bluntly recalled in a London television interview. "I was the girl who was never late to work, and yet I was in big, big trouble." Valerie spoke of being worn out by the rigorous schedule. "We worked really endlessly," she declared in another interview. "Sometimes sixteen hours a day, and we would be at a recording studio and dance rehearsing." Unhappy about having to continue playing a teenager, and wanting to broaden her horizons, Valerie gave the producers an ultimatum. "I just want to come back and direct, I don't want to act," she reported telling them. "And they said if you want to come back and direct you have to act." Valerie made the decision to leave the show at the end of the season. "I think it was painful for me to leave, but I did what I did and I don't regret it. Five months later I got sober." In another interview she later added, "...and I don't know if that would have happened the same way if I had kept going." Valerie did get to direct one episode, called "Reflections," and over the years she has written and directed a number of episodes for several different cable television series.

"Reflections," the episode which Valerie directed, and for which it appears that she took the screen credit of Valerie Landsburg McVay, her married name, dealt with another serious subject matter — anorexia. The

Reikers received the credit for writing the teleplay, but as was generally the case, all of the writing staff was involved in developing the story. Michael McGreevey remembers:

> In that fourth season, I don't know who actually wrote it, but I did all the background on it, we did a show about anorexia. At that point not a lot of stuff had been done on anorexia, but I know an awful lot about it now. And my daughter, who later became a ballet dancer, I sat her down before she went off to the Milwaukee Ballet and made her watch that show.

Once again, divorce in the family has a negative effect on one of the students; this time it is Holly Laird, and she deals with the stress by starving herself. "Cynthia Gibb, who later played Karen Carpenter, was our best candidate for the anorexic because she was the thinnest of all the girls," recalls McGreevey. "I was sort of proud of that show." The subplot involved Doris putting on a luau for the prom and singing "The Haukilau Song" with Nia Peeples. The classic Jack Owens song, written in 1948, was given additional music and lyrics by Gary Scott and Debbie Allen.

Donald Reiker took over the director's reins again on the second to last episode of the season. The show was called "The Ol' Ball Game," and I remember him asking me a lot of questions about staging a baseball game and how to avoid crossing the line. When staging a scene, a director has to maintain the proper screen direction at all times so that the actor doesn't jump from one side of the screen to the other. When that happens it's called crossing the line and can be very distracting for an audience. I gave Donald what advice I could and forgot about it, but later one of the editors told me that Donald still had some problems that made it difficult to edit the show. A couple of years later I had occasion to sympathize with Donald Reiker when I rejoined Chris Beaumont on a new television series for CBS that he was producing called *Downtown*. In spite of a cast of newcomers that would go on to much greater fame in future projects (including Mariska Hargitay, Blair Underwood, David Paymer, Michael Nouri and Robert England of *Freddy Krueger* fame), the show barely got out of the gate before it was cancelled. I was given a script written by the executive producer, Reuben Leder, that used a baseball game as a major plot point — with not one but three separate games, and all of them highly illogical as far as the plot was concerned. I quickly found out just how difficult it was to film a group of players on the field, the opposing teams in their dugouts and the fans in the bleachers, and keep things moving in the right direction. As I said, the script was pretty farfetched in its own right, but I think "Stan the Man," which was the name of the episode, turned out to be the worst job of directing I ever did. Chris Beaumont and I would continue working together on several spec projects that we co-wrote, but which, for various reasons, never came to fruition. Mariska Hargitay and I would laugh about our experiences on *Downtown* as we worked together again on *Falcon Crest*.

One day Ken Ehrlich came into Michael and Ira's office and announced that the boys had to write a farewell episode for Janet Jackson's character, but it had to be a "bottle episode." This term meant that the studio didn't want to spend a lot of money on the episode, and it had to be shot in only two days. Everybody, including Donald Reiker and Patricia Jones, helped to create what would turn out to be the final episode of the fourth season, an episode filled with clips from previous episodes to fill out the time requirements. So Janet Jackson's character of Cleo Hewitt quietly slipped into *Fame* history in an episode entitled "School Is Out," in which she sang only one number, "Dream Street." This episode, as directed by Debbie Allen, was the final chapter in Season Four and also marked Valerie Landsburg's final appearance in the series until she returned two years later for the concluding episode in Season Six.

Janet Jackson continued her recording career over the next few years, with varying degrees of success. However, it would seem that a so-called "wardrobe malfunction" during her brief dance with Justin Timberlake at the 2004 Super Bowl half-time show would be Janet Jackson's definitive claim to fame. The FCC levied a fine of $550,000 against CBS for the incident, but an appeals court panel ruled against the FCC, and CBS was excused from paying the fine. However, on May 4, 2009, the United States Supreme Court reversed the decision and ordered the 3rd U.S. Circuit Court of Appeals in Philadelphia to re-examine its ruling. While Janet Jackson continues performing in concerts all over the country, whenever her health allows, she can't come close to matching the intensity or the crowds created by another *Fame* alumnus — or, rather, a *Fame* reject; Madonna's *Sticky and Sweet* concert tour, and her album *Hard Candy*, have broken records everywhere. The *Los Angeles Times* referred to her Dodger Stadium concert as "a night of triumph and defiance." Jackson's health has forced her to cancel numerous play dates, and her latest album has showed disappointing sales, but Jackson labors on.

19

It's Looking Good,
but Not for Long

Almost immediately after I completed my final assignment during Season Four, things started popping for me. I had recently signed with a new agency, and almost straight away they were in negotiations with MGM for me to direct two more episodes of *Fame* during the upcoming season. This time, I was excited to learn, I would be going back to New York to film location sequences for the two episodes. In addition, I met with Bill Blinn and Chris Beaumont on a new series they were producing for Lorimar called *Bridges to Cross* and got a script assignment. The idea that I had pitched, partly based on history and partly fictitious, involved an old bag lady who claims to be the matriarch of a wealthy family, now reduced to living on the streets while another takes her place. Called "Memories of Molly," a title given to it by Bill Blinn, it guest starred Ann Nelson as Molly the bag lady, a vastly different type of role than Mrs. Berg on *Fame*, but she played it beautifully. I was delighted to learn that Ann would be able to appear in the role while she was on hiatus from *Fame*, since she was now turning up regularly in almost every episode of the show. My *Devil Pups* project had also gained momentum when, after Bill Blinn left the project, my agents put me together with another very successful writer/producer named Paul Monash, who helped pitch the project to Jeffrey Katzenberg at Disney Studios and got us a development deal. While I was writing my *Bridges to Cross* script, David Chisholm was busily writing the *Devil Pups* first draft. And if that wasn't enough, Ken Swofford had talked to his friend Peter Fischer, and, having met with him, I now had an assignment to direct the opening episode of the second season of *Murder, She Wrote*. I was riding high, perhaps too high. I was ready for a fall, and it would come, but not right away.

153

After a short break, Ira Behr, Michael McGreevey and Carol Gary reported for duty and, along with Donald Reiker and Patricia Jones, began writing the episodes for the fifth season. They worked rapidly to complete the scripts that would be needed for the New York location filming, and by the time production started, eight scripts were ready, with each of the scripts featuring scenes that took place on the streets of New York

In addition to Valerie Landsburg and Janet Jackson's departure, further changes were taking place. In an attempt to reduce his involvement and thereby limit the risk of his delaying production, as well as acknowledging his obvious age, Gene Anthony Ray's Leroy was moved over to the faculty side of the school as Lydia Grant's assistant. Time and his lifestyle had begun to take a toll on Gene's once trim physique, and you could see a conspicuous increase in weight, deeper lines around his eyes, a noticeably receding hairline and, in my opinion, a more subdued performance. Perhaps it was Gene's idea of showing maturity, or maybe the fire had just gone out. Whatever it was, I missed the dynamo that was the old Gene.

New cast member, Loretta Chandler, was introduced to the school as Dusty Tyler. As I look back now, Loretta reminds me a lot of Jennifer Hudson. I can almost hear her singing "And I'm Telling You I'm Not Going," which, in fact, she did while appearing in a Los Angeles production of *Dreamgirls*. If there'd been an *American Idol* back in those days there's no question that Loretta would have been a contestant and possibly even won the contest. Loretta started singing when she was six with her family's gospel group in her home town of Pueblo, Colorado. She had the personality and a magnificent voice, but her acting talents were somewhat less impressive, and the producers quickly found ways to minimize the acting and focus on her singing. After performing on *Fame* for the remaining two seasons, Loretta would appear in only one episode of Debbie Allen's *A Different World*. After that she returned to the stage to concentrate on her singing career and appeared in numerous national touring companies, including *Dreamgirls*, where she earned a Drama-Logue Award from that West Coast theater trade publication for her outstanding performance in the lead role of Effie White. In an interview on the *Fame Forever* website in 2000, Loretta explained how she had to leave the business to help take care of her mother who had breast cancer. "But now, my mother has recovered," she told the interviewer, "and I have just moved back to L.A."

Later in the season more changes would occur, with Carrie Hamilton and Page Hannah coming on board as, respectively, Reggie Higgins and

Kate Riley. Ken Swofford would also abruptly leave the cast, but that's a story for a bit later. Both of the new arrivals had relatives in the business; Carrie Hamilton was, of course, Carol Burnett's daughter, and Page Hannah's sister was actress Daryl Hannah. I wouldn't have the opportunity to work with either of these actresses while on *Fame*, but I would later work with Carrie Hamilton when she starred in a music video that I produced and directed for one of the Writers Guild Award Shows. Instead of speaking, the actors sang all of their dialogue. We rehearsed for several weeks with our choreographer in one of the big rehearsal halls at CBS Television City, and then spent several days pre-recording the music tracks. We then filmed for two days at Warner Bros. Studios, and Carrie, who was one of only two professionals in the video (the other performers were all writers), carried the brunt of the work and never complained once. She was marvelous as the haughty actress who refused to read "...these terrible lines. Get the writer!"

Carrie Hamilton was born in New York and grew up in Los Angeles. She studied music and acting at Pepperdine University in Malibu, California, and made her first television appearance, the year before joining *Fame*, in the TV movie *Love Lives On*. Carrie's bubbling personality and boisterous laugh quickly made the character of Reggie Higgins an audience favorite, and in the sixth season the scenes between Michael Cerveris and her revealed a chemistry between them that was undeniable. In the years after she left *Fame*, Carrie divided her time between theater and film, and in the late nineties her playing of the role of Maureen Johnson in the first national tour of the musical *Rent* brought her national attention. She also wrote and directed several short films; and for one of them, *Lunchtime Thomas*, she won the Woman in Film Award at the 2001 Latino Film Festival. Carrie spoke openly of her drug addiction problems and her eventual success at becoming drug-free. "Carrie was a terrific gal," declared Michael McGreevey. "To overcome what she had to face — I mean, this girl was a major drug addict and at the end of her rope, and she came all the way back and then to get the damn cancer."

One of her last creative acts was to come up with the idea of adapting her mother Carol Burnette's best-selling memoir, One More Time, into a play. She and her mother wrote *Hollywood Arms*, but, unfortunately, Carrie would not live to see it performed. The play had its world premiere, under the direction of Hal Prince, in 2002 in Chicago shortly after Carrie's death. When I worked with Carrie in 1992 on the music video, I found her to be much too sweet and vivacious and talented to have had

Rehearsing on the set at Warner Bros. with Robert Yacko and Carrie Hamilton for the WGA video.

to suffer as much as she ultimately did before dying of lung and brain cancer in January of 2002 at the age of 38. In 2006, the former Balcony Theater of the Pasadena Playhouse, where her mother is a board member, was dedicated the Carrie Hamilton Theater in her memory.

Page Hannah, who played Kate Riley, albeit for only one season, is Daryl Hannah's younger sister and somewhat more of an acting novice than her sibling. Michael McGreevey remembers her this way: "Page was an interesting choice and a wonderful actress, but she shared with me a couple of times that she did not feel comfortable with either the dancing or the singing, and I can remember that we often struggled in the writing of that character." Hannah left the business shortly after her season on *Fame* and married the celebrated record producer Lou Adler, with whom she has had four sons. Lately, her appearances on television are more frequently at movie premieres and at the L.A. Lakers basketball games, where she can be seen with her husband sitting courtside with his good friend Jack Nicholson.

With Ken Ehrlich having left the show, a new producer was brought on for Season Five by the name of Claylene Jones. She had spent a great deal of her early career at Lorimar on *The Waltons*, Earl Hamner Jr.'s, immensely popular series about life in Virginia during the Depression. Starting as a production coordinator when the series first began, Jones moved up to associate producer and finally producer over the next seven years. In addition, she produced three *Waltons* reunion movies in 1982. Michael McGreevey, who had worked with Claylene at Lorimar, was very fond of her; however, I never really had a chance to get to know her. Apart from our meeting in the Reikers' office when I came in to discuss the shows I would be directing in Season Five, I probably only saw Claylene a few times.

Until that meeting I felt that I had a good relationship with Donald and Patricia, but something happened that day that changed everything, and I imagine that I was inadvertently to blame. I needed to have a meeting with Bill Blinn and Chris Beaumont to go over notes on the script I was writing for them, and since the Lorimar offices were also on the MGM lot, I scheduled it for one hour before I was supposed to meet with the Reikers. As it turned out, the Blinn meeting took a little longer than I had anticipated, and I was a few minutes late in arriving at the *Fame* offices. This may have annoyed Donald, but nothing was actually said, and we began to discuss "His Majesty Donlon" and "Broadway Danny Amatullo," the two episodes I was to direct. Also present at the meeting, apart from Claylene Jones, was the new choreographer, Jaime Rogers, and Denny Salvaryn, who had moved up to the position of unit production manager a couple of years earlier. Denny had brought with him the production breakdown boards for my two shows. When a script is approved for filming, it is then turned over to the production department to be broken down into a shooting schedule. The assistant director who is assigned to that episode then goes through the script and writes out all of the requirements for every scene on a special form. The information from those pages is then transferred to strips of narrow cardboard that are then inserted into a production board. The strips are individually colored to signify day or night, exterior or interior, and can be moved about the board until a complete shooting schedule for the episode is established. In addition to several dialogue scenes, I had two big production numbers to film in New York. One of those numbers and several dialogue scenes for "His Majesty Donlon" were scripted to be shot outside of the United Nations headquarters on the east side of Midtown Manhattan. The other production number, for "Broadway Danny Amatullo," was to be staged in the Crystal Pavilion of Central Park's Tavern on the Green, followed by a two-page dialogue scene.

Donald Reiker asked me how long I would need to shoot the various scenes, and I demurred, saying I wouldn't know until after I'd had a chance to see the locations and view the choreography for the dances. Jaime admitted that he hadn't as yet come up with the complete routines, but would be working on them with the dancers once they got to New York, and I would have plenty of time to consult with him. Donald again pressed me for an answer, and he seemed to become annoyed when I again refused to give it. Although a director is normally restricted on just how much time he will be allowed to shoot each scene by the production department's shooting schedule, filming on location in a big city can be problematical at best, and I felt that we needed to see what the physical obstructions might be before locking the schedule. Perhaps I was feeling my oats a bit, but I felt that Reiker's demand was unreasonable, and quite obviously he was upset with my answer. The meeting ended on this unfortunate note of disagreement. I wouldn't see any of them again until a few weeks later when I reported for work in New York and discovered that Donald was apparently still angry with me.

Alan Arkush and Ray Danton were already in New York when I arrived, directing location sequences for "A Place to Belong," "Leroy and the Kid," "Bronco Bob Rides Again" and "Selling Out." Alan left almost immediately, but Ray and I would alternate working with the New York film crew for the remainder of our time there. I had first met Ray Danton at Warner Bros. back in 1962 when he appeared as Shelley Winters' lover in *The Chapman Report*, the film that first made me a producer. I remember his distinctive deep, mellow voice and dark good looks; he could have been a successful radio announcer if he hadn't chosen acting as his first career. After having appeared as an actor in a number of television anthology programs, Ray's first big break in features was in *Too Much, Too Soon*, the story of John Barrymore's daughter Diana and her battle with drugs and alcohol. In 1958, after appearing in a supporting role to Andy Griffith in the comedy *Onionhead*, he signed a term contract with Warner Bros. and began appearing in their television series and features, eventually starring in 1960 in *The Rise and Fall of Legs Diamond*, in which he portrayed the title character. In the 1970s he began dividing his time between acting and directing, taking the helm on a few low-budget horror films before giving up acting entirely and moving into television, where he directed more than 40 episodes before his untimely death in 1992.

Ray's son, Mitch Danton's, mother is the actress Julie Adams, who starred in over one hundred and forty films and television shows, but would forever be remembered for starring in *Creature from the Black Lagoon*. Julie Adams also starred in *Tickle Me*, the first of the six Elvis Presley films that I worked on as a writer. Mitch, who grew up watching his father at work and is now a successful film editor in his own right, has kindly shared a story with me about his father's experiences while filming a dance number on one of the streets in Spanish Harlem. They picked the location, as Mitch tells it, because there were no gang members in the area; and since it was an east/west street they'd have daylight continuously from sunrise to sunset, which would eliminate lighting problems for the camera crew. "About one hour before sunrise," Mitch reported, "my Dad, arriving at crew call, looked down the street and saw a city paving crew, an asphalt crew, coming toward the location that they had blocked off. They were maybe about two blocks away." At that point, according to Mitch, his father asked the transportation captain to relocate their large equipment trucks, "the forty footers," and park them at the end of the street to block the paving crew's approach. As the trucks were being moved, the location manager set about making sure that their filming permits were all in order. A vocal confrontation developed between the film company teamsters and their fellow teamsters on the paving crew, and inevitably tempers intensified. "The truck was spraying asphalt," said Mitch, "and as our trucks blocked the street, they sprayed the forty footers with asphalt." This resulted in a shoving match between the two groups of teamsters; meanwhile, down the block, Ray Danton kept filming his scenes, trying to keep on schedule. "I guess, ultimately, about an hour later," Mitch recalled, "the street crew agreed to go to another block." Ray Danton was able to finish his work for the day without further incident. As I said earlier, filming on location in a big city is always a problem; and as if to prove my point, I had my own dilemma a few days later.

The Director's Guild's contract sees to it that directors are treated properly when they travel to a distant location, and I was treated exceptionally well. I'd been flown first-class on TWA from L.A. to New York and put up in a very nice room on the 46th floor of the Sheraton Hotel and Towers on 53rd and Seventh Avenue, just down the block from Carnegie Hall and the famous Carnegie Deli. All of the *Fame* cast and crew were staying at the hotel, and, after checking in, I stopped by the production office to say hello to Denny Salvaryn. Denny introduced me to our New York production manager, Chris Cronyn, who happened to be the son of actor Hume Cronyn and that marvelous actress Jessica Tandy. The Cronyns were old friends of my family's when they all lived in California during the 1940s. Chris offered to take me out to where the company was filming to meet the crew. When a film company travels to New York they are required by the unions to hire almost an entirely local crew, and since I was a complete stranger to the people I would be working with for the next few weeks, I definitely wanted to meet them as soon as possible. We drove in a studio car from the hotel up to 129th street and the section known as Spanish Harlem. I'm not sure if this was the same day that Ray Danton had his problems with the city's street pavers, but it must have been the same location. As I walked from where the car had parked to where the company was filming, I passed Donald Reiker and Patricia Jones, seated in their directors chairs. Reiker made a sarcastic comment about me that was so out of line that I didn't even bother to answer him. I simply turned around and returned to the car and asked the driver to take me back to the hotel. From that point on I had as little to do with Donald Reiker as possible.

Apart from checking out locations with Chris Cronyn and my assistant director Win Phelps, who had come out from Hollywood, I didn't have much to do for the next few days. On a couple of occasions I was scheduled to film in the afternoon, but Ray Danton's work took longer than expected, and my stuff was rescheduled for another day. I did visit the dance studio on West 72nd Street to watch some run-throughs as Jaime Rogers worked with the dancers and cast members on the two production numbers I was going to film. Jaime Rogers was one of a number of featured dancers in the film *West Side Story* who went on to become very successful choreographers in their own right. Jaime had some pretty impressive credits, including having choreographed the legendary Elvis '68 comeback special on NBC and 33 episodes of the original *Sonny and Cher Show*, as well as numerous nightclub acts and Broadway shows. For his choreography on the Mary Tyler Moore special, *Mary's Incredible Dream*, Jaime was nominated for an Emmy in 1976. I loved what he was coming up with, particularly for our version of Prince's "Baby I'm A Star" that Nina, Carlo, Billy, Loretta and Jesse were going to perform in the Crystal Pavilion at the Tavern on the Green. The Tavern was a Manhattan landmark that opened in Central Park in 1934 and has been a popular restaurant ever since, with over half a million visitors each year. After I went out to have a look at it I was a little concerned about filming at this location because, just as its name implied, the Crystal Pavilion was nothing but mirrors and windows, and that's tough to light and film without seeing yourself or your equipment caught in the reflections. As it turned out that problem was solved, thanks to the efficiency of our crew, but the "One Dream" vocal number for "His Majesty Donlon" that we were scheduled to film later in front of the U.N. Building would turn into a nightmare.

20

On Location

So I sat around the hotel cooling my heels and occasionally reporting to the location, ready to go to work, only to be told they were behind schedule and to return to the hotel and they would call me when I was needed. I did get a few calls from Hollywood to break up the monotony. One was from writer David Chisholm reporting on the progress of our *Devil Pups* script, which was going well, and another from Robert O'Neill, the producer on *Murder, She Wrote*. Bob was calling to tell me that I would be going to Hawaii to film my segment almost immediately after I returned from New York. The episode was written to take place in Jamaica, and obviously Universal wasn't going to fly sixty people there. But their original plan had been to film at a fancy hotel in Orange County, so Hawaii was a definite improvement. I hadn't been back to Honolulu since I'd been there for *The MacKenzies of Paradise Cove* in 1979, and I looked forward to returning.

While I was killing time at the hotel, I took advantage of the Club Level Lounge on the 44th floor to read the morning newspapers, watch TV and have a bite of breakfast. It was there one morning that I watched a TV show with Doris Day and her old friend Rock Hudson, whose appearance was shocking. He had lost an enormous amount of weight, and his speech was slurred. In fact, it so shocked everyone that clips from the show were rebroadcast a number of times on the evening newscasts, along with speculation as to what was wrong with him. A week later Hudson released a statement admitting he was suffering from AIDS. Rock Hudson, who would die three months later, was the first well-known personality to publicly admit to the disease, and he helped bring it into the public eye. A tragically high number of our *Fame* colleagues would die of this curse within the next few years.

The Carnegie Deli was just a few blocks from the hotel, and I went there several times to sample their famous sandwiches and be insulted by their equally infamous waiters. Frequently called the "most famous" deli in the United States, the restaurant offers pastrami, corned beef and other sandwiches, with at least a pound of meat, as well as other traditional Jewish fare. Their menu alone is worth the price of admission — if just to read the descriptive names for such items as their famous liver sandwich, named "Fifty Ways to Love Your Liver" after the Paul Simon song "Fifty Ways to Leave Your Lover." Portions of Woody Allen's *Broadway Danny Rose* were filmed at the deli, and I thought it only appropriate for me to lunch there since we were ripping off his title for one of our episodes.

I finally got my hands on the crew and started filming some short dialogue scenes for "Broadway Danny Amatullo" with Carlo, Jesse and Gene on Seventh Avenue near the entrance to the Sheraton Hotel. The following day we filmed the episode's big production number at the Tavern on the Green. The plot of "Broadway Danny Amatullo" starts out with the basic Mickey and Judy gimmick of the kids putting on a show (or, in this case, a number) to get the attention of a famous agent. Danny finagles a job at the restaurant where the agent eats lunch every day so that the gang can do their bit. The kids performed the "Baby I'm a Star" number magnificently, and I was particularly impressed with Loretta Chandler. Loretta, who is not a small person (to put it politely), somersaulted across the room with amazing agility several times during the number and really stole the show. It was, in fact, a standout performance by all of the kids.

When I first saw Jack Kehoe on the set, an actor who I liked and admired very much, and who had been hired to play the agent Moe Starkey, I realized that the producers had cast him without consulting with me. In fact, I hadn't been invited to participate in any of the casting sessions for either of the two shows that I was directing, which was a violation of DGA rules, not to mention damned inconsiderate. I was beginning to feel that continuing on *Fame* under the current executive producers wasn't an appropriate future for me. We shot the number in record time, and then the two-page dialogue scene between Carlo and Jack Kehoe, which played beautifully thanks to the professionalism of both actors and the New York crew. I was so happy with the quality of the work we'd done that day that I returned to the hotel to start preparing for the next day's shoot of the scenes for "His Majesty Donlon," feeling like I could lick the world. As I got out of the studio car and started to enter the hotel I failed to notice the ominous storm clouds that were gathering on the horizon. It started raining just after sunset, but then seemed to let up after a couple of hours.

The production department's weather report assured everyone that the storm would blow over during the night, so, as the schedule called for, the company reported to the United Nations Headquarters the next morning at 7:00 A.M. and found the sun peeking at us through the clouds. We began filming.

"His Majesty Donlon" was a blatant rip-off of Anthony Hope's classic story *The Prisoner of Zenda*, published in 1894, which had already been dramatized as a play and made into at least six films, not to mention a comedy adaptation with Peter Sellers, and a cartoon version. The classic rendering, and a film that I adored, was David O. Selnick's 1937 movie starring Ronald Colman in the dual roles of Rudolf Rassendyll and his twin, King Rudolf V. Unfortunately for me, in my version I had Billy Hufsey playing the dual roles, and I will never forget the day that he came to me complaining that a certain line of dialogue "just wasn't me." I managed to contain myself just long enough to explain to Billy that he was playing the character of Prince Frederic of Vatonia, and it was this character who was speaking the line, not him. I then went behind the set, let out a silent scream and counted to ten. As much as I hated the script, written by Ira Behr, I was excited by the technical challenge of filming two Billy Hufseys in the same scene and having the characters interact with one another.

The United Nations Headquarters complex is located on an 18-acre site overlooking the East River. It consists of four buildings, with the thirty-nine floors of the Secretariat Building dominating the view. Originally built in 1950, it is the headquarters of the General Assembly, where delegates from the 191 member nations gather, and tourists from all over the world come to visit. We had been given permission to set up our cameras on the driveway leading to the main building, and once again I met my guest star for this episode for the very first time as he reported to the set for a rehearsal. I had been a fan of Henry Beckman's for years, first noticing him in 1968 in *Here Come the Brides*, a series for which Bill Blinn was the story consultant. Henry played the irascible ship's captain, Captain Clancey, and he was always a breath of fresh air whenever he appeared. Later, Henry, who was also a writer, would form a production company called Migraine Pictures whose motto was "Every production is a headache." I loved his sense of humor. Henry was playing William Rosenkranz, aide-de-camp to Prince Frederic, and his performance was one of the few joys for me in the whole episode.

We first filmed the sequence where Rosenkranz spots Christopher

Donlon in front of the U.N. Building and recognizes his resemblance to Prince Freddy. The Prince is scheduled to appear before the Assembly the following day and give a speech; but assassins are out to kill him, and Rosenkranz sees a way to use Chris as a decoy. He talks Chris into taking the job without revealing his true motives. Just as we finished filming this sequence and wrapped for lunch, it started raining again, and this time it was a steady downpour. I still had one more short dialogue scene to shoot, in addition to the big production number, and I was concerned that I wouldn't have enough time to finish everything. I started hoping that it would keep raining until the production department would pull the plug and send everyone back to the hotel, and I could tackle the musical number on another day. I remember huddling with Donald Reiker and Denny Salvaryn in the limousine that I had used in the earlier sequence with Billy Hufsey and Henry Beckman, watching the rain pouring down, counting the minutes and longing to hear the words, "It's a wrap!" Unhappily, those cherished words never came. Donald Reiker didn't want to add another day to the schedule, as the company was supposed to finish and fly back to the West Coast and the MGM studios the following day. Wouldn't you know it — the sun did eventually come out. This left me about two hours to finish shooting before the crew went into overtime and we had to wrap. Now, that may seem like a lot of time, but it isn't when you have to move 75 people and tons of equipment from one spot to another and then set up the necessary lights and camera to film two pages of dialogue and a three-and-a-half minute musical number. The dialogue scene went quickly enough, but then what to do with Jaime Rogers' wonderful choreography for "One Dream?" Donald Reiker demanded that I shoot the number in one long take, and Jaime agreed to restage it as best he could. I had previously sent a second camera to the top of a building across the street to get an establishing shot of United Nations Plaza, and we decided to use that camera for the start of the number and then cut to our second camera on the street and slowly widen out as each of the principals joined in singing. It wasn't very effective, since there weren't any close-ups and you could barely tell who was singing. Later, I remembered a trick I had used years before in a similar situation and added close-ups of each of the kids singing against a black cloth background, and superimposed their faces over the exterior shot. I would need to come up with much more complicated tricks when it came time to film Billy Hufsey playing both characters in the same shot.

There would be a fairly long break for me before I would have to report to the studio to film my interiors, while the other two directors finished filming their shows. Since I wasn't scheduled to leave for Honolulu to shoot my *Murder, She Wrote* episode for another week or so, Katie came back to join me, and we went off to her hometown of Shippensburg, Pennsylvania, to visit her family. I arrived back in Los Angeles just in time to sit in on a cast reading of my "Memories of Molly" script for *Bridges to Cross*, before leaving for Honolulu the following day. Bill Blinn had kindly invited me to the read-through, and I had the tremendous pleasure of meeting Jose Ferrer, Roddy McDowall and Eva Gabor. I hadn't seen Suzanne Pleshette, who was starring in the series, since we were both under contract to Warner Bros. and I had attended her wedding to Troy Donahue in 1963. Unfortunately, the wedding ceremony lasted longer than the marriage, as they were quickly divorced. Since then, Suzanne had become a big comedy star on *The Bob Newhart Show*, and she was a perfect choice to play the tough newspaper reporter to Jose Ferrer's managing editor. My father had played Roddy McDowall's father in *The Keys of the Kingdom* in 1944, a film in which Roddy played Gregory Peck as a boy. When we spoke briefly before the read-through began, Roddy remembered my father and had some very nice things to say about him.

The next day I was in Honolulu at the Colony Surf Hotel preparing to film Angela Lansbury playing duel roles in the "Widow, Weep for Me" episode, but this time, thank goodness, Angela was merely impersonating a wealthy widow in order to trap the murderer and had no scenes with herself. As it turned out, Peter Fischer, who was not only the executive producer but had also written the script of what would become the opening episode of *Murder, She Wrote*'s second season, liked my work so much that he spoke to my agent about my directing an episode of a new series he was producing for Universal called *Blacke's Magic*. I wanted very much to do it, even though it would mean giving up finishing "Broadway Danny Amatullo." I had by this point directed six episodes, and I knew that I needed to build my résumé with other shows besides *Fame*. My agent eventually got MGM's permission for me to leave early, which angered Donald Reiker even further. Larry Dobkin, another actor turned director, was hired to replace me on that episode; but in the meantime, I still had to finish "His Majesty Donlon."

In 1952 MGM remade *Prisoner of Zenda* in Technicolor starring Stewart Granger as the King and his doppelganger. There were some amazing shots in this film where Granger would walk behind his other self seated in a chair or shake hands with himself, and I tried to track down anybody

in the MGM special effects department who could tell me how to replicate these shots. Unfortunately, all of the original technicians had died,
and nobody had bothered to keep any records on how the trick shots were
done. What a terrible waste! I ended up finding an excellent photo double to use in over-shoulder and long shots, and resorted to split screen,
the traditional technique of masking one half of the frame in the camera
while filming Billy Hufsey in the opposite side of the frame, then switching the masking to the other side and repeating the process, with Billy in
his other wardrobe. Technically, the show worked beautifully, but thanks
to a weak script, a weak performance by Billy Hufsey and my own con-
tribution, the end result was disappointing. I'll always regret that this
became my last episode on *Fame*; for as much as I enjoyed doing not one
but two episodes of *Blacke's Magic*, which, in turn, brought me more work
at Universal and elsewhere, I would have liked to have finished "Broadway Danny Amatullo." It was a much better script, and I would like to
think that I would have done a much better job on it than I did on "His
Majesty Donlon."

21

Hello and Goodbye

Once again the producers were bringing in name actors, and in some cases future stars, to bolster the flagging ratings. Between October of 1985 and May of 1986, when the season finished, seven well known actors appeared on *Fame*, including John Carradine, Jack Carter, Myron Healey, Leo Gordon, Bebe Neuwirth, Kevin McCarthy and Russ Tamblyn. In addition, lesser known but soon to become better known actors, such as Esai Morales, Don Cheadle, Dermot Mulroney and Stan Shaw (plus two well recognized character actors, Robert Costanzo and Paul Bartel), made guest appearances. According to Michael McGreevey, Don Cheadle, who would return in a second episode, had a personal connection to the show. "It was Don's first thing," reported McGreevey somewhat inaccurately. "He was a friend of Jesse Borrego's, they went to Cal Arts together, and Jesse spoke to Donald [Reiker] about him." Cheadle had already appeared in two short films and had a bit part in a Neal Israel comedy called *Moving Violations* when he auditioned for *Fame* and won the part of Henry Lee, a friend of Leroy's. "Donald loved Don," noted McGreevey. "In fact, I remember there was talk about how to bring him on as a semi-regular." After appearing again in the final episode of the season, Don Cheadle worked his way through several other television shows before being cast as Pvt. Washburn in the Vietnam drama *Hamburger Hill*, which was his breakout role to stardom. Since then, his portrayal of such diverse characters as Mouse Alexander in *Devil in a Blue Dress*, Sammy Davis, Jr., in *The Rat Pack* and Paul Rusesabagina in *Hotel Rwanda* have shown his amazing versatility as an actor. And his star was undoubtedly burnished by his appearances in all three of the less demanding but highly amusing *Ocean's Eleven, Twelve and Thirteen* films.

Russ Tamblyn began in films as a teenager in *The Boy with Green Hair*, and solidified his remarkable career as an actor and a dancer at MGM in

168

such films as *Seven Brides for Seven Brothers* and *Tom Thumb*, and later as Riff in *West Side Story*. He moved into television in the late sixties and guest starred on numerous series, such as *The Name of the Game* and *Nero Wolfe*. He would later play Dr. Lawrence Jacoby on the ground breaking series *Twin Peaks*. Tamblyn would first appear on *Fame* in Season Five as a character appropriately named "The Choreographer" in the same episode as Don Cheadle and Dermot Mulroney and would then return in Season Six as "The Choreographer." Tamblyn appeared once more, in the final episode, but in a totally different role — as a bigtime actor and (here it is again) a "High School of Performing Arts alumni." In that episode, McGreevey, who was the writer, incorporated a brief clip from *Seven Brides for Seven Brothers* showing Tamblyn's wonderfully acrobatic dance in the "Barn-Raising" sequence. In recent years, Tamblyn has devoted most of his time and energy to managing his daughter's, Amber Tamblyn's, career. Amber starred in *Joan of Arcadia* for three seasons on CBS, as well as a number of films, including *The Sisterhood of the Traveling Pants* in 2005 and its sequel in 2008, and is now co-staring in the new series *The Unusuals* for ABC.

Another guest star, or perhaps I should say the ghost of a star, was the appearance of Elvis Presley in episode number eighteen, "Stage Fright." Having previously worked on six Elvis films as a writer, I was naturally curious as to where the inspiration to use Elvis came from. As it turned out, it wasn't from an Elvis film at all. "They had referred several times to the fact that Elvis was Donlon's hero," recalled Michael McGreevey. "And the Reikers said to me, 'You have to do a Donlon, Billy Hufsey story.' I wanted to do *Play It Again, Sam*, so I was really ripping off Woody Allen," he added with a laugh, "and trying to do it with Elvis." As McGreevey explained it, Christopher Donlon was part of a musical number, and after making his entrance too early he becomes flustered and forgets what he is supposed to do. Said McGreevey:

> He went up on stage in a number and he'd never done anything like that before. And he starts to develop palpitations and all that stuff. This was more about confidence and getting back on the horse and feeling confident about yourself. And we used this Elvis character, who would appear out of nowhere when Donlon would look in the mirror and say to himself, "What's wrong with me?" And Elvis would say, "Hey, little buddy, you're gonna be okay."

The show, which was again directed by Debbie Allen, had as its guest star Bebe Neuwirth as another dance instructor, which is interesting because in the new *Fame* movie Neuwirth plays the dance instructor and Debbie Allen plays the school principal.

Speaking of the school principal, there is a sad story involving Ken Swofford and the Mr. Morloch character that took place just after I finished filming on "His Majesty Donlon." I was still at the studio, working with my editor on the director's cut, and one Friday I was sitting by myself having lunch in the commissary, when Ken Swofford joined me. I'd known for some time that Ken was upset with the direction that the series was going, but this day he seemed to be over the top. Perhaps it was because he was just finishing filming the Christmas show, an episode called "Ebenezer Morloch," obviously another rip-off, this time of Dickens's *A Christmas Carol.* Ken didn't eat, but he did order a number of beers as he voiced his anger over what the Reikers had done to Bill Blinn's concept. I tried to calm him down, but couldn't argue with his position, as I felt much the same way myself. Apparently, after lunch Ken returned to the stage and resumed filming the scenes where Quentin Morloch is visited by the "Ghosts of Christmas Past, Present and Christmas Yet to Come." At the end of the day, on the very last shot, when director Nick Sgarro called "cut and print," I guess all of the anger and frustration in him just boiled over. Michael McGreevey picks up the story at that point:

> That was just the saddest thing that happened during my stay. The funny thing is he had already gotten into it with Reiker. He would tell the Reikers that he didn't like what they were doing, but they actually gave him some of the best stuff he had. You know, you're getting good stuff here, and they actually like what you're doing. I thought he was really terrific.

McGreevey went on to set the stage for what happened that Friday night:

> It was the Christmas show, "Ebenezer Morloch." It was his show, and it was the last shot late one night. It was a two-shot, I remember the dailies. They finished it, and Nick Sgarro, who was directing, said "Cut, that was great." and Ken said, "No, no, don't cut, I've got something I want to say." He stood right into the camera, and I don't know his exact words, but basically with some pretty strong profanity he cussed out Donald and Patricia and told them what he thought of them.

Frank Merwald would receive a phone call over the weekend from Denny Salvaryn. "I got a call from the UPM," Merwald remembered, "and he said, 'Frank, something happened last night on the set, and it turned out to be a big deal. Ken Swofford blew up and told off Donald and Patricia. Nobody is to see that footage, it is not to get on dailies, and you're to make one copy of it and bring it to the studio.'" Salvaryn then told Merwald that he was to turn over the one and only copy to an MGM attorney. Other than the cast and crew on the set who had observed the incident in person, Frank and the colorist at the lab were the only other ones to have seen the footage up to that point. "I was flabbergasted," he reported. "He really went off on them."

Michael McGreevey heard about the incident on Monday morning when he ran into Frank Merwald in the hall. "I could tell he was surprised," McGreevy remembers. "He told me that he had just picked up the dailies and 'something's going to happen here.' I never really saw it," McGreevey admitted. "Donald and Patricia and the powers that be at MGM saw it, and I don't think they had any choice." Ken Swofford was released from his contract that very day. "It was the most self-destructive thing I have ever heard of in my life," said McGreevey. "Of the three years that I was there, that was the most upsetting time for me personally." More tragedy would befall Swofford in the next few months, but he would eventually reclaim his life and continue to work steadily during the next fifteen years in films and television, including a continuing appearance as Lt. Catalano on the perennial television favorite *Murder, She Wrote*. Ken Swofford would retire in the late '90s and move to Northern California, where he still lives.

A replacement for Swofford had to be found immediately, and the casting department came in with a list of fifty possible replacements. One name that stood out to Ira Steven Behr was Graham Jarvis. Behr's then girlfriend and future wife, Laura Feder, was a teacher at a ballet school in Los Angeles, and Behr had just seen Jarvis playing Dr. Copellius in a production of *Copellia* that Laura had directed at the school. Behr gave a strong recommendation to the Reikers for Jarvis to be their choice, and he was hired. "I never had to audition for the show," Jarvis claimed in a *Fame Forever* interview in 2000. It probably was an easy sell, inasmuch as Graham Jarvis was already a well established actor at this point, having appeared on Broadway in the original casts of Gore Vidal's *The Best Man* and Arthur Miller's *Incident at Vichy*, and was the narrator in the original production of *The Rocky Horror Show* before making his film debut as Man on Bus in Sidney Lumet's *Bye Bye Braverman*. He would go on to work on other films, such as *In the Heat of the Night* and *What's Up, Doc?* before moving into television and making a name for himself as the obsequious husband of Mary Kay Place's would-be country singer in *Mary Hartman, Mary Hartman* and as John Ehrlichmann in *Blind Ambition*. Graham Jarvis' character of the self-important principal Bob Dyrenforth was hurriedly written into the very next episode, and he would remain with the series for the rest of its run. After *Fame*, Jarvis would continue his busy career in films and television, eventually becoming a regular on the series *7th Heaven*, on which he was still appearing when he died of cancer in 2003.

In addition to Graham Jarvis joining the show, the next episode, "Choices," which is credited to Donald Reiker and Patricia Jones, and was directed by Reiker, was also the episode where Cynthia Gibb would leave. As written, Gibb's Holly Laird leaves the school to accept a role in a day-time soap opera that tapes in Hollywood, something Cindy Gibb had, in fact, done for two years (on *Search for Tomorrow*) prior to joining *Fame*. The episode, which explained Mr. Morloch's sudden departure by saying he had left rather suddenly to take advantage of an offer to coach a semi-pro ball team in upstate New York, also introduced Carrie Hamilton and Page Hannah as two very gifted young students who catch the eye of the faculty during midterm auditions and are invited to join the student body. Another auditioner, a less-than-talented dancer and street friend of Leroy's named Henry Lee (played by newcomer Don Cheadle), tries to use his connection with Leroy to bluff his way through his audition. The story, filled with various characters and their need to make choices, also included Nicole being forced to make a choice between appearing in an off–Broadway production and staying in school.

"As the season progressed," admitted Michael McGreevey, "I thought it went downhill a little bit. We were just doing what I called 'top of the head stories.' You know, they were based on let's rip off *Carmen*, let's rip off *Prisoner of Zenda.*" The real problem was that *Fame*, which had begun as a character-driven show in the early years, had evolved into a plot-driven show, and there were just so many plot derivations to choose from. With four rip-off shows in a row under their belt, "Savage Streets" *(Carmen)*, "His Majesty Donlon," "Broadway Danny Amatullo" and "Ebenezer Morloch," followed by a couple of shows that did deal with personal issues, the Reikers and the writers then used *Huckleberry Finn* as an inspiration to do a show about racial intolerance, censorship and book burning. As heavy as that subject matter was, they still managed to include a dream sequence with Leroy and Jim, the escaped slave from Mark Twain's classic story. Then it was back to more rip-offs with a Sherlock Holmes story, followed by one featuring a Dr. Jekyll and Mr. Hyde motif. Then, suddenly, things turned serious again with a story about teen suicide. Now I must point out that Parke Perrine had already written a forceful story about teen suicide and the Suicide Prevention Center during the second season, called "...Help from My Friends," but at least the Reikers were trying to include serious subjects — and not without resistance from the powers that be. Reported McGreevey:

> The problem that we faced was that there was this edict to not get too seri-
> ous. There was a quote that I always remembered the Swedish buyer had
> said, "We have a very high suicide rate as it is, we want *Fame* to make us
> happy." So that was the joke that was used. I think by the end of the Fourth
> Season we did some good stuff, and the beginning of the Fifth Season there
> were a few really good things. It was that season that we also did the teen
> suicide where Jessie was on the hot-line at the radio station, the high school
> radio station, and the girl calls in.

It was a show called "W.S.O.A.," which was also the name of the school's radio station, and Jesse, who is the DJ for the moment, keeps getting mysterious phone calls from a girl asking him to play the same song over and over. When it's discovered that the girl intends to kill herself, a search is initiated to find her, but fails to turn up anything until the girl calls again and tells Jesse that she has taken pills. In the dramatic climax of the episode, Jesse desperately tries to convince her to live. "W.S.O.A." also marked first assistant director Win Phelps' promotion to full director status. He would ultimately direct eight episodes in the series and do an excellent job in the bargain.

In another episode, also written by Reiker and Jones, the inspiration came from Cervantes's *Don Quixote* and was called "To Tilt at Windmills." A new English teacher is introduced as a substitute for Miss Sherwood, who is ill with a cold. Broadway and Film star Kevin McCarthy plays Mr. William Quigley, a charismatic individual with eccentric ways. McCarthy who is well remembered for his work in the 1951 film adaptation of Arthur Miller's *Death of a Salesman*, as well as the horror cult classic *Invasion of the Body Snatchers*, turned in a superlative performance as the teacher whose odd antics earned him a trip to the asylum, but who still managed to leave a lasting impression on his students.

For an episode called "The Incident," Michael McGreevey went back to the well once again, but at least this time its predecessor merely *inspired* the idea. Declared McGreevey:

> At the end of that fifth season, I was convinced that if we were going to rip
> something off, I wanted to rip off something good, but I really wasn't going
> to rip it off. I said I think we should do a *Rashomon*-type show, a really dra-
> matic show, and it should begin with Jesse Borrego in the hospital and a
> guest teacher accused of assaulting him. We should slowly do *a Rashomon*-
> type thing and find out how it happened. To their credit, I think Donald
> wanted ... "Wow, Kurosawa! Let's do Kurosawa!" That's what happened:
> "Let's do Kurosawa." I said, "No, let's just do *Rashomon*." So I wrote a
> *Rashomon* piece; it was called "The Incident."

Michael McGreevey at his desk (Michael McGreevey Collection).

McGreevey wrote his story, but the filming was pushed back until it became the final episode of the season and he had already been laid off. "Once all the writing was done and the shows were locked down," recalls McGreevey, "Ira and I would be let go about four weeks before the end of production."

One day McGreevey received a phone call from Donald Reiker saying, "I'm just warning you that we had some legal problems with 'The Incident.'" When asked what the problems were, Reiker replied, "Well, MGM said that Michael McGreevey had ripped off an American movie made by Marty Ritt." The film in question, *The Outrage*, made in 1964 and starring Paul Newman, was, in fact, itself an adaptation by Fay and Michael Kanin of the original Kurosawa film. When McGreevey denied ripping off anything from the MGM film, Reiker confessed, "Well, we sort of rewrote your script." McGreevey admitted to being annoyed. "And I said, Well, I've got to see this, because now the WGA is calling me and saying that they're going to arbitrate and that I'm going to have to share a credit with the two other writers.'" McGreevey asked the Writers Guild arbitrators to read his script before they made a decision, but Guild rules required that the Arbitration Panel make its decision based on the contents of the final shooting script, and that script, by Reiker and Jones, did, in fact, resemble *The Outrage*. Not only that, but the episode had already been shot and was in the can. McGreevey called Donald Reiker and asked to view the episode, and Reiker agreed, saying, "Oh yeah, sure, you'll like it." When McGreevey watched the show he was shocked to see how much it resembled *The Outrage*. As McGreevey related:

> He did it shot by shot. Win Phelps directed it, and actually he did a very good job. The show itself was pretty good, but it was an insult to me. It was an interesting show, but why do you have to completely copy what went down? But, you know, I'll give him credit, he did it blatantly. I mean, it starts like the movie in the rain, and it's outside a theater, and Sherwood and Dyrenforth both come in from out of the rain, and as they're talking you pull back and on the theater you see the marquee — and it's a Kurosawa festival. It was an interesting show, there was a wonderful score written for that show by John Debney, who did quite a few scores for *Fame* while I was there. He later went on to do features.

Debney has most recently written the score for Disney's first Hannah Montana movie. "John is a very talented guy," McGreevey continued. "He did terrific stuff and that particular show, "The Incident," he really did a nice job." In the end, McGreevey was forced to share a credit with Fay and Michael Kanin. "It's the only time I ever had to take a teleplay credit," McGreevey reflected. "Teleplay by Michael McGreevey, story ... inspired by, or something like one of those deals. It was the WGA being very careful, and I'm sure they paid out some money to the writers." Of course, Akira Kurosawa and Shinobu Hashimoto, who had written the original screenplay based on stories by Ryunosuke Akutagawa, never saw a dime. As McGreevey put it laughingly, referring to Donald Reiker, "That's who he really ripped off.... And that was the kind of stuff that went on."

Near the end of the fifth season, the Reikers renewed their association with their old friend Gary David Goldberg, who had just created a pilot for Paramount Network Television called *The Bronx Zoo*, another look at a New York City high school that was closer to *Blackboard Jungle* than *Fame*. After *Fame* had completed production, Donald Reiker and Patricia Jones signed on as executive producers of *The Bronx Zoo*, and Reiker was signed to direct the pilot. Although it was a Paramount production, Reiker arranged for all of the classroom sequences in the pilot to be filmed on the *Fame* sets at MGM. When NBC bought the pilot and scheduled the show for a mid-season debut in their 86-87 season, the Reikers ended their association with *Fame* and moved their offices to Paramount Studios. Having remained executive producers for two seasons,

Reiker and Jones relinquished their positions to another husband and wife team, Harry and Renee Longstreet. When *The Bronx Zoo* debuted on NBC on March 19, 1987, John J. O'Connor of the *New York Times*, gave it a lukewarm review, saying in part, "Populated with what looks like a lot of teen-aged Whoopi Goldbergs and John Travoltas, all of them pussycats under their sometimes forbidding exteriors, *The Bronx Zoo* has as much promise as any other well-intentioned new series, the vast bulk of which mercifully drop out of sight." After its March debut, *The Bronx Zoo* returned to the air for a second season in December, but was taken off the schedule the following April. Now retired, the Reikers have an interest in various race horses and live in Malibu, California. In February of 2002 Donald Reiker joined with over 100 other members of the Writers Guild of America as a plaintiff in a groundbreaking class action lawsuit against every major studio and talent agency, charging them with practicing discrimination against older television writers. According to a bulletin in the April/May 2009 issue of *Written By*, the Writers Guild's journal, the writers achieved their first victory last fall with a $4.5 million settlement from two prominent agencies, ICM and the Broder, Kurland, Webb Agency.

22

New Hands
at the Wheel

Since I hadn't worked on the sixth season, I hadn't met Renee and Harry Longstreet, but when I contacted them by email and introduced myself they immediately agreed to be interviewed, expressing their fondness for the time that they had spent on *Fame*. When I interviewed them by phone at their home on Bainbridge Island in the state of Washington, it was coincidentally their wedding anniversary. Harry and Renee were on separate phones, and Harry was eating breakfast at the time. Renee had to ask him not to use the speaker phone because it was hard to understand him. So Harry, saying, "Okay, so I'll one-hand my breakfast," switched to the hand phone. Renee did most of the talking, with Harry breaking in occasionally with an amusing comment or two. I could tell that they were going to be fun to interview, and I wasn't disappointed.

Harry Longstreet was the son of screenwriter Stephen Longstreet, who had begun his career writing screenplays for the Office of War Information during World War II. Longstreet senior, who later wrote the screenplays for *The Jolson Story* and *The Helen Morgan Story*, was also a novelist and adapted his own novels *Stallion Road* and *Silver River* for the screen, as well as writing the libretto for the 1948 hit Broadway musical *High Button Shoes*, which starred Nanette Fabray and Phil Silvers. Harry Longstreet had at first chosen a different path, becoming first a stockbroker and later joining a public relations firm. He was still in corporate P.R. when he met and married Renee, who at the time was a single mother living in Bel Air. They combined their families — her three and his two — becoming, as she put it, a *Room for One More* family. Renee decided that she wanted to take a stab at writing, and Harry financed her efforts, even though, as she explained, she didn't want to be dependent on a man because of her dis-

Harry and Renee Longstreet in happy retirement (courtesy the Longstreets).

astrous previous marriage. Harry broke in to add, "That's because she was married to the wrong man." To this, Renee's retort was, "Honey, now we can't understand you because you have food in your mouth."

Renee began writing an original spec script, and each night when Harry would come home from his public relations office he would critique her work. He eventually began to write it with her until, in the end, it became a collaboration between the two of them. Recalled Renee Longstreet:

> Gerry Isenberg was a good friend of ours, and he was just getting a series started. He read the script, and he said, "You know, I'm getting this series, *Julie Farr, M.D.*, and if this gets a pick-up I'm going to hire you guys to do a backup script." So we got hired to do a backup script, and Harry kept

his job at the corporate P.R. firm. We were so naïve that we didn't know that when you were asked to do a backup script, you took a couple of months to do it. So we did our script in, I guess, a week, turned it in, and they said that they were going to shoot it as their second episode.

According to Harry Longstreet, when he asked them what had happened to all of the scripts that were already there, their answer was, "Oh, none of them were any good."

On the strength of their first script, the Longstreets were asked to come on board as story editors for the series. Reported Renee:

> So Harry kept his job in Century City for about three weeks, and we started. Even though we had five kids to take care of, we were going to take this flyer. Eventually Harry quit his job, and we started as story editors on *Having Babies*, which was the original title for *Julie Farr, M.D.*, and ended up writing almost every episode. From there we went on to — Kenny Johnson was starting *Cliffhangers* at Universal. Although we had only been in the business about six months, we were older; we were in our late thirties at this point, so they hired us to be executive story consultants, and they had about eleven other writers working for us. We didn't know anything, but Kenny let us do a lot of the editing, and we were getting into a lot of writing and producing and running the writing.

After writing a few television movies, the Longstreets started producing episodic television in earnest. Their credits included *Voyagers!*, *Trauma Center*, *Hot Pursuit*, *Shadow Chasers* and *Misfits of Science*. "We were show runners," admitted Renee, "We didn't own anything. I don't think in twenty five years we pitched more than one or two times. We sold two pilots to CBS." As Harry put it, "We were hired guns, and then this *Fame* job came via our William Morris agent."

The Longstreets met with the MGM TV executives about taking over the job of executive producers on *Fame* during the hiatus between Seasons Five and Six, but they weren't hired initially. "They told us that they were looking to —'they' being MGM TV — they wanted to open up for more humor," reported Harry Longstreet. "William Morris said that we didn't get the job, that they hired a sit-com guy."

It's hard to imagine that after two seasons of "brightening up the show" that MGM would still be looking to put more humor into *Fame*, but they did indeed hire a show-runner with sit-com experience. When it appeared that they were going to get the *Fame* assignment, the Longstreets cancelled a planned trip to Europe, and when the job fell through they were very disappointed. In place of reactivating the Europe trip, they decided to go to Hawaii instead, and booked themselves into

the Mauna Lai resort on the Big Island. The day they arrived they received
a phone call from their agent telling them that the other producer had been
fired. Renee Longstreet picks up the story at this point:

> We heard that the guy they hired came on, and the very first day he went
> down to look at the sets and he said, "Where's the booth?" And then he
> asked about where was the writer's room where they can all like sit together?
> And I think immediately MGM said, "Oops, not so fast." So I think he
> was there for two days, that's what I remember.

For those not familiar with the term, the "booth" is the area, usually
above the stage, where a director sits to control the multiple cameras used
in taping a half-hour comedy show. The show is generally taped at night
before a live audience in one or two sessions, thereby allowing the cast and
crew to rehearse and stage the show earlier in the week and on the day of
taping. Since sit-coms are written in tandem by a staff of comedy writers,
they do indeed need a large room to meet each day and talk through their
scripts. Of course, this process is entirely different on a dramatic show such
as *Fame* that is written by one or possibly two writers, and photographed
on film over a period of seven days on various sets by a director using a
single camera.

The Longstreets spent their entire five days at Mauna Lai negotiat-
ing their contract. Renee Longstreet noted the irony in the fact that their
friend Gerry Isenberg was originally supposed to produce the series:

> When he first was doing it some years earlier, he had talked to us about
> maybe coming on and being in the original thing, but then when Bill Blinn
> took over nothing happened. When we told him that we were doing the
> show, he said, "What goes around comes around." So it was just kind of
> ironic that what goes around, comes around and there we were several years
> later doing the show.

They were told "up front," as Harry defined it, "This is the last. Here's
twenty million, make 24 episodes. MGM TV decided that this would give
them enough episodes to syndicate it where they wanted, and this was the
last year." Renee then added more details. "Lee Rich was the head of MGM
when we came in. David Gerber was TV, and Lynn Loring worked for
him and was our boss, and then there was a man named George Paris who
was their syndication guy." Renee Longstreet went on to further explain
the process:

> We came on in April, and we had to be in New York to shoot the exteriors
> in June, and they didn't have any scripts. We came in and we had eight
> scripts ready to go, and I think it was from our experience of working with

Ken Johnson and doing those other series. Of the twenty-four episodes that we did, we would turn out concepts and they would approve it, we would do a script and they would give us notes — and we rarely had a note. George Paris might have had a few. We only had one concept turned down. Ira Behr wanted to do *Road Warrior* in the School of the Arts, where everything is gone. They said, "Oh no, I don't think we're going to do a *Road Warrior*." That's the only time that we got turned down. They were just going to fill out this order. We were going to do it for the money, and they didn't really care that much what we were doing.

"The thing of it is," noted Harry Longstreet, "that for a while we thought we were doing some wonderful stuff." There was a note of pride in Renee's voice as she added, "*TV Guide* said that we brought the show back to Bill Blinn's standards." And from all indications, that was true. Gone, for the most part, were the rip-off shows, replaced by stories that dealt with such hard-hitting subjects as homophobia, reverse discrimination, drunk driving and death.

Ira Steven Behr and Michael McGreevey had been approached about remaining with the series. Recalled McGreevey:

> MGM came to Ira Behr and me. They told us they wanted to go ahead with a sixth season, but they wanted continuity. "We're going to get some new show-runners, but will you guys come on?" And we said yeah, but we have to be producers. So that's really what happened.

McGreevey and Behr would continue writing scripts, but with the added incentive of a producer's title and increased salary. In addition, the Longstreets brought in three other writers with whom they had worked before — Susan Goldberg, who was given the title of executive story consultant, and the writing team of Hans Beimler and Richard Manning, who took over the job of story editors. Christopher Seiter joined the staff as supervising producer, and Denny Salvaryn continued on as co-producer/unit production manager. Although Behr and McGreevey had never produced before, the Longstreets gave them the responsibility. "What we did," declared Renee Longstreet:

> We gave them every other episode that they would produce and work in the editing room with us. We were trying to give them a way into producing, and so they alternated shows. Harry and I also alternated shows, and we had always done that. Harry would be the main guy on one show, and I'd be on the next, and that would be in terms of the dub and the editing and the casting and ... the whole thing.

As usual, there were the prerequisite changes in the cast, with several new characters arriving in the persons of Michael Cerveris as Ian Ware, a

The producing staff for Season Six (clockwise from top left): Ira Steven Behr, Michael McGreevey, Harry Longstreet, associate producer/editor Karina Friend, and Renee Longstreet (Michael McGreevey Collection).

rock 'n' roll major from the U.K., Elisa Heinsohn as student Jillian Becket, the daughter of an over-protective Irish cop, and Eric Pierpoint as drama teacher Paul Segar. Concurrent with these new arrivals was the departure of several other cast members. Once again, the excuse for characters leaving was perfunctory, with Carol Mayo Jenkins' Miss Sherwood moving to Maine as a published author of a titillating romance novel, and Page Hannah's Kate transferring to a school in Boston. In fact, Carol Mayo Jenkins eventually returned to her home town of Knoxville, Tennessee, to become an artist in residence and a member of the faculty of the Theater Department at the University of Tennessee. Page Hannah more or less left the business entirely. As Renee Longstreet explained it, the writers had just run out of ideas for these two characters, particularly Elizabeth Sherwood. "We thought she'd done everything, and there was nothing left to do with her," Longstreet reported. "We brought in a male drama teacher." As it turned out, the new cast members did seem to pump some much needed life into the show.

Eric Pierpoint, who would play Paul Seeger, the disillusioned actor/ cab driver who becomes the school's new drama teacher, was himself an excellent young character actor who had made his debut in the 1984 independent film *Windy City*. He had appeared on a number of television series, including *Hill Street Blues*, and had recently starred for Harry and Renee Longstreet in the short-lived TV series *Hot Pursuit*. "He was a really fine actor," reported Renee Longstreet. "We were really happy with that character." Pierpoint would go on to divide his time between television and film, appearing as the alien detective George Francisco in the TV series *Alien Nation*, and with Anthony Hopkins in *The World's Fastest Indian*. His more recent performances include playing the unemployed chef in the eponymous *Phil Cobb's Dinner for Four* in 2009.

Elisa Heinsohn had done very little before she came in to audition for *Fame*, but her looks and talent impressed everyone. "She was a soprano," noted Renee Longstreet. "She was a completely different type from Nia Peeples and Carrie Hamilton and Loretta Chandler. This was a soprano, and she was an Irish-Catholic with a very protective family, very different from the characters that had already been established." After leaving *Fame*, Heinsohn would travel to Broadway in 1988 to co-star as Meg Giry in the original New York production of *The Phantom of the Opera*.

And then there was Michael Cerveris. Cerveris grew up in Huntington, West Virginia, and studied acting and voice at Yale University, after having graduated in 1979 from Phillips Exeter Academy. Because of his father's requirement that he and his siblings each learn to play at least one musical instrument, Cerveris chose the guitar in his teens and became an accomplished musician. Renee Longstreet remembers the impact that Cerveris made when he first appeared at a *Fame* casting session in New York City:

> When we went to New York to scout locations, Meg Liberman, who was our casting director, went with us. Every afternoon, after we'd location scout, we'd go sit up in an office and we would see kids, and Michael just walked in on an audition. With Michael Cerveris, I have to tell you, there have been times over the years when Harry and I have seen somebody and just go, "Oh my God!" And Michael Cerveris was that. He was a done deal from the minute we looked at him. He came in and he played something, he sang something. He was a drama major, a philosophy major, and we just knew that we wanted to bring him out.

The character of Ian Ware was the result of Ira Steven Behr's frustration with his earlier lack of success with Sam Slovick's Cassidy character in Season Four. So he had tried again, creating the bushy-haired British exchange student with musical ties to the Rolling Stones and the "Fab Four" who joins the school as a freshman. Michael Cerveris was obviously not British, but he carried off the "West End" accent without a hitch. According to Michael McGreevey, who was also at that casting session and was equally impressed with the young actor, Cerveris came in and spoke with a British accent. "We thought he was British," explained McGreevey, "so we gave him the role." The Longstreets jointly exclaimed, "Oh my God, he was wonderful. That kid could do anything." Cerveris would certainly prove them right in later years with his phenomenal successes on Broadway. First playing the role of *Tommy* in the 1992 revival of the Who's rock opera (and being nominated for a Tony for his performance), Cerveris would then star in Stephen Sondheim's *Assassin* and win the 2004 Tony Award as Best Featured Actor in a Musical. Then the 2006 revival of *Sweeney Todd*, with Patty Lupone, would see him nominated for another Tony, and in 2007 he would again be nominated for a Tony for his performance as Kurt Weill in *Lovemusik*.

There was one other complication in the production process for the sixth and final season. Immediately after finishing filming on the fifth season of *Fame*, Debbie Allen had moved to New York City to begin rehearsals as the lead in Bob Fosse's revival of his hit musical *Sweet Charity*. The play opened on April 27, 1986, at the Minskoff Theater and received five Tony Awards, with Debbie Allen receiving her second Tony nomination for her performance in the title role, as well as a Drama Desk nomination. *Sweet Charity* was still running when the *Fame* company moved to Manhattan to begin filming location scenes for the sixth season, and Allen had to divide her time between filming during the day and performing on Broadway at night. To be able to include her in as many episodes as possible, the producers filmed all of her scenes in New York City, which explains why she only appeared in exterior scenes in the early episodes and had no interior scenes until she left the musical in October of 1986 and returned to Hollywood, with Ann Reinking taking over her role in *Sweet Charity*.

23

A Good Beginning

Each year, as cast members came and went, the main title that Michael Levine and I had created back in 1981 would be adjusted to include close-ups of the new arrivals. For the sixth season the title sequence was once again revised, but this time, since Erica Gimpel had been absent from the series since her one-time return appearance in 1985, the Longstreets had Loretta Chandler re-record Michael Gore and Dean Pitchford's by now celebrated title song, as well as considerably re-editing the title sequence, still keeping our original style (and one shot taken from one of my shows of Gene Anthony Ray's feet in red tennis shoes sliding across the floor). For their version they chose not to show Loretta singing on camera, and to use Debbie Allen's "You want fame" speech as a voice-over.

The season got off to a rousing start with a five-and-a-half-minute music and dance number called "Back to Something New," featuring the entire cast and the *Fame* dancers, and filmed all over the streets of New York City. The song, with its driving tempo and upbeat lyrics, was written by Sue Sheridan, John Beasley and *Fame*'s supervising music consultant, Maureen Crowe, and was dynamically choreographed by Jaime Rogers. It was the perfect way to introduce the new season. Written by Ira Steven Behr and directed by Win Phelps, the episode, which bore the same name, "Back to Something New," also showed off new arrival Michael Cerveris' prodigious talent on the guitar, with a taste of rock 'n' roll, bluegrass and flamenco. Some good dramatic moments occurred between Cerveris' Ian Ware and Albert Hague's Mr. Shorofsky, and Hague also had the opportunity to perform one of his melodic piano compositions. The main story line dealt with Christopher Donlon and his struggle to make it on the outside, now that he had graduated; and Billy Hufsey, in a fantasy sequence, danced and sang "Breaking Ground" partially on location in the center of Times Square. Michael McGreevey was in New York and was functioning

185

as the line producer when they shot the location portion of the number. "We made the mistake of setting a number in Times Square, and the shooting regulations there are almost impossible to deal with," McGreevey reported. One of the main problems, according to McGreevey, was coordinating Christopher Donlon's name to appear on the big video screen that dominates Time Square in conjunction with the staging of the action on the street below. "I'm being told by NYPD's finest that at exactly midnight I'm done, no matter what," McGreevey declared. "That they're going to shut off the cameras, and Win Phelps is like two shots away and we've got like ten minutes. We're between shots, and they're letting the traffic through again, and some guy throws a bottle from a cab and hits Billy Hufsey right on the side of the head." Luckily, Hufsey wasn't seriously hurt, and they were able to complete the shot where he steps into the limo. The rest of the number was filmed later on a sound stage at the studio. I know I'm repeating myself, but it's a stone cold fact that filming on location in a big city is always a problem.

Oz Scott, who alternated as director with Win Phelps on the first six episodes that were filmed in Manhattan, was born in Hampton, Virginia, and began his career at the Arena stage in Washington, D.C., before moving to New York and winning a Drama Desk Award for directing *For Colored Girls Who Have Considered Suicide When the Rainbow Is Enuf.* He directed his first feature film, *Bustin' Loose*, starring Richard Pryor and Cicely Tyson, in 1981, and by the time he arrived at *Fame* had already directed numerous television shows, including 40 episodes of *The Jeffersons*. Today, Scott is one of the most successful directors in television. His first episode on *Fame*, "The Last Dance," written by Susan Goldberg, was a good, solid, character-driven piece concerning Nicole and Jesse's on again and off again relationship. Some good dramatic confrontations and somber reflections were abetted by a nicely choreographed fantasy dance that was filmed at night in Central Park and helped to illustrate the Jesse/Nicole dilemma. The subplot introduced Jillian Becket's overbearing father, her two equally bossy brothers, and the family's misgivings about her dating Danny. Sandy McPeak, who played Jillian's father, Officer Becket, was an old friend of mine who had appeared in *Palm Springs Weekend* when we were both under contract to Warners, and the studio had renamed him Sandy Kevin. He had a long and successful career as a character actor before his death in 1997. "The Last Dance" was also the episode that denied Jesse Borrego the opportunity of doing *La Bomba*. Renee Longstreet explained:

We tried and we couldn't make it work. Because we were going to New York, and because those were the episodes that were prepped, we had to take Jesse with us. He was the lead in episode two, and we couldn't ... I remember sitting for a day at least with the board seeing if we could do it, and to this day I feel terribly guilty.... It would have been a huge break for him.

Renee and Harry Longstreet's first script, "New Faces," introduced Eric Pierpoint as Paul Seeger, an old acting friend of Lydia Grant's, who she runs into by accident at a film location near the school. When Seeger, who is playing a bit part in the film, expresses his dissatisfaction with the direction his career is headed, Lydia arranges for Seeger to teach an acting class at the High School of Performing Arts. After some misunderstandings with his students, particularly Jesse, Seeger settles in to become the school's permanent drama teacher.

In the next episode, titled "Judgment Day," one of the members of *Fame*'s original dance company, Lycia Naff, returned in a guest starring role. Lycia had left the series at the end of the third season to pursue an acting career, but continued to be seen in the main title sequence in clips from several dance numbers that she had appeared in during the first season. In 1991, after starring in an ABC Afterschool Special, *The Perfect Date*, and receiving a Daytime Emmy nomination for her performance, Lycia changed professions, becoming a newspaper reporter, and for several years worked for the *National Enquirer*.

Michael McGreevy's script for "Judgment Day" dealt with a serious topic — reverse discrimination. When, as the assistant dance teacher, Leroy picks a black student for a student production, he is challenged by another student, Susan Pareno, played by Lycia Naff, who claims that he has discriminated against white students in favor of black students. McGreevey remembered:

> Gene loved that show. I think he thought it was different, it was a different take. I think he sort of liked being accused of that. He started to doubt himself; he put the white girl in, replaced the poor girl that was originally in, and he had a scene where he finally said, "Bullshit, I'm not listening to you people!" That's a story structure that's dramatic; the characters are being driven by something. Even the white girl who accuses him of this is an interesting character. Someone who wants fame that much that she'll destroy the reputation of a person. And, of course, I made her Danny's girlfriend for this show. And Danny is now pitted against his best friend, whose judgment he's questioning because of his loyalty to the girl. That type of dynamic happened a lot more in the sixth season — not to say that we didn't have our stinkers. We had stinkers every year that I was involved.

Perhaps McGreevey was referring to an episode titled "That Was the Weekend That Was." Featuring one of the weakest scripts in the sixth season, the episode's subplot had Leroy joining an organization known as the Muskrats. In watching it, it was hard to discern whether it was Leroy or Gene Anthony Ray who looked more uncomfortable playing these scenes. Rock musician Lee Ving, best known as the lead singer and rhythm guitarist for the L.A. punk band Fear, guest starred as Miltie's friend Fred, offering an energized vocal rendition of "The Night Rolls On." Ving, who displayed an impressive baritone voice, had also appeared as Fred in "The Monster That Devoured Las Vegas" in 1984, in which he sang "To Dream the Impossible Dream" from *Man of La Mancha*.

And then along came "All Talking, All Singing, All Dancing," arguably the single best episode in the *Fame* anthology. It seemed as if everyone involved, from director Win Phelps to choreographer Jaime Rogers to cinematographer Robert F. Sparks to costumer Nanrose Buchman to editor Jim McElroy and the entire cast, all rose to the challenge of Richard Manning and Hans Beimler's witty adaptation of *42nd Street*. Yes, technically it was another rip-off, but done with such style and energy that you had to forgive them their trespasses. "That was the first show they wrote, and it was a classic," declared Renee Longstreet, referring to writers Manning and Beimler. "We did the entire *42nd Street*," she continued. "The entire cast, everyone was dressed for the entire episode, we did it as if it was the thirties." The episode opened in black and white, with the old MGM logo and Leo the Lion, and then a typical '30s cast intro, with close-ups of each of the players. What followed may have used the old movie plot, but the dialogue was new, sharp and witty. Jesse Borrego was the director, a role played in the original by Warner Baxter, and Elisa Heinsohn was the ingénue, played by Ruby Keeler in 1933, and both sparkled in the acting, singing and dancing categories. The writers, who were clever enough to come up with their own version of "You're going out a youngster, but you've got to come back a star," gave all of the cast members flamboyant roles to play, but one of the principal standouts was Carrie Hamilton as the gum-chewing chorine fashioned after Ginger Rogers' character in the original film. This episode also revealed the marvelous onscreen chemistry between Hamilton and Michael Cerveris in a short sequence where they perform "It's Love I'm After, After All," by Alan Roy Scott. Another highlight was Nia Peeples singing George and Ira Gershwin's "Someone to Watch Over Me." The episode's finale, a tribute to Busby Berkeley, was filmed on the steps of the Metropolitan Museum in Manhattan, with all of the principals and fifty dancers tapping and singing

Harry Warren and Al Dubin's classic "Forty-Second Street." Graham Jarvis, who appeared in the episode, was quoted in a 2000 interview as saying:

> In spite of the fact that *Mary Hartman, Mary Hartman* was my favorite TV series, I've always told anyone who was interested that the single best episode of TV that I was ever a part of was, in my estimation, "All Talking, All Singing, All Dancing" on *Fame*. Michael Cerveris and Carrie Hamilton had a duet in that episode that I just loved. In fact, I loved the whole show, and I'm delighted I managed to tape it for myself when it played.

By comparison, the next few episodes were unremarkable except to fulfill the need to give various cast members shows that would feature them. As Michael McGreevey explained in an interview on the *Fame Forever* website, "We knew that we would have to do a certain amount of shows that would feature each lead character. We usually had to develop three shows apiece for Chris, Nicole, Jesse, Leroy, Reggie and Danny." Renee Longstreet added more detail for me:

> Harry and I had a system, which we had developed, where everybody sat in a room and developed the story on a board before the writer went out to write it. If we were doing a freelancer story, then they would sit with us and do the beating out of the story, and then that writer would go home and write it. We had learned that you can't say to a writer, go home and do a story, come back, give them notes, go home and re-fix the story, come back, give them notes. We did the story together, and this is the way we worked it pretty much on every episode.

Harry Longstreet chimed in to add, "And we'd give the writer full credit."

"A Different Drummer" featured Reggie's attempt to demonstrate her avant-garde way of thinking, and ending up being arrested instead for demonstrating without a license at the Guggenheim Museum. Michael Switzer, the third director to film location footage in New York, had worked with the Longstreets previously on *Misfits of Science* and would ultimately direct three episodes of *Fame* before going on to direct dozens of TV movies and series. As Renee Longstreet explained it, Michael Switzer would always maintain a fondness for his time on *Fame*. "One of the directors that had worked with us before was Michael Switzer," Longstreet reported. "And, of course, that was a wonderful story because he met Susan Goldberg, our story editor, and fell in love, and they just celebrated their twenty-something anniversary." While Switzer was filming location scenes for "A Different Drummer," problems cropped up again with Gene Anthony Ray. As Renee Longstreet reported:

> Gene was in the throws of some very difficult times. Whatever he was doing, the first indication we had was in New York City when Michael Switzer was

directing a scene. It was toward the end of when we had been there, and Gene fell in a bathtub at the hotel. He didn't show up, and they found him unconscious in a bathtub."

When asked if they had been warned about Gene, the Longstreets admitted that they knew that the studio had hired a bodyguard for Gene — or, as Harry Longstreet put it, a watcher. Michael McGreevey described the futility of this action. "We got him a full-time bodyguard, which was problematic because Gene could have a good time, with anybody. So his bodyguard ended up having a good time and we'd be looking for both the bodyguard and Gene." But the problems continued to worsen, said Renee Longstreet:

> I was in contact with Selma Rubin, his agent/manager in New York, because there were problems right within the first couple of weeks, and we had to rely on this man to get him to the set on time. At one point, when we were doing the Christmas show — and that was probably toward September, October, it was one of the first when we got back from New York — he just didn't show up. At that point we suspended Gene, we wrote him out of five episodes. And one of the only ways he could come back was I got him a therapist, and he had to go to therapy three or four times a week, I forget the exact numbers. Years later we had lunch, and he said that he was very appreciative of the way Harry and I dealt with him, because we made him take responsibility, and he actually finished the year. After that suspension we didn't have a problem anymore, and he was going to therapy. He had difficulty with drugs, he had difficulty with the fact that he was gay, he had difficulty with the money issues. He was kind of a lost soul, but Debbie Allen was always in his corner, and she did as much as she could. We really felt for the kid, and we really liked him.

Michael McGreevey echoed those sentiments, but had his own theory of what Gene was going through:

> Debbie Allen was also his mother, and she kept him together over all those years: I watched her do it. She was his friend, and she truly loved him and he loved her. It was just very hard for him. He felt in that last season — I think he knew that it was coming to an end, and he was frightened by that. He was leaving the safety of *Fame* to go out into the world, and I think he was terribly frightened.

But like the familiar phrase says, the show must go on, and so it did, with the writers and the cast laboring to turn out the remaining episodes for the final season. "We had to figure out how to introduce new regular characters to the series, like Ian and Jillian," noted Michael McGreevey, "and write shows about certain characters leaving the show." Such a situation involved the character of Nicole, played by Nia Peeples. Renee Longstreet recalled:

> Nia Peeples wanted to leave the show. And we had to let her out because she had it in her contract. We wanted to do a drunk driving show, and we said to her, if she'd let us kill her in a show in the interest of public safety we'd let her out of her contract. It was about getting into a car with some-one you knew was drinking. It wasn't about driving drunk; it was a whole other thing.

Renee Longstreet wrote the script, "Go Softly into Morning," in which Danny and Nicole mistakenly allow themselves to be driven from a party by a friend who has consumed too much alcohol. There is an accident and Nicole is killed, throwing the entire school into mourning. Jesse, in his anguish, threatens to kill the young man who was driving the car. "Moth-ers Against Drunk Driving loved the show," commented Harry Longstreet, "and they wanted coroners all over America to show this to kids because it was against drunk driving." Michael McGreevey felt that killing Nicole was a mistake. "In retrospect, I think the decision to kill Nicole was made for the wrong reasons," he commented in his interview with *Fame Forever*:

> When we were developing the story we all felt that the impact of teenage drunk driving would not be communicated to our audience strongly enough unless we had somebody die, but would killing off a guest star have enough impact? I don't remember who came up with the idea, but somebody sug-gested that we use Nia's departure as a way of solving our story problem. I truly believed that Nia would say no, but she actually felt good about the idea that her exit from the show might save some lives. I realized the extent of our blunder when I sat down to write the last episode and was confronted with the fact that I couldn't bring Nicole back for the reunion.

24

The Last of the
New Kids

By late autumn, Debbie Allen had returned from her triumphant success in *Sweet Charity* and resumed her chores on *Fame*. Her first assignment was to direct — but not to appear in — another derivative script by Richard Manning and Hans Beimler, "The Crimson Blade," based on a number of costume films of the thirties and forties, but primarily *The Mark of Zorro*. The episode had its moments, first and foremost in the performance of Robert Romanus, returning as Miltie Horowitz. A rousing score by John Debney, and Debbie Allen's energetic direction, also helped; however, even she couldn't hide the over-the-top concept better suited for children's television.

A stage production called *The Crimson Blade*, with Jesse in the title role of a masked avenger, is threatened when a substitute principal, played by Alison La Placa, orders all dancing and singing halted in the hallways, and cancels the play in punishment for the students' opposition to her orders. Miltie assumes the role of the Crimson Blade to protect Maxie, an attractive new student played by Olivia Barash. The script worked when it concentrated itself on Miltie's internal battle between selfishness and his regard for others, but fell apart in a ludicrous sequence that had two students dueling ferociously with swords. Even Debbie Allen resorted to copying old movies by staging part of this fight in silhouette, á la the sword fight in *Robin Hood*.

Olivia Barash, who had joined the cast for the previous episode, "Love Kittens Go to High School," had auditioned at the beginning of the season. "We held open auditions in L.A.," Renee Longstreet recalled. "And it was a big, open cattle call, there were hundreds of kids. Olivia Barash was the one that we liked, but we didn't think that she was the right person, and we knew that we wanted to bring in a couple of kids." So at the New York casting sessions Michael Cerveris and Elisa Heinsohn were selected instead, and it wasn't until episode number twelve that Olivia Barash would be called back to guest star as a young actress who is starring in an exploitation film called *Love Kittens Go to High School*, that is filming on location at the school, and then decides to join the school to further her education in dramatic arts. Michael McGreevey says that part of the concept for Maxie's character came from his own experiences as a young actor who would later study with acting coaches to perfect his craft. "Actually," added McGreevy, "I found out later that Olivia had gone through a similar experience herself, and this helped her identify with Maxie." Olivia Barash would ultimately appear in four episodes during the sixth season, with her last appearance in the finale, "Baby, Remember My Name."

Just before the Christmas break, Harry Longstreet directed his first episode, "The Big Contract." The story featured Russell Johnson, of *Gilligan's Island* fame, as Lou Mackie's nefarious brother Duke, who cons Chris into signing a contract with him for a record album. The Longstreets wanted to give the crew a short break for Christmas, so Harry decided to cut his shooting schedule to five-and-a-half days. "Poor Russell Johnson," said Harry Longstreet. "Most of his scenes were on the last day, and I swear that he had twelve and a half pages. By the time I was shooting the last scene, I had to put him on a couch, I had to sit him down, and I had to get it line by line, he was so tired — and I don't blame him." "Then we got the dailies in the next day," added Renee, "And I asked Harry, 'Why was he sitting through the whole scene?' Harry's answer was, 'He was toast.'"

"Stradi-various" was a fantasy that did seem to work, with various cast members believing that a violin that Mr. Shorofsky receives after it was lost in delivery years before possesses magical powers. After a number of wishes seem to come true, Shorofsky reveals that the violin actually came from a pawn shop, and the magic was all in their minds. According to Michael McGreevey, one of the wishes in the original script called for Jesse to dream about the comedian Henny Youngman, who told jokes while playing his violin. Youngman, who was famous for the line, "Take my wife ... please!" had agreed to appear, but one week before filming was to begin his wife of over fifty years died, and he withdrew from the show. Unable to think of another comedian to take Youngman's place, "We were just about to completely rewrite the script," reported McGreevey in the interview he gave to the website *Fame Forever*. "Then our casting director suggested Morey Amsterdam. Morey had done his old stand-up comedy routine using a cello. It wasn't a violin, but a string instrument is a string instrument, right?" Amsterdam, who had been a gag man and writer for numerous stars in the thirties, such as Jimmy Durante, Will Rogers and Fanny Bryce, and was reportedly able to remember over 100,000 jokes, was also one of the regulars for five years on the old *Dick Van Dyke Show*, with Mary Tyler Moore and Rose Marie. "He was a complete professional," recalled McGreevey. "And he did a wonderful job. In fact, I think "Stradivarious" turned out better than any of us ever imagined."

One of the highlights for everyone in the sixth season was the episode "Reggie and Rose," because it paired Carrie Hamilton with her mother, Carol Burnett. "We were very careful in talking to Carrie about her mother, because Carrie obviously wanted to be accepted on her own grounds," recalled Michael McGreevey. "But by that last season she was very comfortable with her role on the show and had really grown a lot, and we finally convinced her to ask her mother if she would do a show." Burnett played Rose, a cafeteria lady who takes a special interest in Reggie the rebel. When Rose is laid off due to budget cuts, Reggie talks her into entering the school as a student. Burnett does a very funny audition for the teachers that utilizes some of her own material from her hit TV specials. The chemistry between mother and daughter was to be expected, but it still surprises in several touching moments. Renee Longstreet remembers:

> Susan Goldberg wrote that show. That was my show, and I spent some time with Carol and Carrie. It was a very warm, loving, terrific experience. Kevin Sullivan, who directed that episode, was a new director who ended up becoming a major director.

For Kevin Rodney Sullivan, who directed "Reggie and Rose," it was his second directorial effort in series television, having started as an actor and then moved into writing with a script for *Cagney & Lacey* in 1983. In *Fame*'s second and third seasons he had written two episodes, with Ralph Farquhar, for Bill Blinn. Sullivan would direct the Angela Bassett box office hit *How Stella Got Her Groove Back* in 1998, followed by *Barbershop 2: Back in Business*, the equally successful sequel to the comedy *Barbershop*, in 2004.

The episode opens in the school cafeteria with a skillfully choreographed, well edited and photographed number that brought to mind memories of the "Hot Lunch Jam" number in the original *Fame* movie. From there it moves to the lunch counter and introduces Carol Burnett's character of Rose. "I'll tell you how that concept came up." Renee Longstreet recalled:

> At the time that we were there, the MGM commissary was purchased. All of those women that had been there forever all lost their jobs, and they got nothing. Susan Goldberg said, "We're going to do the cafeteria ladies all losing their jobs." We knew that we were looking for something that Carol wanted to do with Carrie, so Susan created that project. It came right from the MGM disaster. We ended up, I think on that show we were twenty minutes over or something on our first cut, and we had to take out the B story.

Harry Longstreet added, "We took it out because we didn't want to rob Carol and Carrie's other story." In the episode, Rose convinces Reggie that she should try out for a summer stock season, and Reggie talks Rose into helping her with the audition piece. The two of them do Irving Berlin's "A Couple of Swells" dressed in tramp costumes and makeup similar to that worn by Judy Garland and Fred Astaire when they did the same number in *Easter Parade*. Recalled Renee Longstreet:

> "After Carrie passed away I had written Carol a letter, and I asked her if she had clips of all of Carrie's spots, and she didn't. So I took my stuff and I went into an editing room in Tarzana, somewhere in the West Valley, and I made her a twenty minute tape of all the highlights of Carrie's years. You couldn't imagine how appreciative she was. And recently we saw the American Masters piece on Carol Burnett, and they used a little clip from it.

Toward the end of the final season, Michael McGreevey and Ira Steven Behr returned from lunch one day to find their office buzzing with excitement. One of the secretaries announced excitedly, "You just missed him." Upon further inquiry, they learned that the "him" in question was Christopher Gore, who had stopped by to say hello. What McGreevey found extremely strange, if not a little heartbreaking, was that Gore had left a copy of his résumé for them. What was the purpose of that? Was the man who had written the screenplay for the film and the pilot for the television series looking for work? Since the show was winding down and there weren't any writing assignments left to hand out, they never found out the true reason for Gore's visit. If you look up Christopher Gore's credits on IMDB (the Internet Movie Data Base), you will find that there are only four entries for his entire career in film and television: the screenplay for the movie *Fame* (1980); a story credit for an animation short, *Faeries* (1981); and the teleplay for "Metamorphosis," the pilot episode for the television series *Fame* (1982). And, of course, his credit as story consultant on the series — a contractual arrangement whereby he received a royalty check for each episode, but for which he never made an appearance.

By the time that *Sweet Charity* dimmed the lights in March of 1987 for its 369th and final performance, Debbie Allen was pregnant again with her second child, son Norman Nixon, Jr., and *Fame* was reaching the end of its run. The Longstreets had always agreed that the final episode would be something special, so they tried to plan ahead for it. "From the very beginning," explained Renee Longstreet, "we knew that the last show was going to be bringing back all of the kids that we could." "We wanted to squirrel away some money," added Harry Longstreet, "because we knew we would have extraordinary cast expenses to bring back as many people as we wanted for the last show." Over the course of the filming season the Longstreets had managed to set aside $160,000 in a special account for the final episode, "Baby, Remember My Name." "About four episodes before the end," remembered Renee Longstreet,

> Lee Rich somehow got wind that there was a hundred and sixty thousand in the account on *Fame*, and called Chris Seiter and said, "What is that?" And Chris said, "Well, we're planning to use that for the last episode." And Lee Rich said, "No you're not, you saved it." And he took it; he took it away from us. Harry was directing the second to the last episode, so we pared that episode down to the bone and Harry shot the episode in five-and-a-half days.

This next to last episode, called "Alice Doesn't Work Here Anymore," featured Ann Nelson's character of Mrs. Berg, who, after receiving a letter from a former beau, unexplainably asks for an indefinite leave of absence from the school. Renee Longstreet elaborates:

> She had been in love when she was a young actress before she was at the school. And there was this Czechoslovakian director, and all the years they had corresponded he thought she was the head of the school — that it was her school — and he was coming to New York. So the kids had to turn the school into Mrs. Berg's school, and they couldn't tell the principal. So we did that on a shoestring, and we got back $80,000 of the 160. We saved it on one episode so that we could still bring all the kids in.

The B plot line for "Alice" was a cute bit involving Carry Hamilton's character, Reggie, and a young student who was squeamish about dissecting a frog in biology class. Gordon, the young student, was played by Renee and Harry Longstreet's son Greg, who is today a publicist for a Beverly Hills PR firm. Wasn't that where Harry started?

Michael McGreevey wrote the script for "Baby, Remember My Name," and, appropriately, Debbie Allen was the director. Utilizing Alumni Week and the students' first video yearbook as its springboard, the story allows the school's current pupils to ask each of the returning alumni

Harry Longstreet directing Carrie Hamilton and his son, Greg Longstreet in "Alice Doesn't Work Here Anymore" (courtesy the Longstreets).

what impact the school had on them. The main plot dealt with another alumnus, Michael Taftner, played by Russ Tamblyn, who is staging a ballet as part of the proceedings and casts Leroy as his lead dancer. Taftner, who was a star of film musicals, but who disparages his own career as worthless, is shown the error of his thinking when Lydia shows a clip from one of his old films — actually a clip from *Seven Brides for Seven Brothers* — to her class, and he watches their positive response. Leroy is forced to make the difficult choice between remaining at the school as a teacher or leaving the nest and trying to make it in the tough world of show business as a dancer. In a touching scene toward the end of the episode that paralleled the reality of Gene Anthony Ray's own feelings, Leroy expresses his love for the school and for his mentor, Miss Grant. It is doubly touching when watched in the context of this being the final episode and the awareness that Gene Anthony Ray is actually saying goodbye.

The Longstreets realized their goal and filled "Baby, Remember My

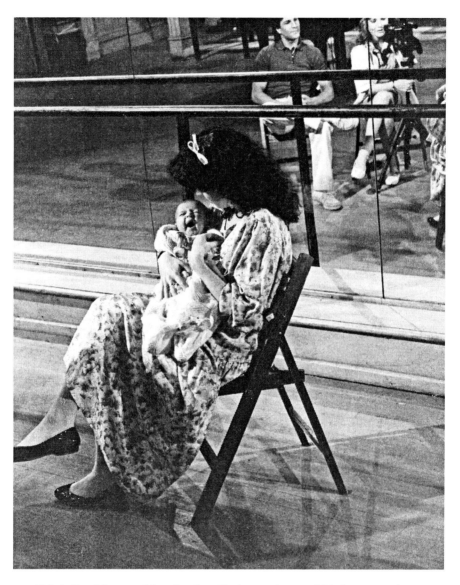

Valerie Landsburg and her daughter Taylor on the set of "Baby, Remember My Name" (Michael McGreevey Collection).

Name" with returning alumni P. R. Paul, Lee Curreri (who also had one of his songs, "Bird Jam," included in the episode), Erica Gimpel, Valerie Landsburg, Cynthia Gibb, Carol Mayo Jenkins and many of the original *Fame* dancers, including Michael DeLorenzo, Bronwyn Thomas, Michael

Left to right: Michael McGreevy, music supervisor Maureen Crowe, Ira Behr, writer/director Robert Caplain, Donald Reiker and Michael DeLorenzo, with Patricia Jones (curly hair) in background (© 1987 Frank Merwald).

Bill Blinn surrounded by the *Fame* family (© 1987 Frank Merwald).

Rooney and many others. Valerie Landsburg spoke of how she felt about returning in an interview she gave some years ago: "It was great when they called me to do the reunion episode, the very last episode. Taylor had just been born, and she is the baby in that scene where Doris comes back." All of the crew and staff were featured throughout the segment, and Ira Steven Behr and Michael McGreevey could be seen wandering through a couple of scenes, dressed in painter's overalls.

On the final day of shooting, the finale was filmed on the cafeteria set on Stage 26, with the entire cast singing and dancing to the exuberant title song. "We were all in that," declared Renee Longstreet:

> We put everybody in it. You know that had been six years of a show that didn't have a lot of drama. There wasn't a temperamental cast, it was a show that everybody who worked on it loved, and I think you feel that at the end. I mean, I loved doing that show.

As the camera swept across the crowd, catching a glimpse of Renee and Harry Longstreet, other alumni appeared, including Donald Reiker and Patricia Jones; and, standing next to Debbie Allen, there was Bill Blinn singing along with the others. What the camera doesn't reveal, but Blinn reported to me later, was that he had a small television monitor strapped to his back so that Debbie the actress could see what Debbie the director's camera was getting. For the final moment, as everyone repeated the phrase "remember, remember, remember," the camera pulled back and up until it had risen over the set, revealing the studio lights and the rigging. The singing slowly faded as the image faded to black. And then, behind each of the end credits, different group photographs of various crew members served as a background and further tribute.

A few days later, Michael McGreevey and art director Ira Diamond walked down to Stage 26 to take one last look at Ira's Emmy Award–winning school set before it was to be torn down. After six seasons the time had finally come to say goodbye. But it wasn't easy — too many memories filled the empty halls of the school and the classrooms, now devoid of furnishings. All of the set dressings had been returned to the prop department; the overhead lights that had illuminated so many magical moments had been taken down and returned to the electrical department; the makeup tables and dressing rooms had been taken away; and all that was left were the echoes of songs and laughter and tears. Michael and Ira turned and walk out of the stage as the studio guard placed the locks on the doors for the final time. The next day, the swing gang would begin to tear down the sets and return the flats to the scene dock. Forever had finally arrived.

As if to underscore the finality of this moment, a few months later, on February 13, 1988, the landmark building that was the original home to the High School of Performing Arts was destroyed in a five-alarm fire. The school had merged three years earlier with the High School of Music and moved to a new location near 64th Street, and the old building had become Liberty High School and was used to teach English to immigrant students.

There was to be one last tribute for *Fame*. On September 12, 1987, at the Pasadena Civic Auditorium, Nanrose Buchman received *Fame*'s ninth and final Emmy for Outstanding Achievement in Costuming for a Series for her work on "All Talking, All Singing, All Dancing."

25

And So It Is Over

Frank Merwald would stay on for several weeks to complete the final post-production chores. One day, shortly after he had finished his task and left the studio, he received a phone call asking him to come in to the studio and discuss re-editing the shows for syndication. "George Paris called me up and had me come in. He told me, 'I have sold *Fame* as a half-hour drama. What you have to do is you have to cut out all the music and all of the dance.' I was sitting across from George and my jaw dropped." This ridiculous idea didn't go very far, since no audience wanted to watch the show without the one element that made it unique. Merwald was able to re-edit the shows and, by dropping the B story and cutting the numbers down from three minutes to a minute-and-a-half, give Paris a show that fit his time requirements. Even so, as Frank Merwald pointed out, since *Fame* had already been in syndication for four years, what you had was basically a re-run of a re-run, and the show didn't sell well, nor last very long.

In the early summer of 1997, MGM began production on *Fame L.A.* and put it into syndication in an attempt to update the old format. The series ran for 21 episodes between October of '97 and March of '98, but was not renewed. It did win two Emmys that year, one for its choreographer, ex–*Fame* dancer Marguerite Pomerhn Derricks, along with Peggy Holmes, for their work on the pilot episode. In 2003 MGM tried again with a different format, this time a live talent contest, with Debbie Allen as producer and host, that ran on NBC for one season.

Even as he continued working in the industry as an associate producer and co-producer on a long list of television productions, Frank Merwald kept playing with the idea of doing a *Fame* reunion. One day he ran into Lee Curreri at a Starbucks and tried the idea out on him. Recalled Merwald:

It was four or five years ago. They were doing the *Happy Days* reunion, *Dallas* reunion, and *Knot's Landing* reunion, and I ran into Lee Curreri and we started talking. And I said, "You know, I've got this idea about a *Fame* reunion, and I know that MGM would probably give us a pitch meeting." So I called up Hudson Hickman, who was a production executive at MGM. And Lee and I got together in a couple of cafés in Santa Monica and we talked about it, and we both went in and we pitched them.

Apparently, MGM wasn't interested at the time in a reunion show, and nothing came of the meeting. Merwald went on to become associate producer on *Two and a Half Men*, and is currently working on a new television pilot.

And what of some of the other original staff and crewmembers; what has happened to them?

Mel Swope would produce several television movies for MGM TV, including two sequels to *The Dirty Dozen*, before becoming Executive in Charge of Production for Wilshire Court Productions, a wholly owned subsidiary of Paramount Pictures. He would supervise the making of thirty-one TV movies over the next four years before moving over to Paramount Television in the same position for the next two years. In 1995 he would rejoin MGM TV as Executive in Charge of Production, and in that capacity he would supervise the unsuccessful attempt to resuscitate the *Fame* franchise, *Fame L.A.*

Parke Perine would leave the series at the end of the third season and later rejoin Bill Blinn as a producer on *Our House*, as well as writing five episodes for the series. He would also write a number of scripts for Michael Landon's *Highway to Heaven*, and was the story editor on *Knot's Landing*, before moving into live television as a writer/story editor on the daytime soap *Port Charles*. Perine is now retired and living with his wife Flavia in Sherman Oaks, California.

Robert Scheerer, who won his first Emmy for directing *The Danny Kaye Show* in 1964, was nominated eight times for Emmys, including three consecutive years for his directing on *Fame*. Scheerer would continue his successful career by directing and producing such diverse shows as *Live from Lincoln Center: New York City Opera's Candide*, six episodes of *Our House* for Bill Blinn, and several episodes of *Star Trek: Deep Space Nine* and *Star Trek Voyager*.

Chris Beaumont would also leave *Fame* after the third season to continue working with Bill Blinn as a producer on *Bridges to Cross*, and to write several episodes of *Aaron's Way* and *Our House*. He would also write episodes of *Highway to Heaven* and several television movies, and produce the short-lived series *Downtown*. He has been living in Oregon with his wife Casey, but has recently returned to Los Angeles to sign with the Creative Artist Agency and pursue his writing career.

Donna Lee would become the administrator for the DGA and the Motion Picture Association of America's Contract Basic Agreement Administration that monitors contracts for production managers and assistant directors in the motion picture and television industry. She still lives in Burbank, California, in the house where she grew up.

Ira Diamond, who in 1982 won an Emmy Award for his design of the sets of *Fame*'s High School of Performing Arts, would earn two more Emmy nominations in 1983 and 1984, and would go on to become the production designer on the sci-fi series *Alien Nation*, as well as *Dr. Quinn, Medicine Woman* and *Diagnosis Murder*.

William Goldstein, who had written the lovely tune "A Special Place" as well as incidental music for countless episodes of *Fame*, and received an Emmy nomination for his scoring of "Not in Kansas Anymore," would continue writing the scores for over fifty TV movies and series, including the 2000 television adaptation of William Gibson's *The Miracle Worker*.

Meg Liberman, who cast the original *Fame* pilot and continued to cast the series as head of casting for MGM, became one of the leading casting directors in film and television. She has been nominated ten times for Emmys, and won in 1998 for Steven Spielberg and Tom Hanks' *From the Earth to the Moon*. In November of 2008 Liberman became Senior Vice President, Casting at CBS Paramount Network Television.

Denny Salvaryn, who began as one of our assistant directors and ultimately moved up to production manager and then to producer, went on to *The Larry Sanders Show* after *Fame*'s final season, and eventually became the coordinating producer on *L.A. Law* for three seasons. He is still active as a unit production manager.

Otis Sallid, who co-choreographed a number of episodes of *Fame*, and co-produced *The Heart of Rock 'n' Roll* concerts, would choreograph features such as *Girls Just Want to Have Fun*, *Sister Act 2: Back in the Habit*, and *Malcolm X*, and direct several television series. He would win an American Choreography Award for *Swing Kids* in 1994, and in 1995 he co-authored the long-running Broadway musical *Smokey Joe's Café: The Songs of Leiber and Stoller*.

Gloria Montemayor, whose sister was actress Yvette Mimieux, was already well established when she became *Fame*'s hairdresser in 1981. She was nominated for an Emmy for her work on the first season, and has continued to remain very active in films and television on shows such as *Star Trek: Voyager*. She would later become Angela Lansbury's personal hairdresser on three *Murder, She Wrote* TV movie specials.

Jack Wilson, who had been David Jansen's makeup artist on *The Fugitive* before joining *Fame*, was nominated in 1983 for his makeup design on "Not in Kansas Anymore." Jack continued working with Gloria Montemayor on several other series after they finished on *Fame*, before retiring after two seasons on Carroll O'Connor's *In the Heat of the Night*.

Marilyn Matthews, one of the first of our group to win an Emmy in 1982 for her amazing work as our costumer, has gone on to earn three more Emmy nominations (for her work on the pilot for *thirtysomething* and the TV Special *Stompin' at the Savoy*). More recently, she has become the costume designer on the feature *The Truman Show*, with Jim Carrey and Laura Linney, and the associate costume designer on *Master and Commander: The Far Side of the World*, starring Russell Crowe.

Tony Amatullo, our location manger for the first season, who had also worked with us at Blinn/Thorpe Productions, would continue as a location manager for several more years before moving up to the unit production manager position on four features. He would then become a producer on one of my favorite black comedies, *2 Days in the Valley*. He is still producing and executive producing in both films and television.

Tommy Klines, our redheaded second assistant cameraman, who stayed with the show from the first episode to the last, has now developed an impressive list of credits as a first assistant cameraman over the years, including *The Princess Diaries*, *Terminator 3: Rise of the Machines*, *Spider Man 2* and *The Last Samurai*.

Gary Scott, who was our music producer and occasional composer, went on to compose the music for many other television series, including the theme and background music for Donald Reiker and Patricia Jones' *The Bronx Zoo*. Other series he composed for were *7th Heaven* and *Beverly Hills 90210*.

Maureen Crowe would remain in music and continue as a music supervisor on numerous features, including such big hits as *Wayne's World*, *The Perfect Storm*, *Chicago* and *The Pink Panther*, with Steve Martin. She is busily working on several more films as of this writing.

Mark Melnick would leave the series at the end of the second season, but because of his Emmy nomination for his editing of the episode "Musical Bridge" in the first season of *Fame*, he was immediately signed to join editors Don Zimmerman and Mark Warner in editing Sylvester Stallone's unsuccessful sequel to *Saturday Night Fever*, *Staying Alive*. Not letting that stop him, Melnick would go on to edit numerous films and television movies. In 1997 he would direct the independent feature, *Jamaica Beat*.

Bud Hayes, our other original film editor, and I would work together on several projects after *Fame*, including *Asteroid*, a mini-series that aired on two consecutive nights in February of 1997 on NBC and, according to their figures, drew over 75 million viewers. Bud would receive an Emmy nomination for his editing of "Part One" of *Asteroid*, and would later win an ACE Eddie Award for his work on the television series *In the Heat of the Night*. Bud is now retired and living in Oregon with his wife Diane.

As for me, I would do a bunch of things, like directing for *Murder, She Wrote*, *Dallas*, *Falcon Crest* and *Downtown*; being elected in 1997 to the Board of Governors of the Television Academy; and executive producing the *Creative Arts Emmy Awards* from 1998 to 2006. My wife Katie and I would then retire to the lovely little beach community of San Clemente, where I started writing books such as this one.

26

Fame Lives On

Certainly one of *Fame*'s tragedies was the scourge of AIDS, which repeatedly spread its dark shadow over the participants of this series, including Christopher Gore, who succumbed to AIDS in Santa Monica, California, on May 18, 1988. But David de Silva's original idea goes on and on, and may, in fact, live forever, if only in its numerous manifestations. De Silva's stage production of *Fame—The Musical*, with music by Steve Marcoshes, lyrics by Jacques Levy and stage adaptation by Christopher Sergel, has been seen by nearly four million people since its West End premiere in 1995. In October of 2008 a workshop presentation of *Fame— The Musical* was presented at the Beijing Central Academy, which was followed in early 2009 by a professional touring company of Chinese actors performing in the Mandarin language. The sequel, *Fame Forever*, will tell the story of the original characters thirty years later. The musical *Fame* was an inspiration to young people all over the world. It represented the great promise of the American Dream by saying that they must never give up on their big dreams — but that dreams don't come easily, and to achieve them you had to *start paying in sweat*! The wonderful thing is that *Fame* is still indirectly inspiring new generations of young people, empowering them to follow their dreams, 30 years after the award-winning 1980 movie classic hit the silver screen, 20 years after the series finished its award-winning run on television, and 15 years after the record-breaking launch of a live stage musical based on the High School of Performing Arts. There's little question that the current phenomenally successful Disney franchise of *High School Musical* films, with the third installment earning a record $91 million at the box office so far, and Disney already planning a fourth sequel — not to mention their *Hannah Montana* TV series and feature film, plus MTV's television series *The American Mall*, that takes place in a mall music store popular with teens — proves that the teen musical is experiencing a revival, and that the inspiration and style for all of this began with *Fame*. Fan clubs all over the world continue to keep the memory of those over-achieving kids alive, and in a way, one could say that even *American Idol* and its many manifestations owes its allegiance to *Fame*. MGM released a remake of the *Fame* movie, starring Kelsey Grammer, Bebe Neuwirth, Megan Mullally, Charles Dutton and Debbie, Allen in September of 2009, and once again the halls of the High School of Performing Arts resonated with the sounds of music and dancing. The Fox network has a new series called *Glee*, in which a school's Spanish teacher tries to mold a failing glee club into a championship winner, and the series includes four musical numbers per episode. Then there are the legions of Performing Arts Academies throughout the United States, as well as David De Silva's Father Fame Foundation. Says De Silva:

> The mission of that is really to promote theater art in schools, especially in public schools. Thirty years ago, when the movie came out, there weren't many. The High School of Performing Arts in New York was an unusual thing. Now, every major city seems to have a performing arts school. I'd like to think that in a small way, *Fame* helped to promote these schools.

In the United States there is a fan club with a website called *Fame Forever* that is run by Pamela Rosensteel of Pennsylvania. Pam was very helpful in allowing me to quote from her website and in helping me connect with *Fame* fans all over the world. Here are some comments from some of those fans who still remain loyal to *Fame* after all these years.

Shannon Grinaway (Location unknown):

> I was 8 years old when the show came on the air and 13 when it ended, and now, all these years later, it remains my all-time favorite TV program. I was totally hooked! It was everything — the dynamic dance numbers, to the fun original songs, to the endearing characters that were so easy to care about.

Brian Mattocks (England):

> I was a horrifically bullied child at school, and here was this school on TV where kids got on, they sang and they danced and it looked magical. I was thirteen and wanted friends like these kids so badly. I believed in *Fame*.

Derek O'Sullivan (Dublin, Ireland):

> When growing up in Dublin back in the '80s, life was quite gray, dull and depressing. I was 14 years of age ... going through adolescence and discovering myself and desperately trying to be comfortable in my own skin ... trying to deal with being gay in a society which, back then, would never accept or tolerate such a lifestyle. Then one Thursday evening ... the TV screen came to life with incredible sound, colour and an energy that I'd never

seen before. I was literally transfixed, nearly hypnotized by what I saw — the colours. energy. dancing and school kids working together to achieve one ultimate gain — Fame.

Elaine Prescott (Essex, England):

Fame meant a lot to me almost from the start of the first series shown over here in the U.K. in 1982. It was a show that had a quality of its own, and at the time, I couldn't quite work out how a series like that could have so many different, fabulous stories every week, that included music and dance as well! I had the chance to meet Val when she came to London in 2001.

Karen Cartmill (London, England) (from a newspaper article that she sent me):

It was so amazing when mum and dad bought our first coloured TV and I got to watch *Fame* in colour, that is something I will never forget.... I would sit there taking it all in and with my audio cassette player ready to tape any songs that came on each week. I think I managed to tape every song from all six series this way, and I still have the tapes today.

Mark Perkins (England):

Fame was first screened in the U.K in June 1982, and I was a lonely, confused, 14 year old who felt he had no place in the World. I never wanted to be an actor, singer or dancer, but the show had so much to say to me. A group of characters who perhaps weren't always the smartest or best looking or most confident helped me realize that everyone has something special inside them, including me. The characters became like friends to me, and the show completely took over my life.

Teresa Parks (Michigan):

Thank you so much for this opportunity to share my love for *Fame*. Living in a small mid-western town in the state of Michigan, I have had several encounters associated with *Fame*. Michael Cerveris was the first star I had direct correspondence with in a hand-written letter from him and an autographed 8 x 10. I was finally face to face with a star of the show when Billy Hufsey decided to do a musical stage show near his home town of Akron, Ohio. It was amazing to see him in the same room, singing and dancing.

Mark Dodds (Toronto, Canada):

Fame meant a lot for me for various reasons: Helped me to escape to a place after my twin sister passed away. As a gay person (even though I was a child at the time), it really did teach me acceptance and that it was okay to be different. Taught me that nothing is handed to you in life ... you have to go out and get it.

So it was over. Perhaps, besides admonishing that *fame costs*, Lydia Grant should have also acknowledged that fame is fleeting. For most of the *Fame* cast, with the obvious exceptions of Debbie Allen, Michael Cerveris and Janet Jackson, very few of them would ever again experience the same degree of recognition.

The theme song repeats a staccato six note phrase followed by a sustained chord — it still plays in my memory over and over — like the mournful resonance of a lonesome trumpet that reiterates through the final notes of an old Sinatra ballad, or the distant wail of a police siren echoing through the empty streets at midnight. It stimulates my mind to conjure up memories of other times and places. Of friends who have left us and those who are still with us.

Debbie Allen continues to act and direct in film and television, including directing her sister Phylicia Rashad in two films at Disney based on the Polly stories by Eleanor H. Porter, which were written and produced by Bill Blinn. She and her husband, Norm Nixon, founded the Debbie Allen Dance Academy in Culver City, California, where young dancers could learn their craft, and in 1997 she produced Steven Spielberg's *Amistad*. In March of 2008 she made her Broadway directorial debut, and again directed her sister and James Earl Jones in an all–African American production of Tennessee William's *Cat on a Hot Tin Roof*. She lives in Santa Monica with her husband and has two grown children, daughter Vivian Nichole, who has become a performer like her mother, and son Norman Jr., who has followed his father into sports.

Lee Curreri married Sherry Dean, the sister of his co-star in the original *Fame* movie, Laura Dean, and they have two children. Although no longer acting, he remains very active in the music industry through his company Xacca Sounds, Inc., as a composer on several television series and video games, and as a record producer for such artists as Natalie Cole and King Creole & the Coconuts. He recently released his first full-length album of original music, *Aquabox*.

Valerie Landsburg has continued her acting career, appearing in several TV series and movies for television, and has just recently appeared with Cybill Shepherd in a TV movie called *Mrs. Washington Goes to Smith*. In 2005 Valerie was the director of a direct-to-video erotic thriller called *Bound by Lies*, for which her husband James McVay wrote the music. I caught the movie recently on cable television and thought that both Valerie and James did an excellent job. James has become a very successful composer for television, with over thirty TV shows and specials on his résumé. He collaborated with Valerie and Lee Curreri on a new album of songs by Valerie called *Grownup*. Married for over twenty-five years, they live in the Santa Monica Mountains and have two grown daughters, Taylor and Brooklyn.

Carlo Imperato would continue to try his hand at acting after *Fame*, with little success, eventually turning to real estate investing and later opening a studio prop-making company. After two failed marriages in ten years he seems to have settled happily into his third marriage with wife Angela and a son and daughter, in addition to another son from his first marriage. Angela operates a beauty spa in Toluca Lake, California, that Carlo bought and renovated for her.

Billy Hufsey has recently reappeared on the VH1 reality program *Confessions of a Teen Idol*, an embarrassing piece of television hogwash that purports to examine the lives of six actors whose careers have gone downhill since they starred as teenagers on popular TV shows. I watched a promo for the show and found myself wincing in embarrassment as Billy Hufsey humiliated himself before the other actors and a "celebrity psychology expert" named Cooper Lawrence, as he sobbed out his desire for fame. After watching the premiere episode, *L.A. Times* reviewer Mary McNamara wrote that "it's difficult to know whether to laugh or cry." She finished her review by saying, "Watching these guys preen ... all I could think of were the countless hardworking, dedicated actors in this town who have watched their fees slip away and their opportunities dry up as reality shows like this one have steadily replaced all the comedies and dramas and procedurals that once kept them employed."

Erica Gimpel, whose first love was and always would be the theater, returned to it after leaving *Fame*, starring opposite John Malkovich in the off–Broadway production of *States of Shock*. She also appeared in regional theater as Sally Hemmings in *Dusky Sally*. By the early '90s, her career in television began heating up again, and over the past nineteen years she has appeared in over 100 television series and movies, including featured roles on *Profiler*, *E.R.*, *Veronica Mars* and *Boston Legal*.

Lori Singer went on to star in a number of films in the late '80s and early '90s, including *Footloose*, *The Falcon and the Snowman*, *The Man with One Red Shoe* and Robert Altman's *Short Cuts*. As a member of this all-star cast, Singer performed on the cello with singer Annie Ross. In her final appearance in films for more than eight years she played Dr. Angela France in Atom Ergoyan's 1997 *Bach Cello Suite #4: Sarabande*, and once again she performed on the cello, this time with famed cellist Yo-Yo Ma. She returned briefly to films in 2005 in the quirky independent *Little Victim*, and in January of 2008, Lori Singer was the soloist for the premiere presentation of Karl Jenkins' *Hymn for Martin Luther King* at Carnegie Hall in New York City.

Cynthia Gibb has continued working as an actress since leaving *Fame*. In addition to portraying Karen Carpenter in *The Karen Carpenter Story*, she played the grown-up Gypsy Rose Lee opposite Bette Midler in the television version of *Gypsy*, and has appeared in a number of other TV movies and series. Cindy has three children by her ex-husband Scott Kramer and is still very active, her most recent television appearances were in *Criminal Minds* and *Without a Trace*.

Morgan Stevens continued working as guest star on various series, including a continuing role in six episodes of *Melrose Place* and another in several episodes, of *Murder One*. I lost contact with Morgan after we finished our *Blacke's Magic* episode and his IMDB credits end abruptly with a single appearance on *Walker, Texas Ranger* in 1999. From that point on there is no record of Morgan Stevens the actor, nor have any of us, including Bill Blinn, Michael McGreevey, or Chris Beaumont, who used to live near him, heard anything about him. Wherever Morgan is I truly hope that he is well and successfully pursuing his acting career or whatever is now his heart's desire. He was and is a true gentleman

Michael Cerveris, the bushy haired and handsome music student on *Fame*, is now the bald and handsome major Broadway star, having shaved his head after losing much of his hair as the years went by. He has starred in such New York productions as *Titanic*, *Assassins*, and *Sweeney Todd*, and in the Los Angeles and London productions of *Hedwig and the Angry Inch*. Currently he is creating quite a stir starring in the Broadway revival of Ibsen's *Hedda Gabler* opposite Mary Louis Parker. Recently his mysterious character of the Observer on the Fox sci-fi series *Fringe* could also be seen at various national sporting events and sitting in the audience at *American Idol*, all part of a network promotion for the series' season finale.

Nia Peeples found herself immediately starring and singing in her first feature film just months after leaving *Fame* when she replaced another actress in the Universal Pictures 1987 surfing drama *North Shore*. She followed this up with another feature, *DeepStar Six*, and then returned to television to appear in numerous TV movies and series. She has been featured in several series, including *Crisis Center* and *Courthouse*, and for three years co-starred on *Walker, Texas Ranger*. In 2007 she joined the cast of *The Young and the Restless*, and in 2009 she was nominated for an Image Award for her performance on the daytime series.

Jesse Borrego would go on to portray several diverse characters in films and television, including recurring roles on *24, ER* and *Dexter*. His most recent film, *La Mission*, made its world premier at the Sundance Film Festival in February of 2009. He frequently returns to his hometown and recently created the Cine Studio San Antonio, a nonprofit foundation committed to helping developing artists and filmmakers. Jesse's father, sister and brother are all musicians, and they have frequently joined Jesse in a group called Conjunto Borrego, performing traditional Mexican-American Conjunto music.

Michael DeLorenzo worked his way up from a small role in the feature *Fatal Beauty* in 1987, through guest appearances on over a dozen series, to co-starring as Rosie Perez's love interest in the independent feature *Somebody to Love* in 1994, a role in which his character ironically couldn't dance. After co-starring for three years on *New York Undercover*, he would continue appearing as a guest star in numerous series and TV movies. His most recent credits include co-starring roles in the features *Contradictions of the Heart* and *Not Forgotten.*

Dick Miller has divided his time since leaving *Fame* between doing voice-over work in animation and commercials, and acting in films and television. With over sixty credits earned just since 1987, he is still one of the most active performers in the business, even though he will be celebrating his 81st birthday on Christmas Day of 2009. His track record reflects his well-earned ranking as an icon of exploitation films, with his most recent credit as evidence — *Trail of the Screaming Forehead.*

Robert Romanus, after completing the final season of *Fame*, would very shortly thereafter join the cast of *The Facts of Life* in the reoccurring role of Snake Robinson. He would continue in television and films, racking up an impressive list of nearly forty separate credits, with his most recent being *My Own Worst Enemy*, with Christian Slater. As of this writing, he is currently filming the fifth chapter in the *American Pie* franchise.

27

A Final Goodbye

There is still one cast member that I have intentionally waited until now to discuss, as his tragic story needs to be told in some detail, and that is our beloved Gene Anthony Ray.

After *Fame* ended, Gene attempted to re-establish his dance career in Hollywood, but was unsuccessful. Traveling to Europe, he appeared in a British stage production of *Carrie* in 1988 and then tried unsuccessfully to organize a European dance tour and open a dance school in Milan. By 1992 his use of drugs and alcohol was out of control; he was broke and living on the street. After being arrested in 1995 for drunkenly attacking two men who were taunting him, and after a rumor began to spread that he had died of AIDS, Gene decided to return to the United States and attempt to straighten out his life. His old mentor, Debbie Allen, cast him in a small role in a film she was directing and appearing in called *Out-of-Sync*. It was sometime after that that I ran into Gene at the Bistro Gardens in Beverly Hills. Katie and I had been to see a play with some friends at a theater across the street, and we were having a late dinner when Katie spotted Gene walking back to his table. I looked over at the same moment that Gene saw me, and we both moved quickly to greet each other. He was truly happy to see me as we gave each other a big hug and spoke briefly. I had heard all of the rumors, but Gene looked like his old self, and he was full of enthusiasm, telling me about several projects he would soon be doing, including an idea for a new television series. We said goodbye, promising to get together very soon. Sadly, I only saw Gene one more time, at a party at Bill Blinn's, and again we spoke only briefly. Donna Lee was also at that event. "I hadn't seen him for a while," she recalled. "And then I saw him at Bill's and I said, 'Gene, there's some Angel sitting on a sofa smoking a cigarette and going, "Man, this kid is wearing me out." But look at you you're still here, because I really didn't expect you to be here.'" Soon, he was, in fact, diagnosed with AIDS, and things started to get worse. The treatment of highly toxic drugs caused his condition to weaken. "A woman in my church worked in a hospice off of Santa Monica Boulevard in West Hollywood," Donna Lee continued. "She came to me and said, 'Donna, do you remember the show *Fame* and the actor who played Leroy?' She had no idea that I was involved with the show." The woman told Donna that Gene had just been admitted to her hospice. "So I went to see him, and he'd found Jesus," Donna reported. "He'd been doing cruise ship shows and he arrived at LAX, got a cab and started talking gibberish and was sweating, and the cab driver freaked and got him to, I think, Cedars-Sinai Emergency, and that's how it happened." Donna Lee contacted Chris Beaumont to tell him about Gene. Beaumont recalled:

> He kind of reached out to Donna Lee and Carol Mayo when he got sick. And they got in touch with me, and he was in a facility somewhere in West Hollywood. He still had the old energy — you know, over-the-top, wide-eyed energy — but he was sick. He still looked good, but there was a weakness in his voice. There was a relationship with Jesus that I think came out of coming face to face with his own mortality. I think he was very much in touch with his condition, and he knew that it was probably going to be fatal, and he cried a couple of times. But then he would come back and ... I think the drugs that he was on then, the proper drugs that he was on — not illicit drugs — created some mood swings. I visited him twice, and one time I was there for about an hour, then next time I was there for about a half an hour and then he grew tired.

In April of 2003, some seven months before his death, Gene joined several of his fellow cast members — Valerie Landsburg, Lee Curreri, Carlo Imperato and Erica Gimpel — at Debbie Allen's dance studio in Culver City, California, for a filmed reunion special for the BBC. Gene looked in ill health, he spoke slowly and seemed to be having difficulty in forming his words, but he had no difficulty in showing his love for Debbie. "Debbie's a powerful human being," he declared. "And the fact that she took to me and loved me like she does and like she did before is more of a blessing than actually doing *Fame*. *Fame* has ended, figuratively, but not Debbie. She'll never go away. Never."

He tried gamely to be the Gene that everyone remembered, but it was obvious that he had changed. In watching Gene in the TV special I was reminded of watching Elvis in another special filmed years before, during his final concert tour. Elvis had also appeared ill, but what had shocked me most of all was a close-up near the end of the film showing a bloated Elvis standing backstage in Omaha, Nebraska, waiting to go on.

My favorite picture of Gene Anthony Ray. That questioning look was always there.

His eyes were absolutely lifeless, with the fat jowls and sweat running down his forehead only helping to accent his ghastly appearance. This was filmed only a few short months before he died, and when the story broke of his death I have to admit I wasn't terribly surprised. Gene's eyes had that same lifelessness in them, as if his soul had just given up. It would be his last public appearance; Gene would die of complications from a stroke seven months later on November 14, 2003.

Someone has put together a marvelous tribute to Gene on the internet that they call *Dancing with Angels.* It is extremely well edited, but, more importantly, it conjures up the essence of what Gene Anthony Ray was — a free spirit that could dance with the wind and make you believe that every moment he was dancing was a special moment for him, as indeed it was for you. Gene once said in an interview:

> Everybody who remembered the film and the series, especially people who wanted to be actors and singers and went on to do that, said I inspired them. That *Fame* really inspired them, *Fame* meaning the whole cast. When

you inspire somebody, if your work, what you've done, has inspired somebody to do well and do something positive in this crazy world today, it's worth it. I'd do it again.

Sometimes when Gene was dancing you'd see a smile of pure joy illuminate his face. It was as though he had been transported to another plane where nothing mattered except the rhythms of the dance. I have seen that same expression on jazz musicians' faces when they were trading licks and a particularly skillful extemporaneous section pleased them. At the end of the tribute there is a written comment from one of his fans:

> Today, February 20, 2004, I found out about the death of Mr. Gene Anthony Ray. Ironically, I heard this from his mother, Jean. She was standing beside me in a Harlem restaurant wearing a sweatshirt bearing his image. He was engaged in a magnificent leap. As such, I was fortunate to be able to deliver condolences to her in person. You will be pleased to know that she seems well. I will share with all of you her words to me regarding his death: "He is now dancing with angels — without pain."

Epilogue

But the story isn't quite over yet. On a rainy night in early February of 2009 the Writers Guild of America awarded William Blinn the Paddy Chayefsky Laurel Award for Television. Named after one of the most lauded writers in entertainment history, the award, according to the Guild's own description, is the "highest award for television writing, given to writers who have advanced the literature of television."

The event was held at the Hyatt Regency Century Plaza Hotel in Century City, Los Angeles, and several of Bill's friends and associates from *Fame* decided to attend and whoop it up for him. Chris Beaumont and his wife Casey, Parke and Flavia Perine, Michael and Jan Gleason, and Katie and I shared a table. When I spoke with Bill just before the dinner was served he seemed a trifle nervous, but when called to the stage to accept his award, after receiving a standing ovation from his fellow writers, he gave a hard-hitting and amusing acceptance speech. His opening line was an example of his self-effacing sense of humor. "When this first came about," he said, "the Guild came up with a press release, and the first sentence in the press release said, 'William Blinn's work has changed the face of television.'" Bill paused for a beat, and then, looking mockingly at the audience, he added, "So it's my fault?" Actually, it was a bittersweet moment for Bill, for John Robinson, his dear friend and fellow classmate from the Academy of Dramatic Art, had succumbed to cancer the week before, and, as he admitted later, John had been on his mind all through the evening. Before he spoke, a video was screened showing highlights of Blinn's career, including moments from *Roots*, *Brian's Song*, and *Starsky & Hutch*, and ending with a clip of Debbie and Gene and the dancers in a sequence from the "Passing Grade" episode from *Fame*. I found myself smiling. Here I was watching the man who had been more responsible than anyone else for making *Fame* the success that it was receiving a lifetime achievement award from

218

Bill Blinn with his Paddy Chayefsky Laurel Award (courtesy Getty Images/WGA).

his peers, while the very first piece of film that I had ever edited for *Fame* was being displayed on the screen. Spanning the twenty-eight years that had transpired, it seemed a fitting coda to the entire fabulous experience.

Sources

Beaumont, Christopher — interview 8/7/08.

Blinn, William — interviews 3/4/08 and 7/15/08; phone interview 4/22/09.

Danton, Mitch — phone interview 2/27/09; email correspondence 3/9/09.

De Silva, David — phone interview 8/1/08.

Edelson, Elizabeth, re: Barry Robins material — email correspondence 6/24/08, 6/25/08, 6/26/08, 6/30/08, 7/4/08 and 8/1/08.

Ehrlich, Ken — interview 4/3/08.

Lee, Donna — interview 9/13/08; email correspondence 9/14/08; and interview 4/18/09.

Longstreet, Harry and Renee — phone interview 1/9/09; email correspondence 3/25/09 and 5/11/09.

McGreevey, Michael — interview 7/11/08; email correspondence 8/7/08, 9/29/08 and 2/23/09.

Merwald, Frank — phone interview 3/5/09; email correspondence 4/13/09 and 4/24/09.

Perine, Parke — interview 2/27/08.

Reisberg, Richard — interview 10/14/08.

Rosensteel, Pamela — various quotes of cast members and staff courtesy of her website Fame Forever; email correspondence 6/10/08, 6/13/08 and 3/27/09.

Rubell, Paul — email correspondence 9/14/08.

Zachary, Ted — interview 3/26/08.

Index

Numbers in **bold italics** indicate pages with illustrations.
Names of people in *italics* indicate characters.